Panama in Black

Panama in Black

Afro-Caribbean World Making in the Twentieth Century

KAYSHA CORINEALDI

DUKE UNIVERSITY PRESS
Durham and London 2022

© 2022 DUKE UNIVERSITY PRESS

All rights reserved

Printed in the United States of America on acid-free paper ∞

Designed by A. Mattson Gallagher

Typeset in Garamond Premier Pro by Westchester
Publishing Services

Library of Congress Cataloging-in-Publication Data
Names: Corinealdi, Kaysha, [date] author.
Title: Panama in black : Afro-Caribbean world making in the
twentieth century / Kaysha Corinealdi.
Description: Durham : Duke University Press, 2022. | Includes
bibliographical references and index.
Identifiers: LCCN 2021050341 (print)
LCCN 2021050342 (ebook)
ISBN 9781478015895 (hardcover)
ISBN 9781478018513 (paperback)
ISBN 9781478023128 (ebook)
Subjects: LCSH: Blacks—Panama—History. | Blacks—
Panama—Social conditions. | Blacks—Panama—Migrations—
History. | Blacks—Race identity—Panama. | Blacks—Politics
and government. | Race discrimination—Panama. | Panama—
Emigration and immigration—Social aspects. | Panama—Race
relations. | BISAC: HISTORY / Latin America / Central America
| SOCIAL SCIENCE / Black Studies (Global)
Classification: LCC F1577.B55 C675 2022 (print) | LCC F1577.B55
(ebook) | DDC 305.896/07287—dc23/eng/20220126
LC record available at https://lccn.loc.gov/2021050341
LC ebook record available at https://lccn.loc.gov/2021050342
Cover art: Giana De Dier, *Devenir*, 2021. Collage, 30 × 23 cm.
Courtesy of the artist.

For my mother and all the dreamers
who paved the way

Contents

Abbreviations

AFL	American Federation of Labor
CIO	Congress of International Organizations
CZCS	Canal Zone colored schools
CZCTA	Canal Zone Colored Teacher's Association
CZWU	Canal Zone Workers Union
GCEOC	Government and Civic Employees Organizing Committee
ISB	Internal Security Branch
LCN	Liga Cívica Nacional / National Civic League
PCAC	Panamanian Cultural Action Committee / Comité de Acción Cultural Panameño
PCWIEA	Panama Canal West Indian Employees Association
PPP	Panamá Para los Panameños / Panama for the Panamanians
SAMAAP	Sociedad de Amigos del Museo Afroantillano de Panamá / Society of Friends of the West Indian Museum of Panama
UNIA	Universal Negro Improvement Association
UPWA	United Public Workers of America

Acknowledgments

Writing this book has been a journey of love and patience. It began as a kernel of an idea over a decade ago and blossomed into something that I am proud to share with the world today. I am deeply grateful to the wide network of people who throughout the years offered me support and encouragement at each stage of the research and writing process. Your engagement has made my work that much richer and stronger.

I am lucky to count on the friendship of an amazing array of scholars who have been deeply generous with their time. For their detailed attention and comments to drafts of various portions of this book, I thank Elizabeth Son, Kimberly Juanita Brown, Tao Leigh Goffe, Martine Jean, Patricia Lott, Tasha Hawthorne, Nicole Ivy, and Javiela Evangelista. Liz, thank you for being one of my earliest readers and for coordinating great one-day writing retreats. Kimberly, you are my model for mentorship, support, and wicked humor. I especially thank you for creating the Dark Room and allowing me to be a part of this space. Tao, exchanging ideas and drafts with you has been one of the highlights for this entire writing endeavor. Thank you for always asking the hard questions. Martine, thank you for reading the roughest of my drafts. You have been my rock for accountability and productivity. Patricia, Tasha, Nicole, and Javiela, I thank you each for your brilliance, your kindness, and being the most amazing hypewomen anyone could ever ask for. Sharing space with you all through the Humanities Working Group has been a breath of fresh air when I needed it most.

Colleagues in the fields of African diaspora studies, Panamanian history, Caribbean studies, Latin American studies, US history, American studies, and Afro-Latinx studies have also provided rich feedback to papers, presentations, and proposal ideas connected to the book. In addition to those already noted, my thanks go to Melva Lowe de Goodin, Lara Putnam, Katherine Zien, Gerardo Maloney, Alberto Barrow, Lori Flores, Marixa Lasso, Amy

Chazkel, Erika Williams, Katerina Gonzalez Seligmann, Claudia Castañeda, Claire Andrade-Watkins, Ariana Curtis, Melissa Stuckey, Reena Goldthree, Natanya Duncan, Jessi Bardill, Minkah Makalani, Deborah Thomas, Maya Doig-Acuña, George Reid Andrews, Jorge Giovannetti-Torres, Julie Greene, J. Marlena Edwards, Joan Flores-Villalobos, Katherine Marino, Frances Peace Sullivan, Javier Wallace, Emma Amador, Wellinthon García, Nancy Appelbaum, Deborah Thomas, Fiona Vernal, Rhonda Cobham-Sander, Aims McGuiness, G. Melissa García, Paul Joseph Lopez-Oro, Sandy Placido, Natasha Lightfoot, and the late George Priestley. A special thank you as well to my longtime mentor, Gilbert M. Joseph.

Material and organizational support at institutional levels also allowed me to bring this book to fruition. A Faculty Advancement Fund Grant from Emerson College provided me with a course release at a crucial point in the book proposal process. Through a Career Enhancement Fellowship provided by the Institute for Citizens and Scholars, I was able to finalize key revisions to the manuscript. A yearlong fellowship from the Afro-Latin American Research Institute and the Du Bois Research Institute at the Hutchins Center at Harvard University enabled me to interact with a dynamic set of scholars invested in centering Black life in the Americas. My thanks go to Henry Louis Gates Jr., Alejandro de la Fuente, Bronia Greskovicova-Chang, and Krishnakali Lewis for all your organizational and intellectual work. The librarians and archivists at the Archivo Nacional de Panamá, the Ministerio de Relaciones Exteriores, the Biblioteca Nacional de Panamá, the Schomburg Center for Research in Black Culture, the National Archives in College Park, Maryland, Tamiment Library at New York University, and Harvard University's Widener and Lamont Libraries receive my heartfelt thanks for all their assistance. I am particularly indebted to Mirella Castillo, Yesenia Espinosa, and Sabina Bethancourt for providing key guidance in navigating the Archivo Nacional. I also thank the leadership and membership of the Dedicators, Club El Pacífico, and SAMAAP for taking the time to meet with me and share organizational histories and memories. Finally, I extend my thanks to the Duke University Press team for their commitment to the project. I appreciate the attention given by the external readers to the manuscript and Alejandra Mejía for all the coordination in the posteditorial stage. Gisela Fosado, thank you for shepherding my project from the proposal stage to the publication process.

Support from friends and family outside my immediate academic world has been essential in seeing this project from beginning to end. Ria, Imo, Bubu, and Sade, I thank you each for friendship and love that has sustained me across geographies and time. For always believing in me, even when I doubted myself, I thank my mother, Sonia Green, and my sisters, Saskia and Idorsha. From Colón to Brooklyn and now Jersey, we have loved hard and plotted new adventures. Idorsha, you will always be the best promoter I'll ever have. For making me laugh, discover new card and board games, read YA novels, and memorize a ridiculous number of children songs, I thank my nieces and nephews, Shannon, Omar, Amelia, Alexis, Hailey, Zaya, and Alexander. For keeping me well fed and rooting for my success, I thank my expanded Brooklyn family: Rima, Reuven, and Monica. Michael, words are not enough to thank you for your abundant support throughout the writing process and everything that preceded it. I feel lucky to have you as a companion in life. For your sage advice and the beautiful memories we have created over the years, I am deeply grateful.

Introduction

Legacies of Exclusion and Afro-Caribbean Diasporic World Making

On December 11, 1966, the staff of the *Panama Tribune* came together to celebrate the opening of Parque Young in Río Abajo, a working-class neighborhood in Panama City. The park was the first of its kind in Panama to honor the work of an Afro-Caribbean Panamanian. Its inauguration also came seven years after the death of Sidney Young, its namesake. Young, born in Jamaica and raised in Panama, created the *Tribune* in 1928. By the time of his death, the newsweekly held the title of the longest-running Black newsweekly in Central America. Figure Intro.1 features some of the key members of the *Tribune* team, including editors, office managers and assistants, columnists, and area representatives.

The presence of only one woman in this group, Claudina McIntosh (Sidney Young's adopted daughter), attests to the gendered hierarchy of the newsweekly. This hierarchy also affected other aspects of community formation and diasporic activism among Afro-Caribbean Panamanians within and outside Panama. Sidney Young's son, David Young, the tall young man to the right in the frame, was also in attendance. He traveled from New York, where he and his mother had relocated after 1959, joining thousands of other Afro-Caribbean Panamanians in this space. George Westerman, the director and chief editor of the *Tribune* following Young's death, also joined the commemoration. Westerman, born and raised in Panama, like many of those pictured, also had ancestors from the Anglophone Caribbean. I begin with this photograph because it offers one example of Afro-Caribbean diasporic world making spanning from the late 1920s to the late 1960s. This

FIGURE INTRO.1 Parque Young Inauguration, 1966. *Left to right*: George Thomas (sports columnist), Arthur G. Jacobs (associate editor), Otis Smith (office assistant), Victor T. Smith (assistant to the editor), Harold W. Williams (labor specialist), Lorenzo H. Rose (columnist), Hector Gadpaille (guest columnist), Claude L. Walter (Canal Zone representative), Claudina McIntosh (office manager), George Westerman (chief editor), and David Young. From George Westerman, *Los inmigrantes antillanos en Panamá* (Panama City: INAC, 1980), 121.

world making, grounded in histories of migration, gendered hierarchies, citizenship exclusion, and survival, linked the Caribbean, Central America, and the United States and necessitated networks that both claimed and went beyond imperial and nation-state borders. Those gathered to celebrate the inauguration of Parque Young not only posthumously honored a notable member of Panama's Afro-Caribbean community but also through their presence offered visual reminders of the extent, multigenerational nature, and materiality of this world making.

Crucial to how this diasporic world making played out in Panama is that it directly coincided with twentieth-century campaigns to define Panama as a space, idea, and nation. By the early 1920s competing narratives regarding who could claim Panama permeated the isthmian landscape. One such narrative called for a recognition that through their presence and activism Afro-Caribbean Panamanians could and would affirm Panama as the center of Afro-diasporic life and possibility in the circum-Caribbean world. Another narrative privileged Panama as an inherently Iberian American space, specifically an anti-Black Hispanic space, where the "sons of the fatherland" held the responsibility of protecting both the republic and the Latin race. Still another narrative, and one that shared similarities with the Iberian American narrative through its specific exclusion of an othered group, highlighted the Panama Canal Zone as a new space in which to develop US empire making. In this introduction I discuss all these competing narratives and their implications for the late and post-1920s histories that I map in this study, highlighting how the call to demarcate Panama as a culturally Iberian nation in the Americas that required protection against "undesirable" Black foreigners was part of the republic's early legal structure. This anti-Black foreigner discourse evolved throughout the twentieth century with parallels that connected it to US empire building and nationalist campaigns throughout the hemisphere, yet it developed in distinct ways within the Panamanian context.

The worldview imagined and promoted by Afro-Caribbean Panamanians advanced in ways that made direct connections to the Panamanian isthmus, while also remaining attuned to inescapable imperial and hemispheric realities. My examination of this worldview begins with the late 1920s Black press in a xenophobic Panamanian milieu. It next explores the community networks created in the US-controlled Panama Canal Zone by Afro-Caribbeans born in this place. The narrative then probes the anticommunism and hemispheric democracy discourse engulfing the mid-twentieth-century Americas. Later it locates Afro-Caribbean Panamanian activism in the Civil Rights movement of 1960s New York and ends with public intellectual networks connecting Panama and the United States, with an eye to the broader Afro-Americas. Afro-Caribbean diasporic world making, I contend, unlike narratives centered on Iberian American traditions or US empire, demanded a more inclusive understanding of citizenship and belonging precisely because it forced honest yet uncomfortable discussions about the reach of anti-Blackness in nationalist, imperial, and hemispheric discourses throughout the twentieth century. This worldview necessitated a recognition of how the centrality and denigration of Black life and experience framed discourses of modernity in Panama and in many other parts of the hemisphere.

The diasporic world making championed by Afro-Caribbean Panamanians explicitly challenged a history of outsider vs. insider that had long shaped the experiences of African descendants, Indigenous peoples, and migrants of color in Panama and other parts of the Americas. This outsider-insider history, which in turn created perpetual outsiders, depended on Europeanized elites segregating themselves from poor and working-class people of color and rendering Indigenous populations invisible or in need of assimilation. Such a project called for the promotion of cultural and linguistic homogeneity, the push for white European migration as the solution to alleged racial problems, and the scapegoating of migrants of color and their descendants during economic and political crises. Even more daunting about this project was the way in which it, in the words of Stuart Hall, normalized "dominant regimes of representation," demanding that Black and colonized people "see and experience ourselves as 'Other.'"[1]

This book centers Black people, not as afterthoughts or fetishized others, but as people who survived multiple forced and voluntary migrations, colonial and national expulsion campaigns, and brutal and discriminatory working conditions. It assesses how and why Afro-Caribbean Panamanians dared to invent new worlds, the challenges of this endeavor, and the multigenerational nature of this world making. Crucially, it focuses on the words, ideas, and actions of men and women who self-identified as members of a Black diaspora and pushes against a narrative of rescuing Black voices trapped in the shadows of mestizaje.[2]

The men and women I follow in this study refused invisibility and the isolation of being othered by creating diasporically oriented newspapers, businesses, community organizations, schools, churches, labor unions, and libraries, in addition to engaging in other forms of making community. It is precisely because they dared to openly and adamantly create their own worldviews that they faced systematic hostilities. Yet, Caribbean diasporic life, "through its transformation and difference," continued to typify major spaces throughout the isthmus.[3] In fact, through their twentieth-century writings, activism, and travel, Afro-Caribbean Panamanians engaged in a process of world making that connected them to a past and future of Afro-diasporic life within and beyond Panama. In this way they engaged in a macropractice of what Courtney Desiree Morris, in her study of the life of Pan-Africanist Madame Maymie Leona Turpeau de Mena, described as "diasporic self-making."[4] This self-making provided Afro-Caribbeans with multiple opportunities to define Blackness, to define Panama, and to define diaspora.

By creating these cultural and political spaces in the shadow of systemic hostilities, Afro-Caribbean Panamanians engaged in what Tiffany Patterson and Robin D. G. Kelley have outlined as the "process and condition" of diaspora creation.[5] The "process" of diaspora required invention, but the "condition" of diaspora recognized that this ability to invent, renew, and survive was tied to local and geopolitical conditions. Systemic discrimination based on race, gender, ancestry, sexuality, language, official and unofficial segregation, white supremacy, and the denial of citizenship formed part of the local and global "condition" surrounding Afro-Caribbean diasporic world making. Ignoring these realities was not possible, yet invention called for imagining a world not yet fully present. It required recognizing that they were "not merely inheritors of a culture [or a practice] but its makers."[6] This was the challenge and the promise of diasporic world making.

The condition of citizenship, understood through cultural, juridical, racial, and migrant frameworks, also affected this world making. In early twentieth-century Panama, Afro-Caribbeans created their own vernacular practices of citizenship, which acknowledged localized differences between Black migrants yet used language, empire, and culture to unite tens of thousands of men and women from throughout the circum-Caribbean. Vernacular citizenship entailed being a migrant and a citizen of Panama, being a subject and an afterthought of empire, and forming part of generational conversations regarding the promise of diaspora.[7] This practice of vernacular citizenship took place alongside juridical debates regarding access to state-specific citizenship rights. Panama, as in much of the Americas, assumed a birth-based (jus soli) juridical citizenship model, yet eugenicist discussions about racial purity and a discontent with the idea of the children of "undesirable" migrants becoming citizens challenged this birth-based model. Afro-Caribbeans, particularly those born and raised in Panama, sought to balance vernacular citizenship approaches with securing nation-state-specific citizenship access. Engaging with the thoughts and ideas of African descendants from other parts of the world, people who shared divergent citizenship conditions yet had to navigate similar racial hierarchies further added to this complex understanding of citizenship as an invention, a practice, and a right. Expanding notions of citizenship in this way, not limiting its access, formed a core part of the diasporic world making bourgeoning within Panama.

Unpacking and understanding the contours of Afro-Caribbean Panamanian diasporic world making demands urgency given that exclusionist narratives centered on anti-Blackness and xenophobic nationalism remain strong political and cultural ideologies around the world. The denationalization of thousands of Haitian descendants in the Dominican Republic via legislative changes initiated in 2004 and enshrined by a 2013 constitutional tribunal decision is but one poignant example. Dominican legislators used the same language of desirability, cultural homogeneity, and sovereign rights as their political peers in 1940s Panama. The struggle to reverse this policy in the Dominican Republic continues.[8] In the case of Afro-Caribbean denationalization in Panama, twenty years would pass before exclusionist citizenship laws were fully eliminated. In the interim, those affected fought locally but thought globally, rejecting the white supremacist premise that their ethnic or racial backgrounds made them less deserving of full civic and political rights.

Paying attention to the work of Afro-Caribbean Panamanians as world builders, and not only as citizens or noncitizens of Panama, the United States, or various other parts of the Americas, also offers a distinct opportunity to understand activism, community, and diaspora formation from the ground up. The men and women at the core of this book engaged in what Michelle Stephens has described as a materialist approach to Black internationalism.[9] They brought together immediate needs for economic and political access, alongside a vision of the world made possible through Black activism and leadership. Claiming Panama as part of a Black diasporic world was one part of this process. Another included a forceful rejection, through localized activism, of the call to cede the very idea of the nation-state to proponents of anti-Blackness. Through this activism Afro-Caribbean Panamanians engaged in what I term *local internationalism*; that is, they created localized platforms for transformative change that affirmed the centrality of Afro-diasporic life in national and global politics. Through this focus on Afro-Caribbean Panamanians as producers of knowledge, as innovators, and as diasporic world makers, *Panama in Black* affirms the importance of moving away from discourses that present Black communities as merely reactionary and instead suggests that the thoughts, hopes, and expectations that emerge from these communities merit rigorous study.

Early Stages of Afro-Caribbean Diasporic World Making

When considering diasporic world making among Afro-Caribbean Panamanians, it is vital to understand the centrality of the Panamanian isthmus as a major hub of Black migration and Afro-diasporic activism. Sustained Afro-Caribbean migration to Panama began in the mid-nineteenth century.[10] Five thousand migrants made their way to Panama from the British- and French-ruled Caribbean for the building of the Panama railroad in the 1850s. More than fifty thousand followed during French attempts in the 1880s to build an interoceanic canal and as part of the banana cultivation industry dominated by the US-owned United Fruit Company. As noted by Velma

Newton and Olive Senior, many of those making these migrant journeys sought an alternative to unemployment, limited economic mobility, as a well as a postemancipation economy that kept them bound to plantations without any prospect of land ownership.[11] Migrants from Jamaica, the most populated British colony in the Caribbean, made up the majority of those recruited during these early construction and agricultural efforts. Railroad and interoceanic canal construction proved particularly dangerous, resulting in tens of thousands of deaths, but after the successful completion of the first and the failed attempts at the latter, thousands of Caribbean migrants chose to remain on the isthmus. In the cities of Colón, Panamá, and Bocas del Toro, they built schools, churches, and small businesses.

By the time of the US-financed Panama Canal building efforts in the first fifteen years of the twentieth century, a small but strong community of Afro-Caribbean migrants and their descendants already had an established presence on the isthmus. This presence would significantly expand during and after the construction period. Migrants also arrived during the first decade of Panama's existence as an independent nation and as the reality of US control of the canal area dawned on those who had envisioned an independent nation buttressed by the canal but *not* dependent on the priorities of US officials. In all, during the building of the canal (1904–14), between 150,000 and 200,000 Caribbean migrants made their way to Panama. This figure doubled the total Panamanian population at the time. Most migrants were from Barbados, followed by others from Jamaica, Saint Lucia, Martinique, and other parts of the British- and French-controlled Caribbean. As with previous migrants, many sought opportunity, were attracted by the prospect of earning enough money to both thrive and send back to their relatives, and, unlike earlier migrants, had heard of Panama before and to a certain extent knew what to expect. Many nonetheless died in the building of the canal; suffered grave injuries resulting in amputations, chronic respiratory problems, and blindness; and had to contend with a highly regimented system of segregation and discrimination.[12] The violence of this building effort marked entire generations. The canal itself, while becoming a bridge for the world, was also the site of death and loss.

Following the end of canal construction, almost half of those contracted as workers, in addition to the tens of thousands of others who made the journey on their own, opted to stay. Some also had children whom they raised in Panama. The lives and activism of this and subsequent generations, in the Panamanian Republic, in the US-controlled Canal Zone, and in the United States, frame the bulk of this book. As for early twentieth-century Panama, by 1920, Afro-Caribbeans were the majority population of the province of Colón and had a significant presence in the provinces of Panamá and Bocas del Toro. Caribbean migrants also established roots in Panama by founding independent newspapers like the *Independent* and the *Workman*, in addition to editing West Indian sections in English-language dailies and creating private schools and academies open to all in the republic. They also established lodges and mutual aid associations, such as the Colón Federal Credit Union, the Panama Canal Lodge, and the Isthmian League of British West Indians. Members of this community also built dozens of Protestant churches that featured a wide array of social events and festivities. Some migrants opened small shops and businesses, among which food and bus services proved particularly popular. A small number of migrant professionals worked as dentists, teachers, seamstresses, pharmacists, lawyers, nurses, accountants, and engineers. Others made their mark as playwrights, musicians, athletes, and performers.[13]

Moreover, unlike other Afro-Caribbean migrant and migrant-descendant communities that emerged in other parts of Central America, those who made their home in Panama created a unique Afro-Caribbean world. Island-specific identifiers remained, as did class and skin color hierarchies, but the unprecedented nature of migration to Panama meant that people from far-off Caribbean islands actually met one another. In Panama they shared stories about their local governance structure, argued about which island made a particular dish the best, joined in leagues where they jointly identified as West Indian, and had an opportunity to collectively make note of the limits of British colonial rule. In fact, for those whose pleas to British consular officials in Colón and Panamá remained unaddressed, or for those informed that colonial citizenship could not be passed down to children born in Panama, the reality of this limit became paramount. Thus, finding recourses outside the boundaries of British imperial rule in ways that validated Anglophone Caribbean life and culture, while acknowledging the new world made possible in and through Panama, held tremendous appeal and promise.

This emergent view likewise propelled Afro-Caribbeans in early twentieth-century Panama to pursue local internationalist and diasporic projects that connected them to other Black people in the hemisphere. One such project included the creation of local branches of Marcus Garvey and Amy Ashwood's Universal Negro Improvement Association (UNIA) as early as December 1918, a year after the opening of the UNIA headquarters in New York City. By the mid-1920s Panama had one of the largest UNIA branches outside the United States, and the UNIA main journalistic organ, the *Negro World*, circulated freely. Given the vast Caribbean migrant community of the isthmus, the popularity of the UNIA was not surprising. Many understood that postemancipation promises remained unfulfilled and acknowledged that access to capital appeared to determine power and independence. As migrants they especially appreciated the discourse of self-making and Negro pride that shaped the UNIA movement. An example of this self-making included a UNIA branch in Colón that operated a school and a bakery, owned several pieces of real estate, and hosted weekly organization meetings.[14] Some fissures would eventually appear between the parent UNIA and local branches. Marcus Garvey's arrest and conviction caused particularly heated debates and ruptures. Nevertheless, the appeal of forming part of a collective within and outside the isthmus, one grounded in a message of Black pride and Black innovation, proved especially attractive. In chapter 5, I discuss how the appeal of such a collective would also encourage the creation of a scholarship-granting organization in Brooklyn by Afro-Caribbean Panamanian women. The organization, through its activities and platforms, reflected the growing diversity of a Caribbean New York while also reasserting the centrality of the isthmus in the making of Afro-Caribbean diasporic worlds.

In the early 1920s the ideological power of the UNIA helped shape another diasporic and internationalist venture: the staging of the longest running labor strike in the history of Panama Canal operations, and the first such major strike in the history of the isthmus.[15] Beginning on February 24, 1920, and ending nine days later, between twelve thousand and sixteen thousand Afro-Caribbean workers joined the strike. The strikers were members of the predominantly white Detroit-based United Brotherhood of Maintenance of Way Employees and Railroad Shop Laborers. Barbadian-born William Preston Stoute, a teacher in the Canal Zone and vice president of the local union, with the assistance of Cuban-born and Panama-raised Eduardo Morales, a field clerk for the canal and one of the founding members of the first UNIA branches in Panama, led the strikers. Both men did so without any US United Brotherhood officials present on the isthmus. Prior to and during the strike, both men also used newspapers like the *Workman*, published by Barbadian-born Hubert N. Walrond, who also included his own pro-union editorials, to communicate with strike participants, canal officials, and any other parties interested in the strike. The strike was unsuccessful because of intense policing by canal officials, including the confiscation of telegrams sent by the United Brotherhood's Detroit headquarters. Due to this intercepted communication, local union leaders received no response to their request for strike funds.[16] Future attempts at labor organizing by workers of color on the canal would routinely refer to the potentials and missed opportunities of this 1920 strike.

In all, by the late 1920s, the vast presence of the UNIA and attempts at international labor unionism, coupled with rich community networks created by Caribbean migrants as far back as the mid-nineteenth century, attested to the extent to which Panama had become the Caribbean and the Caribbean had been extended to Panama. To speak of Panama in the early 1920s without making note of the tens of thousands of Afro-Caribbeans who called the isthmus home was impossible. Not only had they proved pivotal in the construction of major transit technologies that effectively opened Panama to the world, they also added to the life of a young nation embarking on the project of writing its own foundational narratives. These narratives, however, rather than embracing Caribbean migrant life and an Afro-diasporic spirit, pitted the dream of an Iberian Panama against the apparent nightmare of a Black and increasingly English-speaking nation.

Creating the Myth of an Iberian Nation in the Americas

A campaign among Panama's political and intellectual elite to disrupt the vision of Panama as a Black English-speaking nation borrowed from and expanded on racial hierarchies of the nineteenth century. According to this narrative, African descendants, the largest population on the isthmus by the nineteenth century, while recognized as prospective members of the body politic, were increasingly isolated from the centers of political and economic power.[17] The abolition of slavery and the extension of male suffrage in 1851 by the Colombian Congress promised the full inclusion of Black men in Panama and other parts of Nueva Granada. Through efforts waged by the Liberal Party, a political party that in Panama was colloquially described as the Partido Liberal Negro (Black Liberal Party) because of its large Black membership, Panama by 1855 secured federation status, which ostensibly allowed men, regardless of class or race, to exercise greater local political power. Black Panamanians, especially arrabaleros, those living in Panamá outside the fortress-like communities created by their white peers, challenged the top-down decisions of the Liberal Party. This access to political power changed by 1886 with the inclusion of literacy and property requirements for male suffrage, a legislative move that disenfranchised most men in the country, especially those a generation or two removed from slavery. This Regeneración period (1886–1903) also marked the end of federalist autonomy and saw a rise in violent action against mostly Black popular (nonelite) sectors throughout Colombia.[18]

Despite this pushback, educated Black men, who formed part of a professional elite, remained active in the Liberal Party in Panama and, through a focus on clientelist politics, encouraged continued popular support of the party. Their goals included achieving independence from Colombia. Fear of a Haiti-like revolution in Panama, a fear shared by other Eurocentric elites in various parts of the nineteenth-century Americas, likely suppressed active support for a Black-led independence effort.[19] The province's white oligarchy, along with a few educated Black leaders, retained political and cultural power after 1885. They capitalized on the region's unique geography as a commercial transit zone to reassert control away from the centralized Colombian government. These men formed a long tradition among local elites who viewed the isthmus as their own "commercial imperium," a space where their "utopic imaginary" of a homogenous and civilized nation with ongoing links to Europe and the United States could materialize. French and eventual US attempts to build a canal, beginning in 1881 and 1904, respectively, were thus welcomed, as was the recruitment of workers, given the enormity of the project.[20]

In time, though, a disjuncture grew between the desire for a canal and concerns about the proper cultural and racial identity of the isthmus. By the 1880s, as large numbers of Afro-Caribbeans were recruited for the French canal building effort, commentary about Panama becoming a "new Jamaica" and epithets like "chombo" (undesirable Black foreigner) appeared in isthmian dailies.[21] This pejorative term would continue to inform anti-Black and xenophobic policies and prejudices into the twentieth century. Afro-Caribbean migrants also faced pervasive ill treatment at the hands of Colombian officials on the isthmus. This treatment included police and judicial misconduct targeting them as "foreigners," which resulted in violent assaults, false arrests, exorbitant fines, and prolonged jail sentences.[22] These attacks came at a time when Black people on the isthmus, regardless of place of birth, faced greater economic and political limitations. This antagonism, which played out throughout the nineteenth and much of the twentieth century, informed how elites, whether white or of color, engaged with groups they defined as outsiders to the nation. Following independence from Colombia in 1903 and the signing of the Hay-Bunau-Varilla Treaty, which granted the United States the right to build the canal and control the ten-mile-wide area surrounding it, concern over Afro-Caribbean migrants, who constituted the majority of the construction workforce, grew in intensity. This intensity led local elites to define Panama as neither a "new United States" nor a "new Jamaica" but as a quintessentially Iberian nation in culture and racial composition.

One way to drive this agenda included restricting the number of Black people in high-ranking political offices. The removal of Carlos A. Mendoza after less than a year into his presidency exemplified this agenda. Mendoza was a member of the Liberal Party and one of the writers of the 1903 Declaration of Independence from Colombia. He assumed the presidency in 1910, following the deaths of President José Domingo de Obaldía and first alternate José Agustín Arango. Those opposed to Mendoza appealed directly to Washington for intervention, citing Mendoza's African ancestry in their complaints. Given that Mendoza had opposed Article 136 of the 1904 Panamanian Constitution, which allowed for US intervention in Panama for the protection of the canal (an amendment that passed), US officials backed Mendoza's opponents. In October 1910, the Panamanian National Assembly voted Mendoza out of office, and thus ended the longest tenure of an African descendant president in Panama.[23]

Government campaigns to forge closer cultural ties with Spain also helped to facilitate the growing depiction of Panama as an Iberian or a Hispanic nation. These campaigns also sought to diminish all cultural and imperial connections to Colombia and the United States, an important mandate for a new nation whose very independence remained a topic of debate throughout the hemisphere. During the first two decades of the republic, government buildings were constructed in a neoclassical style, modeling those found on the Iberian Peninsula. Elites in Panamá copied this architecture. In 1913 President Belisario Porras approached Spanish King Alfonso XIII with the hope of building a statue of Vasco Núñez de Balboa, the first Spaniard to colonize the isthmus and the man whose name decorated Panama's currency starting in 1904. Porras hoped that Balboa's statue would rival the Statue of Liberty in New York in both size and symbolic resonance. Ten years later, with aid from the Spanish monarchy and select municipalities in Spain, a much smaller version of the statue was finally erected. This did not stop the frenzy to incorporate and embrace all things Spanish, from the construction of a bronze statue of Miguel Cervantes to a young cadre of writers, many financed by the government, linking places like Panamá Viejo to Spanish colonialism and pursuing advanced studies in Spain.[24] This version of the republic had no room for any African ancestry, Afro-diasporic experiences, or languages other than Spanish. Even the country's vast Indigenous populations found little room in this imagined narrative of the nation.

The celebration of mestizaje as embraced in other Latin American nations did not arise in Panama until the 1930s. Still, it shared two key similarities with earlier twentieth-century developments of this ideology: The first was a heavy reliance on notions of Spanish nobility, Catholic divine right, and a spirit of adventure. Vasco Núñez de Balboa emerged as such a figure in the Panamanian context. The second was a focus on sexual unions between Spanish conquistadores and Indigenous women. The myth of a Spanish-Indigenous romance that led to the creation of a mixed-race Hispanic people (who apparently grew whiter with each generation) typified the Panamanian elite's approach to racial improvement via mestizaje. The total exclusion of Black people from this supposed mixing, as argued by Gerardo Maloney, further supported the discourse of a whitened mestizaje.[25]

This did not mean that all those who used or came under the category of mestizo promoted mestizaje as *blanqueamiento*, that is, mestizaje as the ultimate whitening of the Panamanian population. In this regard I avoid a "blanket conceit of blancophilia," or the glorification of whiteness, when discussing race and racism in Panama.[26] What I suggest instead is that the power of mestizaje as blanqueamiento rested in its normalization. Too many Panamanians readily embraced a category that excluded Indigenous and African descendant life. Instead mestizaje was always connected to white European (Iberian/Hispanic) ancestry, a negation of Blackness, and a mythologizing of an Indigenous past. This type of mestizaje became the desired outcome of cross-racial sexual relations and came to epitomize *panameñidad*, or a Panamanian essence.

Eugenics ideologies focused on white superiority, and the need to improve the populations of the "tropics" also shaped this approach to mestizaje. Panama could not become Spain, but through rigorous public hygiene campaigns, particularly in Colón and Panamá, as well as through the recruitment of white Europeans, the republic could attempt a *mejoramiento de la raza*. Panamanian elites, through their focus on hygiene, found ideological allies in US Zone officials equally obsessed with using science and architecture to "conquer the tropics." In tandem with these hygiene campaigns, a bourgeoning *ruralismo* movement focused on the country's white and mestizo interior in Azuero and Chiriquí as the cultural bedrock of the country in contrast to the "foreign coastal cities" tainted by an imported Blackness.[27] As I argue throughout the book, panameñidad and its iterations, which included "defending the Latin race," "upholding true Panamanians," "*panameñismo*," and "*ser panameño*," overtly or covertly reinforced the rhetoric of an Iberian-centered mestizaje predicated on cultural hierarchies and anti-Blackness.

Demarcating Race, Space, and Opportunity through and against the Canal Zone

Another factor shaping discussions of Panamanian national identity in the first decades of the twentieth century was the presence of the United States on the isthmus. In addition to financing the building of the Panama Canal and controlling the Canal Zone area, US officials adopted their own system of governance in the zone and excluded Panamanians from this process. The Canal Zone developed its own system of courts, a police force, commissaries (for food and basic goods), and schooling and recreational departments that made the area a self-sustained space. In no other independent country in the hemisphere did the United States enjoy such complete sovereignty. Although the canal and the zone were in Panamanian territory, the 1903 treaty, as interpreted and executed by US officials, provided the United States with complete control of this area. The treaty also outlined the annuities Panama would receive for the operation of the canal and affirmed the right of US intervention into Panamanian territory for the purposes of protecting the canal. A version of this clause, Article 136, also appeared in Panama's first constitution. Because the canal became the major waterway for transit and commerce on the isthmus, this doubled Panamanian dependency on the canal and the zone area.[28]

US officials also set about making the Canal Zone an extension of the United States, culturally and racially, upholding Jim Crow segregationist policies there. According to these policies, which were cemented by the end of canal construction, whites and workers of color were separated in terms of jobs, housing, schooling, and recreation. Race and citizenship also determined salaries. The "gold and silver rolls" system in the zone paid US citizens on par with jobs in the United States (the gold roll) and based non-US citizen salaries on those in the Caribbean basin (the silver roll). Under these criteria, a "gold" worker earned four times as much as a "silver" worker. Given that most Canal Zone "silver" workers were Afro-Caribbean migrants, the gold-silver system resulted in white US citizens earning much higher wages than Black non-US citizens.[29]

These hierarchies in the Canal Zone held significance, given that Afro-Caribbeans and their descendants represented more than 50 percent of the population in the zone by the 1920s and would constitute the bulk of the canal and zone workforce throughout the twentieth century.[30] For this reason, privileging US citizenship, recruiting white workers from the mainland United States, and creating schooling and recreational outlets that trained white US citizens born or raised in the zone (Zonians) how to be American grew in importance.[31] This also explained why US citizenship was never extended to the children of Afro-Caribbean workers born in the zone. In US officials' efforts to maintain a white US citizenship stronghold in the zone, they also limited the recruitment of African American workers.[32] By segregating the largest group of workers in the area into the silver roll and by limiting most gold roll jobs to US citizens, US officials helped feed into the narrative that Afro-Caribbeans had special access to canal jobs and were the cause of lower wages. This rhetoric effectively removed any burden from US officials and instead presented Afro-Caribbeans as complicit in an imperialist project that subsumed Panamanians into the silver/nonwhite category, further "blackening" the Panamanian nation.

Also crucial in the development of this socioeconomic status quo was the creation of racially segregated towns within the Canal Zone. Seven gold (whites-only) towns, three on each the Pacific and Atlantic sides of the isthmus, and one at the midpoint of the zone, were erected. The largest such town was Balboa, on the Pacific side, which was also the central command post for the zone administration. The naming of the largest whites-only town as Balboa connected white US citizens and white Panamanian elites invested in the myth of Balboa, one that further supported their respective claims to the isthmus, one as an Iberian mestizo nation and the other as a conquering US empire. Five silver (nonwhite) towns were likewise constructed, three on the Pacific side and two on the Atlantic side.[33] La Boca, on the Pacific side of the isthmus, was the most populous of these. Chapters 2 and 3 expand on how La Boca became an important site for some of the educational and labor activism that emerged among Afro-Caribbean Panamanians in the 1930s and into the 1950s.

An almost total exclusion of Panamanians from whites-only zone areas, save for a few white elites, and frustration with US control over the isthmian transit economy also propelled critiques about the reach of the United States into Panamanian affairs. One issue that drew the ire of an increasingly vocal mestizo middle class, which unlike the white elite had no access to the nation's political machinery, involved the presence of Afro-Caribbeans in the republic's two major cities, Panamá and Colón. Recruiting Afro-Caribbeans to build the canal, they insisted, had been unfortunate but necessary. Having to share the same spaces, especially in the nation's capital, with this group was unacceptable. Disrupting the growth of these communities became the goal of those opposed to US influence on the isthmus and the oligarchy that in their estimation had facilitated the country's dependence on US empire.

One group that emerged at the forefront of this agenda was Acción Comunal (Community Action). Created in 1923 by a cadre of young white and mestizo professionals, including graduates of the Instituto Nacional de Panamá, the nation's premier private secondary school, Acción Comunal combined the Iberian-focused enthusiasm of white elites with an added push to define Panama against foreign peoples and cultures. The group called for teaching children to love their country and flag, upholding the Spanish language as the country's sole language, and popularizing the use of balboas (rather than US dollars, although the balboa remained tied to the US dollar). They also addressed what they saw as the country's growing race problem, typified in the foreign populations of Colón and Panamá, by boycotting any stores or establishments that advertised in English or did not employ Panamanians. The membership of Acción Comunal remained small into the late 1920s, but the group went on to lead the nation's first ever political coup in 1931. Several Acción Comunal members also, by the early 1930s, secured high government positions, including the presidency. Arnulfo Arias, a white Panamanian and the leader of the 1931 coup, assumed the presidency in 1940 and led efforts to denationalize Afro-Caribbean Panamanians.[34] By the early 1920s, though, Acción Comunal signaled the beginning of an expanded antiforeigner and hypernationalist discourse that would focus on Afro-Caribbeans as the nation's most pressing problem.

The "West Indian Danger" in Prose and Law

In October 1926 the Panamanian National Assembly passed Law 13, which categorized "blacks from the Antilles or Guyanas whose original language was not Spanish" as "prohibited immigrants."[35] The law demonstrated the extent to which racist rhetoric targeting Afro-Caribbeans had found legitimacy in mid-1920s Panama. Manifestos such as Olmedo Alfaro's *El peligro antillano en la América Central: La defensa de la raza* (The West Indian danger in Central America: The defense of the race), published two years earlier by Panama's official national press, further attested to this legitimacy.[36] *El peligro antillano* mapped out three potent strains of anti–West Indian discourse, all couched in eugenicist language, which would be regurgitated in defense of Law 13 and similarly framed laws. These strains included assertions that the "problem" with Afro-Caribbeans was cultural and not racial, that members of this group posed an unfair economic competition against honest Panamanian workers, and that Afro-Caribbeans embodied an undesirable and inferior type of Blackness.

According to the cultural incompatibility argument, because Afro-Caribbeans spoke English and practiced Protestantism, customs diametrically opposed to Castilian Spanish and the Catholic faith that characterized Panamanian and Iberian American tradition in general, these migrants and their offspring could never become authentic Panamanians.[37] For hypernationalists, proper patriotism required the shunning of "foreign elements." Yet, this shunning did not include white US citizens or white migrants from Europe. A glorification of whiteness united their assessments of these groups and trumped any presumed cultural incompatibility. This distorted patriotism refused to acknowledge that multilingualism and religious diversity were not alien to Panama but part of an ongoing, if criticized, reality. The decision to target Afro-Caribbeans on the basis of cultural incompatibility spoke more to fears of a whitened mestizo nation that might never be and less to what these cultural practices meant regarding Panamanian identity.

Another critique claimed that unfair economic competition by Afro-Caribbeans resulted in the displacement of Panamanian workers and that the Panamanian government, fearful of upsetting imperial interests, refused to repatriate these workers.[38] By the 1920s the Panama Canal was the largest employer in Panamá and Colón, and Afro-Caribbeans represented the bulk of this workforce. Yet, they did not set the terms for recruitment or compensation in this space. The US government, as noted by Michael Conniff, used a third-country labor structure, which underpaid migrant workers to reduce compensation for Panamanian workers while maintaining steady salaries for US citizens.[39] This created a highly discriminatory wage structure that benefited only those earning US-based wages, while allowing canal officials to cut costs. Alfaro and other cultural nationalists had reasons for their critiques. But rather than envision a working-class struggle that would unite Afro-Caribbeans and others seeking wage equality, perhaps using the experience of Afro-Caribbeans as strike organizers, they demonized Afro-Caribbeans as sinister economic competitors. Such hostility was not limited to an intellectual elite. Even the labor organizations that emerged in the 1920s focused on Afro-Caribbeans as the enemy or ignored their existence entirely.[40]

The last strain of this mid-1920s anti–West Indian discourse, the supposed incompatibility and undesirability of a certain type of Blackness, served a dual purpose—to deflect possible accusations of racism and to present a narrative of acceptable African ancestry within an Iberian American mestizo imaginary. Rooted in this narrative was the myth of "kind" Spanish slave masters, who unlike their British and American counterparts imparted proper morals and values, via Catholicism, to their enslaved populations. For this reason, Black Panamanians from the colonial era adhered to the Catholic religion and were morally superior to Afro-Caribbeans. The number of Afro-Caribbeans in the republic's jails, hospitals, and madhouses purportedly proved this ranking.[41] This maligning of Afro-Caribbeans as criminals and deviants had roots in the nineteenth century and by the early twentieth century merged with racist views that they formed impediments to Panamanian modernity. Their failure or inability to "assimilate," via language, mannerism, or clientelist politics, as other African descendants had, provoked consternation. This pattern of pitting Black people of Caribbean ancestry (Afro-antillanos) and Black people with roots from the Spanish colonial era (Afro-coloniales) against one another, would continue throughout the twentieth century, with Black men replacing white men as key propagators of this message. This dichotomy threatened the idea of diasporic world making by dismissing the possibility of commonalities between Black people across nation-state borders or ethnic lines.

Texts such as *El peligro antillano* succeeded in presenting Afro-Caribbeans as the cultural, economic, racial, and social enemies of the Panamanian nation, a theme that Panamanian legislators found useful. Law 13 of 1926 for the first time listed Afro-Caribbeans as "prohibited immigrants," a status subjecting this group to additional surveillance, regulation, and removal. By specifying that only non-Spanish-speaking Black people would be excluded, the National Assembly upheld the mantras of cultural incompatibility and foreign Blackness. Addressing the "West Indian problem" was hence not about racism but about culture. Not all Black people would be excluded, only those whose ethnicity and social practices proved incompatible. Space could be made for Spanish-speaking Black migrants, but their numbers were so few that legislators did not need address the issue. With Law 13, Afro-Caribbeans, the largest migrant group in the country, joined Chinese, Syrian, and Turkish migrants, who since the earliest years of the republic had also been placed in this category.[42] Added to this group were Japanese and South Asian migrants. The law imposed a fine of $500 balboas/US dollars, an exorbitant amount for the time, or one year of forced labor to "prohibited immigrants" caught reentering the country.[43] While racist and xenophobic immigration laws were not new in the 1920s, what stood out about this moment was the ability to coalesce all these laws in ways that benefited the dream of a whitened mestizo nation, to which Afro-Caribbeans were the most pressing obstacle.

Panamanian officials were not alone in their targeting of migrants. By 1926, Costa Rica, Honduras, El Salvador, Guatemala, Canada, and Venezuela also excluded various immigrants. The passage of anti–West Indian, anti-African, and anti-Asian legislation throughout Central America and parts of South and North America responded to exclusionist immigration policies buttressed by the internationalization of the eugenics movement throughout the hemisphere.[44] As noted by Lara Putnam, through the passage of exclusionist legislation, Latin American nations sought to cement their role as "collaborators in rather than targets of [a] U.S.-led project of eugenic exclusion."[45] A focus on Afro-Caribbeans as a unique Latin American problem, in addition to Asians and Africans as a shared hemispheric problem, affirmed this collaboration. The bureaucratization of travel through passports, visas, and quota systems allowed governments to regimentalize eugenics-inspired policies in the name of "protecting national interests."[46]

Implementation of Law 13 proved difficult given the dependence on Afro-Caribbean laborers by the United Fruit Company (in Bocas del Toro) and complaints by business owners and renters in Panamá and Colón.[47] This clash between business interests and immigration policies would not be unique to Panama. Cuba, Costa Rica, and the Dominican Republic, all countries with business sectors largely dependent on US capital, sought to appease both hypernationalists and capitalists during the early decades of the twentieth century.[48] In the case of Panama, the assembly passed Law 15, which allowed the immigration of "prohibited immigrants" for select agricultural and industrial work as long as qualified workers could not be found in the republic. Because of US-controlled immigration in the Canal Zone, the recruitment of workers to this area was never questioned. This particular feature of immigration policy distinguished Panama from its Central American and Caribbean neighbors. Law 15 also demanded that all industries operating in the republic gradually begin to replace most foreign workers with Panamanian workers, with the goal of a 75 percent Panamanian workforce in all industries by 1932. Enforcement proved challenging, but overall Law 15 responded to the demands raised by Acción Comunal members and proponents of an "Iberian-American mestizo Panama" regarding the need to retake the Panamanian economy.[49]

Not long after the passage of Law 15, the assembly passed Law 16, which clarified that "prohibited immigrants" included those born in or naturalized in countries other than those of "their origin."[50] *Origin* here demarcated a perpetual racialized "other" incapable of belonging to the Panamanian family. Such a focus on origin held parallels to what Mai Ngai, in her study of US immigration policy, termed the creation of "impossible subjects," that is, the use of hereditarianism to exclude nonwhites as immigrants and full citizens.[51] In the specific case of Panama, this thinking motivated legislators to denationalize birth-based citizens as a means of policing the descendants of "undesirable" immigrants.

The existence of such a policy in Panama drove the urgency of continued diasporic world making among Afro-Caribbeans. In no other part of the Americas did Afro-Caribbean descendants find themselves both stateless and vital participants in nation-building processes. In and through the isthmus, they constructed new cultural, intellectual, and political formations that highlighted the intertwined nature of national, imperial, and diasporic frameworks. By centering Black life and possibilities around these frameworks, Afro-Caribbean Panamanians challenged geopolitical debates that presented African descendants as racialized others merely at the service of imperial and national structures.

Why Afro-Caribbean Diasporic World Making?

In examining competing claims to Panama alongside questions of diasporic world making, *Panama in Black* acknowledges the reach of the nation-state in the twentieth century, while recognizing how factors such as migration and diasporic possibilities routinely pushed the boundaries of this construct. Scholars of intra-Caribbean migration and migration to Central America in the first half of the twentieth century have noted the discrimination and exclusion migrants to Spanish-speaking republics faced. These scholars have pointed to continuous attempts by migrants to peacefully coexist or increasingly assimilate into their new national realities, often with mixed results.[52] This work pushes the scholarship further by eschewing the idea of a fixed national model in which Black migrants and those born in these republics either fought against or sought integration. Instead these men and women created many of the key components of what we assume to be "Costa Rican," "Panamanian," "Cuban," or "Dominican" nationality and culture. Their bodies, their words, and their ability to connect with people and places beyond the boundaries of the nation-state provided them with the very tools needed to map complex national belongings. The case of Panama is unique because early nation building, migration, and postmigration diaspora networks all happened simultaneously. This reality made attempts to exclude Afro-Caribbean descendants both difficult but also especially appealing.

Indeed, Panama was a multilingual Afro-Caribbean nation even as proponents championed the isthmus as the heart of an Iberian-centric mestizo America. State officials could be punitive and exclusionary, and these actions did affect the day-to-day experiences of individuals. But officials could not completely eliminate the knowledge about the world and community that migration and diasporic networking made possible. Afro-Caribbean Panamanians knew about educational, labor, organizational, cultural, and economic ventures bringing together Black people in every part of the world. They drew inspiration from these ventures and founded their own newspapers, became trailblazing educators, and championed international labor organizing. They also demanded equality through civic associations, chastised state officials for failing at their duties, and made themselves indispensable in transnational and diplomatic conversations regarding the future of the Panamanian nation.

History, in other words, did not merely happen to Afro-Caribbean Panamanians. Their actions, silences, aspirations, and personal and professional losses shaped their responses to a plethora of unjust and discriminatory policies intended to strip them of their personhood and communal ambitions. Afro-Caribbean Panamanians knew that they were not alone in the world, even as governmental officials sought to police their presence; segregate them on the basis of race, ancestry, and nationality; and eventually strip them of citizenship rights to cement this message of exceptionality and exclusion.

So as not to entrench this discourse of exclusion, *Panama in Black* pays heed to Michel-Rolph Trouillot's affirmation that "in history, power begins at the source."[53] Thus, the records produced by Afro-Caribbean Panamanian journalists, teachers, lawyers, labor union leaders, and community organizers, not the writings or policy proposals of elected officials and financiers, receive central attention in this study. This is not to say that presidents, ambassadors, police and military officials, and business magnates from both Panama and the United States are not important players in this study. They are, but I mainly focus on how their actions or inactions coincide with the larger story of Afro-Caribbean diasporic world making. As such, writings from the Black press, yearbooks, petitions, radio addresses, and event programs receive as much attention as government decrees, presidential speeches, and the writings found in elite-owned national newspapers. *Panama in Black* is grounded in the assertion that if we are to take the making of an

Afro-Caribbean diasporic world seriously, we must begin with the full understanding of Afro-Caribbean descendants as producers of knowledge. Anything short of this enterprise risks the danger of superficially engaging with Black populations, whereby African diaspora histories are used as a complement or add-on to "existing historical traditions."[54]

In looking to teachers, journalists, community organizers, and other professional advocates, I also recognize that this discussion of knowledge production privileges the work of an emergent middle class. While this emergent class proved vital, working-class realities also informed this knowledge production. Most people from this community were the first in their families to obtain an elementary or secondary education, to practice a trade, to start their own business, to have steady income to support others, and to enjoy travel not bound to contract labor. These realities were only possible because of siblings, parents, grandparents, and adopted relatives who took on backbreaking labor and who sacrificed their time and sometimes their very lives. Women especially took on continuous care work, deferring their own needs for future generations. The recognition of this sacrifice shaped the worldview of the activists in this study. They understood that they owed a great debt to those who came before them. A 1960s Brooklyn organization, for example, would take on the title of Las Servidoras, or "those who serve," harkening back to an Afro-Caribbean newspaper founded in 1928 Panamá whose mantra was "service to the community." This work of service did not supplant the fact that poor and working-class Afro-Caribbeans had their own understandings of community sacrifice and spoke out against elitist postulations of diasporic world making.

Attention to the gendered nature of these class and generational demarcations is also an important part of this study. Afro-Caribbean women, unlike their male counterparts, had fewer opportunities to attain postelementary education, to travel on their own terms, and to eschew familial obligations. They likewise had to contend with universalized patriarchal standards that called on women to be subservient even as their labor within and outside the home allowed for the family's and community's overall class mobility. As noted by Black feminist scholars, Black women in the Americas continuously encountered demands to choose one nexus of oppression and identity or face relegation into silence. To produce knowledge, women had to challenge this hierarchization of oppression and identity, a process that proved daunting though not impossible.[55] Understanding these class tensions, gendered hierarchies, and generational expectations is crucial to a full assessment of how Afro-Caribbean Panamanians emerged as producers of knowledge.

Through this focus on Afro-Caribbean Panamanians as knowledge producers and world makers, I join scholars of African diaspora studies and Black internationalism who have called for greater studies placing the thoughts, words, and actions of globally minded African descendants at the center of our scholarly inquiry. Their findings hold especial cogency regarding transformation and mobility in African diaspora histories, the gendered nature of diaspora creation, and the importance of the print medium and bilingualism in the development of Black internationalist culture.[56] My attention to local internationalism foregrounds knowledge production at a local level as a necessary first step in understanding diasporic world making. What Afro-Caribbean Panamanians created in Colón, La Boca, and Brooklyn was site specific yet deeply informed by a knowledge of Black life AROUND THE WORLD.

Through an intentional Afro-Caribbean diasporic framework that begins in the Global South, in Panama, and examines diasporic links nurtured therein that emanated to other parts of the Americas, I expand on the hemispheric approach of scholars of Black transnationalism, Afro Latin American studies, and Afrolatinidades.[57] I also build on the work of Black scholars in Panama, who starting in the 1970s focused on highlighting the histories of Afro-Caribbeans within and outside the isthmus.[58] *Panama in Black* also acknowledges the unavoidable reality of US empire in Afro-Caribbean world making, and the extent to which working with or against US empire complicated attempts at Black internationalist solidarities. As chapter 5 explores, US citizenship in the hands of migrants also held the potential for other forms of Afro-diasporic solidarity.

Why Panama and the United States?

A close engagement with the diasporic world making undertaken by Afro-Caribbean Panamanians requires addressing US-Panamanian relations, in addition to exploring the history of Caribbean migration in both spaces. Scholarship on US-Panamanian relations has tended to focus either on Afro-Caribbean Panamanians as discreet communities or on geopolitical dynamics and power structures, but rarely both.[59] *Panama in Black* takes a closer look at the public intellectual and activist work of Afro-Caribbean Panamanians, asserting that these men and women were not simply bystanders or occasional subversives to imperial, neocolonial, and national policies but rather, active observers and participants in the making or supplanting of these policies.

Afro-Caribbean Panamanians stood at the forefront of developing, editing, and popularizing proposals later embraced by Panamanian and US officials, which made them crucial to nation building and imperial processes and also hypervisible during antiforeigner and anti-Black campaigns. Chapters 1 through 3 offer examples of these proposals, which included promoting English-language and bilingual English-Spanish language training, as well as fighting for worker equality in the Canal Zone. While their diasporic positionality made Afro-Caribbean Panamanians appealing ambassadors, they routinely had to contend with a long history of anti-Black exclusionist nationalism that continued to dominate daily life in the Americas. To these exclusions, they brought a unique brand of world making, one that drew from a long history of migration, community building, and activism.

Similarities in Caribbean migration patterns also connects Afro-Caribbean descendant experiences in twentieth-century Panama and the United States. In this introduction I have noted how Afro-Caribbean Panamanians forever transformed the Panamanian geographic, political, and cultural landscape in both the republic and the Canal Zone. Caribbean migrants and their descendants also led major civic, legislative, labor, and human rights campaigns in the twentieth-century United States. It is not surprising, then, that Afro-Caribbean Panamanians would look to spaces like Brooklyn to further their campaigns for a more inclusive vision of diasporic belonging in Panama and the United States. Indeed, migrants from Jamaica and Barbados, along with those from Haiti, Puerto Rico, and the Dominican Republic that formed part of mid-twentieth-century New York, proved crucial in leading and supporting Black solidarity and civil rights campaigns there.[60]

No history of Caribbean or Afro-Latinx New York is complete without an understanding of how Afro-Caribbean Panamanians, with their direct experiences of US imperialism, bilingualism, and multiple migration histories, brought together disparate regional, diasporic, and national histories. From the individual pursuit of studies in the United States, to speaking on behalf of the Panamanian nation on a Brooklyn radio station, to creating organizations within the United States to support Black youth of migrant and nonmigrant backgrounds, Afro-Caribbean Panamanians connected New York spaces to the Panamanian isthmus and the broader Caribbean world.

Rather than Afro-Caribbean Panamanians being just another migrant wave to the United States that added Black diasporic consciousness, their experiences reveal a unique migratory and colonial history. This study is less about the geographic boundaries of Panama and the United States, and more about how Afro-Caribbean Panamanians created, in the words of Katherine McKittrick, "alternative geographic formulations," which challenged discourses of erasure and displacement.[61] That they advanced these formulations with and without the protections of state-specific citizenship rights further adds to the complexity of their activist experiences.

Chapter Overview

I have divided the book into five chapters, each building around a particular moment, event, or policy that proved vital to the development of diasporic world making among Afro-Caribbean Panamanians. Chapter 1 explores debates over the meaning and ownership of Panama as revealed among Afro-Caribbean Panamanian newspaper publishers, journalists, and members of the reading public from the late 1920s to the late 1930s. In this chapter I focus on specific articulations of diaspora possibilities and their connections to ongoing attempts to define Panama. The creation of the *Panama Tribune*, an English-language newsweekly operated by Afro-Caribbean Panamanians, opens my discussion. This chapter provides the first ever detailed examination of the *Tribune*'s work and fills a crucial gap left by those studies that have ignored it as a key site of diasporic world making.[62] Through a review of editorials, letters to the editor, and reports on local and international policies targeting Black people, I demonstrate how the paper offered a key space in which to discuss community achievements and concerns, especially as an anti–West Indian discourse intensified on the isthmus. The *Tribune*, overall, positioned itself as, of, and from Panama, though through its coverage; it connected the isthmus and its diasporic formations with the global experiences of people of color.

The second chapter focuses on the use of citizenship policies and ideologies, by and against Afro-Caribbean Panamanians during the 1940s, as official and popular debates about who could claim Panamanian nationality grew in intensity. The chapter examines the rise of an Afro-Caribbean Panamanian activist core of lawyers, journalists, teachers, and aspiring politicians focused on challenging constitutional changes denationalizing Afro-Caribbean descendants, while also condemning segregationist policies in the Canal Zone. A wide array of neglected sources—letters, petitions, records from civic organizations, proposals initiated by teachers in the zone colored schools, and reports by labor leaders—reveal the breadth of the coalition against denationalization and segregation. Combined, these sources highlight the connected nature of activism in the republic and the

Canal Zone, as well as the bourgeoning tensions between nationalist and diasporic approaches. Uniting nationalist and diasporic approaches was a shared understanding of the isthmus as home, a recognition of the dangers of anti-Black rhetoric, and a desire for more inclusive visions of citizenship.

Chapter 3 connects mid-twentieth-century debates on communism, democracy, and hemispheric diplomacy to discussions of state-specific and internationalist understandings of home and belonging. Afro-Caribbean Panamanians who took on positions as national and international leaders in the 1950s strove to present Panama both as a partner in the fight to protect democracy and as a modern nation deserving of equal treatment from the United States. In this moment, community and labor leaders coalesced along an anti-imperialist discourse that focused on US inequities within and beyond the Canal Zone, and the potentials of a growing Panamanian nation. The policing of Afro-Caribbean Panamanians on the grounds of their alleged lack of assimilation and patriotism nonetheless continued. This policing belied a racist and exclusionist notion of nationalism predicated on Afro-Caribbean Panamanians being asked to renounce diasporic experiences, even as their membership in the nation faced constant scrutiny. Such stances negated activist agendas by this community anchored around establishing pluralistic understandings of identity, home, and belonging.

The book's fourth chapter further dissects the building of activist networks in 1950s Panama through campaigns for labor and citizenship justice against an exclusionist government hostile to Afro-Caribbean Panamanians in the Canal Zone. Government officials and nationalist newspapers questioned the patriotism of Afro-Caribbean Panamanians, who complained about the implementation of the Remón-Eisenhower Treaty and resisted the attempts to erase their activism in the struggle for labor and citizenship rights. In these hypernationalist narratives, Afro-Caribbeans living and working in the zone typified ungratefulness, dangers to a homogenous nation, and a lack of patriotic ethos. Afro-Caribbean Panamanians rejected calls for selfless sacrifice on behalf of the nation. The end to discriminatory citizenship laws at this point came too late for those unwilling or uninterested in "proving" their merit as Panamanians. They sought opportunities outside the isthmus to create their own forms of citizenship and belonging.

Chapter 5 follows Afro-Caribbean Panamanians who opted to leave Panama during the 1940s and 1950s and connects their migration to another phase of diasporic world making. These migrants' agency challenged attempts to rewrite and sanitize histories of activism and diasporic possibilities within the isthmus. This final chapter returns to many of the questions that shape the book's first chapter: What does it mean to create diaspora? How does the label of *outsider* affect the ability to create and sustain community? And what is at stake in defining a particular space as the center of an Afro-Caribbean diasporic world? Unlike previous chapters, this final one closely follows select people to resituate conversations about diasporic possibilities with the intricacies of their day-to-day lives. Afro-Caribbean Panamanian women who created Las Servidoras, a scholarship-granting organization, in 1950s Brooklyn are at the core of the chapter. In New York, Las Servidoras connected with other members of the diaspora engaged in activist struggle. By taking on a leadership position, they also pushed against stereotypes of who had the capacity to lead, move, and become active global citizens.

The book ends by exploring the proceedings of the First US Conference of Panamanians, held in 1974 in the Poconos in Pennsylvania. The conference brought together several US-based organizations created by Panamanian migrants with the goal of exploring how Panamanians living abroad could continue engagement in political, economic, and social happenings on the isthmus. The conference, like the work of Las Servidoras, connected places like New York and Panama, but more so than Las Servidoras, it sought to capitalize on the professionalization of Afro-Caribbean Panamanians and other Panamanians living in the United States to explore the role of these groups in the future of Panama. Conference organizers expanded the legacy of diasporic world making begun by the *Tribune*, embraced by select citizenship and labor rights advocates, and continued by Las Servidoras. The meeting, especially when compared with the agendas of local and hemispherically oriented Black organizations in Panama during the 1970s and beyond, pointed to a disjuncture between US-based and isthmian-based understandings of Afro-Caribbean world making. This disjuncture in turn posed new questions regarding ongoing claims to Panama and the potentials of Afro-diasporic alliances and opportunities across the Americas.

A Note on Terminology and Scope

In this introduction and throughout the book, I privilege the terms Afro-Caribbean and Afro-Caribbean Panamanian. The men and women whose lives shape the bulk of this book used terms like *Negroes, Panamanian, Isthmian, West Indian, British West Indian, Black Panamanian,* and *West Indian Panamanian* to describe themselves and other members of their community. These terms appear throughout the book, but most of my assessments and conclusions utilize the terms Afro-Caribbean and Afro-Caribbean

Panamanian. In doing so I move away from historiography that only reserves the term *Caribbean* for the Spanish-speaking islands, calling the remainder of the area "the West Indies." This term also affirms the centrality of African descendants to the history of these spaces. My use of the term Afro-Caribbean Panamanian does not encompass all people of African descent on the isthmus. The history of Blackness in Panama, Central America, and the circum-Caribbean includes complex ethnic, regional, linguistic, and migratory histories. Afro-Caribbean Panamanians form one aspect of this rich history of race and diasporic formation.

In engaging with Afro-Caribbean diasporic world making as a counter to exclusionist Iberian/Hispanicized depictions of Panama and US imperial claims to the isthmus, my study does not incorporate the worldviews of other groups and communities who challenged these exclusionist platforms. In choosing to focus on Afro-Caribbeans, my aim is not to dismiss these coexisting worldviews, but to highlight what can be learned from one specific approach to creating community within and across national and imperial boundaries.

Panama as Diaspora

Documenting Afro-Caribbean Panamanian Histories, 1928–1936

Writing in November 1928 as chief editor of the newly launched *Panama Tribune*, Sidney Young (figure 1.1) described the newsweekly's aim as providing a "service" to a fledging community. "We bring light," he wrote, "to help our struggling people find their way on the universal road to progress. This is the foundation rock on which we stand, on which we begin to build our superstructure of an able, influential and successful community newspaper."[1] Young's was a bold mandate, but as founding publisher and chief editor, he believed he could accomplish this mandate, particularly through the support of his staff and contributors. Young was also not new to leadership in the newspaper business. He had served as the chief editor of the West Indian section of the English-language daily the *Panama American* from 1926 to 1928. What made the *Tribune* unique was that it was wholly envisioned and staffed by Caribbean migrants who had made Panama home from the beginning of the century. These writers formed part of the first and second generation of Afro-Caribbean Panamanians—men and women either raised or born in Panama—who like their contemporaries sought to protect their communal rights while also keeping an eye on happenings in the broader African diaspora. The *Tribune* provided a voice for and chronicled the experiences of tens of thousands who viewed the isthmus as both home and a possible site for ongoing and future diasporic opportunities.

FIGURE I.I
Sidney A. Young,
1928. From Sidney
A. Young, ed.,
*Isthmian Echoes:
A Selection of the
Literary Endeavors
of the West Indian
Colony in the
Republic of Panama*
(Panama City:
Benedetti Hnos,
1928), i.

The Debut of the Panama Tribune

The inauguration of the *Panama Tribune* brought together years of journalistic efforts by Afro-Caribbean Panamanians desirous to articulate their
presence in and claims to the isthmus. *Isthmian Echoes*, a compilation edited
by Young, which appeared in the same year as the advent of the *Tribune*,
offers a preliminary mapping of these efforts. The compilation brought
together articles contributed to the West Indian section of the *Panama
American* during Young's tenure as the section's editor.[2] One such contribution, authored by Young in February 1926, addressed the very idea of
Afro-Caribbean Panamanian journalism. Did such a thing exist, he asked.
Young's answer was a cautious one and emphasized that the term *journalism*
would not apply "until we can have journals and periodicals of our own

that can compare favorably with those of the other local groups and not shoddy and disgusting apologies for news organs."[3] To him, a section within a newspaper and hastily put-together leaflets did not constitute journalism.

Prior to the creation of West Indian sections in English-language US-run dailies such as the *Panama American* and the *Star and Herald*, the news-weekly the *Workman*, inaugurated by Barbadian-born Hubert N. Walrond in 1916, had offered the most consistent coverage on the Afro-Caribbean community in Panama. By the late 1920s, partly as a result of increased competition from West Indian sections, the popularity of the paper had dwindled significantly. With the *Tribune*, Young and his collaborators proposed to continue with the work that had made these West Indian sections successful. Such work included a focus on the opinions of a growing Afro-Caribbean professional base with literacy rates that surpassed most others on the isthmus, excluding members of the oligarchy and white US Canal Zone residents (Zonians). In the provinces of Colón and Panamá, two areas in the republic with the largest Afro-Caribbean population, 72 percent and 71 percent of the population, respectively, had completed primary school education, compared with the national average of 40 percent.[4]

As an independent paper, the *Tribune* could offer the kind of isthmian and hemispheric attention to the issues connecting African descendants that a single section could not. These issues included the unrelenting presence of anti-Blackness and xenophobia, race-conscious activism and civic work, and debates over questions of assimilation, race or ethnic pride, colonial citizenship, and the parameters of republican citizenship. Operating a community newspaper also required adequate representation of communal needs, staffing from within the community, securing a readership base, and maintaining a careful balance between offering a space for ordinary working people to see themselves reflected on the page and using the newsweekly as a platform to demand and envision a more robust community.

Young's personal history, one he shared with fellow Afro-Caribbean journalists at the *Panama American*, also factored into his decision to start the *Tribune*. Young was born in Jamaica in 1898 and migrated to Panama with his family in 1906. He obtained his elementary and secondary schooling in Kingston, Jamaica. In his eventual editorial pieces for the *Tribune*, Young spoke with pride of the intellectual opportunities in the Anglophone Caribbean. He noted the members of the Panamanian upper class who had benefited from this training.[5] In the early 1920s, Young, like his eventual fellow collaborators, was looking for his big break. It arrived in 1924 when he became assistant manager of the *Central American News*, a US-operated news outlet in Panamá. A year later he joined the *Panama Star and Herald* as a reporter and soon became the cable editor for the *Panama American*. It was there that he pitched the idea of creating a West Indian section and then served as its editor until 1928.[6] Young left the *Panama American* in protest over the unequal pay he received compared to his white peers.[7]

Like the other journalists he attracted to the *Panama American*'s West Indian section, Young was eager to offer an alternative voice to the apathy and discrimination found in the white US-dominated English-language press. Opposing the growing anti-Black and anti-immigrant coverage in the Spanish-language dailies, mostly owned by white Panamanians, also formed part of Young's agenda. The rise of discriminatory immigration policies in Panama further added to the urgency of his mission. By 1926 the Panamanian National Assembly had passed laws excluding or restricting migrants from Asia, the non-Spanish-speaking Caribbean, and the Middle East. In October 1928, the assembly voted to change Article 6 of the Panamanian Constitution, which pertained to citizenship. All those with foreign-born parents would have to petition for their citizenship a year after their twenty-first birthday. They would also have to prove that they had lived in the country continuously for the previous six years.[8] Failure to acquire this certification would deny applicants Panamanian nationality cards (*cédulas de nacionalidad*), which made gaining employment or a passport impossible.

This change in birth-based citizenship, like the 1927 immigration policy discussed in the introduction, excluded "prohibited immigrants" on the basis of "origin" notwithstanding their place of birth or naturalization. It corresponded with a growing idea of "foreign status" being "in the blood" that is, biologically determined, and inherited. The new 1928 petitioning process created a dangerous precedent for future policing of citizenship acquisition. As the largest migrant descendant group in the republic, Afro-Caribbean Panamanians worried about their access to national citizenship and their ability to move in the world with other people of color seeking equality. This petition process was only the beginning of punitive policies related to birth-based citizenship.

Young published *Isthmian Echoes*, a collection of writings by Afro-Caribbean Panamanian journalists, and shortly thereafter inaugurated the *Panama Tribune* in the shadow of these shifting geopolitical tides. Young dedicated his *Isthmian Echoes* volume to "the unity, welfare and progress of the West Indian community in the Republic of Panama and the advancement of colored people throughout the world."[9] Articles in the collection focused on problems of insularity among Caribbean migrants, the increase in discriminatory immigration legislation in Panama and other Central America states, and the dearth of educational and business opportunities for children of color on the isthmus. Most of the writers commenting on the future of the Afro-Caribbean diaspora in Panama were men. Some even took it on themselves to speak on behalf of the women in the community, mainly to bemoan the latter's moral degradation.[10]

For writers like Linda Smart Chubb, one of the five women who contributed to *Isthmian Echoes*, the problem of inequality facing Afro-Caribbeans in Panama went beyond questions of moral propriety, uniting as a group, or remaining in Panama. Smart Chubb, a feminist and an active member of Colón social and civic circles, challenged her peers to consider the multiple exclusions facing Afro-Caribbean women.[11] Women throughout much of the Caribbean did not have the right to vote or run for political office, and male leaders in the community accepted this reality.[12] "Must women always be content to express their views through proxies," Smart Chubb asked her peers. "Why should they not, if they are qualified and are willing, exercise their civil rights in their own person."[13] She understood progress in a way that escaped many of her male counterparts.

Smart Chubb's contributions raised the important question of how an Afro-Caribbean Panamanian newsweekly might differ from other papers. Her work suggested that such a newspaper could challenge hemispheric assumptions regarding gender-specific leadership roles. A community paper would have to acknowledge all members of the community, men and women alike, and treat them as equals. Pursuing this agenda would make the newspaper a true beacon of equality.

Progress as defined by Young and the writers he recruited to his newspaper had much more to do with men in the community recognizing the newsweekly's intellectual service and innovation. Cespedes Burke (figure 1.2), an eventual *Tribune* columnist, described Young's goal as a "stupendous" one. Burke equated the task of providing coverage on the Caribbean community in Panama to that of the "modern historian," working against a plethora of negative and offensive depictions. Young's ability to lead this effort, he insisted, reflected his commitment to "boldly serv[e]" his community.[14]

For L. Christy Williams (figure 1.3), another contributor to the *Tribune*, the paper worked to address the socioeconomic priorities of the community. Such a goal had been difficult with just a single section of a paper. As Williams affirmed: "The various ramifications of our daily lives must be investigated, cultivated and encouraged towards a progressive ideal. There

FIGURE 1.2 Cespedes Burke, 1928. From Sidney A. Young, ed., *Isthmian Echoes: A Selection of the Literary Endeavors of the West Indian Colony in the Republic of Panama* (Panama City: Benedetti Hnos, 1928), 96.

is necessity for a *Tribune*."[15] In this way the paper could encapsulate the challenges and goals of the community.

At least one woman in the community also celebrated the *Tribune*'s inauguration, albeit using a different approach. Mrs. St. Hill expressed hope that the "Baby Tribune w[ould] develop into womanhood" and called on the community to protect this emergent womanhood. "Let this not be an abortion, but a full developed nourished and grown paper, so that we will be more educated in the welfare of our people and learn the things we need to know."[16] Comparing a successful newspaper to womanhood, though, contrasted sharply with the staffing decisions of the paper. With the exception of one woman, all the section editors and most invited contributors were men. In this regard the *Tribune* shared an established pattern of male-dominated leadership in the Black international press.[17]

FIGURE 1.3 L. Christy Williams, 1928. From Sidney A. Young, ed., *Isthmian Echoes: A Selection of the Literary Endeavors of the West Indian Colony in the Republic of Panama* (Panama City: Benedetti Hnos, 1928), 97.

For the Service of the Race

Within the first six months of publication the *Tribune* had a circulation of three thousand copies. Given that by 1930, about twenty-three thousand people, or 5 percent of the republic's population, were born in the Anglophone Caribbean, in addition to the tens of thousands of Afro-Caribbean Panamanians born on the isthmus who read and spoke English, the paper no doubt had many more readers than subscribers.[18] The paper circulated not only in Panama but in major cities in Costa Rica, Honduras, Guatemala, the United States, and Jamaica.[19] Based on letters to the editor, at least one copy of the paper made its way to Peru. Karl Schillos, writing from Negritos, Peru, expressed his delight at the literary advancement of "our Isthmian West Indian community."[20] Schillos spoke as a member of the larger diasporic community in the Americas. The progress projected through the pages of the *Tribune*, which cost five cents a copy, found wide appeal both among Afro-Caribbean Panamanians seeking to make their claims to the isthmus and among those outside Panama who were curious about livelihoods on the isthmus.

This wide-reaching readership affirmed the connection between the local and the hemispheric: local internationalism that formed the everyday realities of Afro-Caribbean Panamanians. Community formation on the isthmus meant paying attention to events in Panama while recognizing the far-reaching implications of this community's influence. The *Tribune* shone a light on how Afro-Caribbean descendants made diaspora and the challenges of this endeavor for men and women who shared similar narratives of migration, social formation, and racial identity. Through this hemispheric lens, Afro-Caribbean Panamanians made the isthmus their own, and they could, if they so desired, picture other men and women throughout the hemisphere embarking on similar journeys of diasporic formation.

In terms of content, the first issues of the paper provided a rich road map of the connections between the local and the diasporic as it unfolded over the years. Featured sections of the paper reported on news and events from the Atlantic side of the isthmus (Colón), which had the country's largest African descendant population, as well as happenings in the Canal Zone colored towns and the Anglophone Caribbean. In connecting these three spaces, the paper mapped the isthmus in a way that pushed against the Panama City–specific or whites-only focus of most Spanish- and English-language news publications.

The newsweekly's Happenings in the Zone Towns section exemplified this push for new perspectives. Almost forty thousand Afro-Caribbeans called the Canal Zone home by the late 1920s, but rarely were their day-to-day lives featured in local or national newspapers.[21] With weekly contributors based in various towns, the *Tribune* shifted this discourse. Residents and curious readers could now follow the progress of baseball teams like the Tom Boys of Red Tank and the Imperial Nine of La Boca and learn about the activities of the Paramount Social Club of La Boca, the Gatun Literary and Debating Society, and the Women's Missionary Society of Red Tank. They could take in reviews and notices of dramas, comedies, and musical shows performed by young and old alike, ladies' nights, dances, and educational picture nights. The *Tribune*'s Happenings section staked out the Canal Zone as an Afro-Caribbean space emblematic of the potential of Black diaspora communities.[22]

Other sections of the newsweekly expanded on developments in the Panamanian and international Black press to undergird this message of isthmian and diasporic life. Like older newspapers, the *Tribune* featured an editorial section, with editorials by Young, a section of letters to the editor, and a sports section (edited by George Westerman, who would become an associate editor by the late 1940s). The paper also reported on local, national, and international news. With its Of Interest to Women section, introduced two months after the paper's first issue, the *Tribune* expanded on a feature that grew in popularity among newspapers on the isthmus. Campaigns by women readers had resulted in the creation of women's sections or pages in select papers in the international Black press starting in the mid-1920s. The *Tribune*'s women's section, like its predecessors and contemporaries, featured recipes, fashion tips, and relationship advice, although the section's editor, Amy Denniston, the only woman on the editorial staff, pushed beyond this standard coverage.[23]

Like its diasporic contemporaries throughout the hemisphere, the newsweekly also culled stories from the international wire services as well as the global Black press. Many of these stories focused on growing anti-Black policies and sentiments in Europe, successes by African American teachers in the United States, and the rise of white supremacist groups in the Caribbean. Stories about New York received particular attention, since New York City was a favored destination for those with the means and opportunity to depart the isthmus. This migrant presence, in conjunction with the coverage provided by the *Tribune*, would provide familiarity for Afro-Caribbean Panamanians migrating to New York starting in the 1940s.[24]

In addition to inspiring future migrations, newspapers like the *Tribune* held other radical potentials. As noted by Brent Hayes Edwards, Black periodicals of the 1920s and 1930s were "a threat above all because of the transnational and anti-imperialist linkages and alliances they practiced."[25] Newspapers like the *Tribune* provided information about the Black world that was underreported or did not appear at all in mainstream dailies. This made the content of these pages unique and dangerous, especially to those with biased ideas on citizenship, race, and national identity. Rather than creating "community in anonymity," to borrow from Benedict Anderson's formulation of the links between newspapers and the fictive narrative of modern nations, these papers emphasized diaspora and race consciousness to make visible the Black people crucial to yet erased in most nationalist and imperial narratives.[26]

A focus on Marcus Garvey's activities and the ongoing efforts of the Universal Negro Improvement Association (UNIA) allowed for papers like the *Tribune* to document, celebrate, and critique bourgeoning ideas such as an African-centered empire. Young and his staff had much to say about Garvey's accomplishments, his failures, and his living legacy. These commentaries ranged from deep admiration of Garvey's race pride message and the popularity of UNIA international conferences to criticisms of Garvey's continued arrests, his egomania, and the unfulfilled promises of the UNIA.[27] Alongside these commentaries, the newspaper also documented the participation of Afro-Caribbean Panamanians in UNIA events in Jamaica and reported on Garvey Day celebrations as well as racial uplift classes coordinated by local UNIA branches. This indicated competing stances regarding the goals and accomplishments of Garvey and the UNIA.[28] In all, by featuring the experiences of a global Black diaspora, in conversation with local events and opinions, the *Tribune* purposefully connected Panama to the world and vice versa. In doing so, the paper asserted that Afro-Caribbean Panamanians had rich cultural, activist, and entrepreneurial links that expanded beyond the isthmus and could serve as sources of inspiration and reflection.

While making these global and diasporic connections, the paper prided itself on publicizing the successes of the local Afro-Caribbean community. High-achieving students, for example, could count on having their names and photos featured in the newspaper and, at least for a day, relish receiving the same treatment afforded to national and international leaders.[29] Sidney Young and his staff took very seriously their role of educating and leading the community. A section of the paper concentrated on the contributions made by Caribbean migrants and their descendants in Panama.[30] Parts of the paper, especially the editorial section, strongly condemned policies that targeted Afro-Caribbean Panamanians.

Through its coverage of the community's achievements and hurdles blocking its progress, the paper at times took a paternalist approach. This was most evident in Young's editorials. In one example, Young critiqued fraternal and benevolent societies for impeding the hard work of community building. The money amassed by these societies, Young insisted, would be better used assisting the unemployed and reducing the community's dependence "on the capital and initiative of persons of another race."[31] While benevolent and fraternal associations could refute criticisms of Afro-Caribbean Panamanians as perpetual outsiders by forming places of belonging, they did not offer, at least according to their critics, a financial road map for communal growth and prosperity. As Young understood it, the economic future of his community would be determined by greater unity in the form of financial strength and support of entrepreneurial ventures like the *Tribune*.

Readers of the newsweekly did not silently accept such instruction. They had their own ideas about their place in Panama and what practices and policies most affected the building of a cohesive isthmian identity. One such reader, identified as A New Providence Reader, complained about a piece by Hector Connor claiming that poverty, more so than hair and skin color, was the source of discrimination faced by Black people. A New Providence Reader accused Connor of ignoring *Tribune* articles detailing the discrimination faced by Black professionals in the United States, England, and France. "Instead of penning such falsehoods," the reader complained, "[Connor] might have rested his weapon that week."[32]

A New Providence Reader reminded Connor of instances when, as in the 1920 Canal Zone labor strike, members of the community rose up seeking professional advancement and equality. White prejudice, not poverty, insisted the letter writer, was to blame for that particular activist loss. Taking on Connor and other bourgeois leaders, the reader concluded, "during the past ten years or more, we have been trying to better our condition from every point of view, and by now would have succeeded had not it been for the educated parasites of our race."[33] Education, as presented by the letter writer, had clear class connotations. Those with formal education presented themselves as speakers for "the race," yet this highly educated circle often ignored the experiential and activist education of those who preceded them. For this older generation of working-class men and women, "the canal builders," as they often proudly called themselves, their very presence and activism on the isthmus made them key authorities in the claiming and defining of Panama for generations to come.

Even if not always apparent through the paper's content, the staff of the *Tribune* shared this common goal with A New Providence Reader. The inauguration of the newsweekly and its first years of publication marked the rise of a generation eager to write about and envision the isthmus on their own terms. For the *Tribune* team this entailed putting pages to the diasporic, internationalist, and uniquely Panamanian realities of their community. It also included lecturing to the community when necessary and at times using the paper to represent the entire community.

The comments raised by community members like A New Providence Reader pointed to a topic that would only grow in volume in subsequent years. This concern was education—the nature of it, the access to it, and both the discrimination and the opportunities that would shape the educational experiences of the new generation. Parents sought to provide their children with technical and professional training that could secure them jobs as electricians, stenographers, teachers, journalists, and engineers, jobs that provided economic stability. Teachers and other sectors of the middle class also wanted children to grow in pride as intellectuals, thinkers, and visionaries. Education, as understood by all parties, would decide whether their people would have the vocabulary, tools, and modes of self-subsistence to affirm their claims to the isthmus and an internationalist Black diaspora.

The Need for an Educated Population

The educational options from elementary to secondary level available to Afro-Caribbean Panamanians in the late 1920s and early 1930s included the republic's public schools (the largest enrollment option), the Canal Zone colored schools (CZCS; also public), English-language private schools (known as West Indian schools) operated by Afro-Caribbean migrants, and a return to Jamaica or Barbados for training. Because most private Spanish-language schools in the republic were exorbitantly priced, they remained outside the reach of not only Afro-Caribbean Panamanians but also most other Panamanians of color. Returning to the Anglophone Caribbean was not an option for most Afro-Caribbeans on the isthmus, even for those who secured higher paying Canal Zone jobs.[34] Consequently, most of the attention given to education in the *Tribune* focused on public education and West Indian private schools.

Among those consistently writing about the CZCS, which by the late 1920s enrolled almost four thousand students, was Sidney Young.[35] One of Young's earliest editorials commended recent junior high graduates and pointed to the enormous work ahead of them in educational advancement: "It cannot be too strongly emphasized that the education of these youths has just commenced. That no matter how beautifully framed, the diplomas awarded have no value except in serving as an inspiration for the acquiring of broader knowledge. Only the bare foundations have been laid.... The children now stand with uncertain footsteps on the first rung of the ladder. Either they can climb upward or step back and remain forever in the fields of mediocrity."[36] To survive in the modern world, young people would need to expand their knowledge and look to all possible avenues for advanced education. Finding such avenues proved particularly important in a climate in which "the dominant race ha[d] imposed limitations to opportunities in the local field." If Afro-Caribbean Panamanians sought to thrive on the isthmus, they needed to harness bright minds and push through with a spirit of determination. Young urged "the entire community [to] join in a great 'commencement' exercise. Commence to think seriously and to accept the realities of life without the false glow of ignorance and vanity."[37] Young had no qualms both congratulating and chastising his readers.

While Young used the commencement to challenge the preparedness of recent graduates and the community as a whole, educators emphasized the holistic and communal benefits of higher education. Leonor Jump was one such educator. She was born and raised in Panama City, educated there at the Escuela Normal de Institutoras (a teacher training school for women), and became a teacher in the CZCS.[38] As Jump insisted in her contribution to the Of Interest to Women section in the *Tribune*, institutions of higher learning instilled valuable lessons about ethical and cultural survival. "Due importance is given to the things that bear most directly on the preservation of life and health, on our moral relations and duties, on the cultivation of the taste and imagination which derive pleasure from music, painting, poetry, and good works of fiction. We are composed of what we know, what we feel and what we believe. In response to these things we act, in respect to ourselves and to others."[39] Institutions of higher education, to her, sought not only to teach students material skills to forge a livelihood but also to instill deep and intimate knowledge of integrity, creativity, and leadership. In this way, the lessons learned in the classroom could affect how entire generations thought of themselves and their communities.

In her contribution to the newspaper, Jump also focused on the role of the wider community in emphasizing higher education. But rather than condemning her peers and neighbors as vain or ignorant, she called on them to encourage the ambitious young people around them. "There is a time," she averred, "when every boy and girl feels admiration for those who have triumphed and the desire to also fight and conquer. Your duty it is, to meet him on the ground, stirring the desire to be something, leading him in the field of commerce, industry and science, selecting achievements of our own people who fought greater battles with fewer instruments as inspirations toward his goal."[40] In this way community members could use their knowledge of Black diaspora history to inspire youths about the growing professional possibilities and the forebears who fought to make them a reality.

Jump used the medium of the paper to offer motivation and inspiration to a growing generation. This approach differentiated the *Tribune* from other newspapers on the isthmus. Many articles seemed to understand that readers of the newsweekly were more than just casual readers but people willing to tackle questions such as the value of education, access to education, and the making of community leaders. Jump's article relied on an understanding of community and education that did not dictate but assumed a base of curious and eager readers.

In addition to offering encouragement to prospective students and the entire community, Jump's contribution broadened the goals of the paper's women's section. The section was inaugurated in January 1929, with Amy Denniston serving as editor. From the first printing of the section, Denniston called on women in the community to contribute their thoughts on issues of the day. As she noted in her introduction, with the "whole-hearted co-operation of the large number of women who read [the] paper," she hoped to urge her readers "a little further on the road to progress."[41] Contributions like those by Jump advanced this goal and called on women's engagement with the key issues that affected the entire community.

Denniston also contributed editorials addressing educational aspirations on the isthmus. Her first focused on "commercial teaching" or technical training in Jamaica and its possible applicability in Panama. Denniston wrote the editorial following a one-month visit to Jamaica, her first since departing as a child.[42] In referencing Jamaica, Denniston drew on a regional history of migration and exchange between the island and Panama that was familiar to *Tribune* readers. Several of them acknowledged the vastness of secondary training on the island, compared to other parts of the Caribbean and the Central American republics.[43]

In her editorial, Denniston expressed admiration for the preparation provided in Jamaica's commercial schools and their gender equality. "It was very refreshing to see boys and girls, young men and women attending these schools. They are opened from 7 AM until 8 PM for the convenience of students who work during the days. Typewriting, shorthand, bookkeeping, business correspondence and Spanish are taught. The young people are very enthusiastic over their lessons and as a result are very efficient."[44] Boys and girls, young men and women, she stressed, had access to technical training in Jamaica. Few students in Panama, she noted, were enrolled in such schools.

By the time of Denniston's editorial, a school for commerce (and the arts) already existed at the Instituto Nacional (National Institute), one of the country's first comprehensive educational institutions. Until 1919, however, only men could enroll, on a tuition basis, in the institute. Outside the institute and select industrial and teacher training schools throughout the republic, few credible avenues existed for professional training.[45] A shortage in technical training also typified Canal Zone instruction. During the early 1930s, zone education for students in segregated nonwhite schools terminated at the eighth grade. While providing students with English-language skills, this education offered few options for employment, which parents and students increasingly complained about. They hoped this shortcoming would be rectified by a 1930 survey group from Columbia University Teacher's College tasked with assessing the czcs system.[46]

Rather than focusing on higher education as emphasized by Jump, or looking to technical training as Denniston suggested, the report called for vocational instruction that helped czcs graduates get manual jobs. This included the introduction of classes in gardening, housekeeping, tailoring, sewing, and carpentry. Practical careers, the survey group concluded, made sense for a group with limited opportunities in and outside the Canal Zone.[47] In her editorial, written the same year as the study, Denniston questioned these limitations on the future of the community. Professional success required access and training. A refusal to provide either naturalized the idea of Afro-Caribbeans as manual laborers. Members of the community, especially old-timers, had secured stability for their families with these manual jobs. This sacrifice was intended to secure less physically taxing labor and greater pay and respect for future generations. The survey results dismissed this possibility.

Through her editorials, Denniston also critiqued initiatives by Afro-Caribbean Panamanians that devalued their community's potential. She questioned the qualifications and long-term applicability of West Indian private schools. These schools had formed part of isthmian life since the start of the century, and although not as abundant as public schools, they remained an option for parents and guardians who embraced the British colonial model of instruction for their children. According to Denniston, the majority of the teachers in these schools "should be pupils instead of teachers." She accused them of failing the two central aims of education: "transmit[ing] to each subsequent generation the best knowledge gained from the previous generation" and providing pupils with needed knowledge to face "the battles of life and to contribute worthily to [their] heritage."[48] These private schools, instead, promoted the emergence of an undereducated and unmotivated generation ignorant of the need for communal growth.

As an alternative, Denniston suggested that parents send their children to public schools in the republic. Here, in addition to having qualified instructors, they could further strengthen their Spanish-language skills, necessary for any professional success.[49] For supporters of West Indian private schools, Denniston's suggestion ignored the cultural role played by these institutions. According to a letter to the editor by A. S. G., the youth enrolled in these schools "do not want Spanish instruction before they are ready for it."

A. S. G. insisted, "neither should it be deemed necessary for Spanish speaking children to acquire an English education before mastering the mother tongue." Language acquisition should be tied to ancestry and comfort. This separated language skills from professional ones by presenting the former as culturally fixed and the latter as malleable. In conclusion, A. S. G. also called on the *Tribune* to work at "influencing parents to give their offspring the benefit of their own language first, before attempting to learn another."[50]

A. S. G.'s letter and Denniston's editorial revealed the key role of language and education in ongoing claims to the isthmus. For people like A. S. G., English formed the core identity of Afro-Caribbean Panamanians. English, as a spoken idiom and for pedagogical instruction, bonded the tens of thousands of men and women who could trace their ancestry back to the Anglophone Caribbean. For people like Denniston though, a compromise between this Anglophone-centric perspective of diaspora and one that recognized the importance of bilingualism in Panama needed to be reached. New models, she averred, even if inspired by those from other parts of the Caribbean, had to be anchored in Panamanian realities. To secure Canal Zone jobs and even commercial jobs in Panamá and Colón, knowledge of English remained a prerequisite. Yet, lack of Spanish-language skills could impede the community's full participation in all aspects of isthmian life. It could also further stoke the intolerance of white and mestizo Panamanians who accused Afro-Caribbeans of refusing to learn Spanish. Denniston did not speak to this latter point in her West Indian schools editorial, but through other editorials, she spoke of the undue burden of "that stigma 'undesirable.'"[51] Whether others agreed with Denniston regarding bilingualism and the republic's public schools remains unclear, particularly since she ceased being an editor for the *Tribune* after her editorial on West Indian private schools. No explanation was provided for Denniston's departure. The role of editor for the Of Interest to Women section also remained permanently vacant. Perhaps Denniston went beyond the section's expected confines by addressing a sensitive matter of interest to men and women alike.

The Isthmus as Home?

Even as debates about what kind of education best served Afro-Caribbean Panamanians unfolded in the *Tribune* sans Denniston, a pressing concern soon galvanized its readers and writers: the rise of exclusionist and repatriation campaigns. By 1929 legislative changes already sought to police Afro-Caribbean Panamanians and others viewed as descendants of "undesirable" migrants. In the early 1930s, with a global economic depression underway, "prohibited immigrants" and Afro-Caribbean Panamanians emerged as economic scapegoats supposedly stealing jobs that should go to unemployed white and mestizo Panamanian workers.

The first manifestation of this included the passing of a ban against Asian, Middle Eastern, and non-Spanish-speaking Black immigrants. These groups already formed part of the "prohibited immigrant" category and were closely monitored within the republic, with limits placed on the number of them allowed in the country. The new 1932 ban now called for a full stop to their immigration. As noted by the *Tribune*, the ban represented "the most drastic immigration ban to date." The government permanently denied entry to Chinese, Lebanese, Palestinian, Syrian, Turk, and "non-Spanish speaking Negro" immigrants. The ban stipulated that "prohibited immigrants" already in Panama wishing to exit and reenter would need to pay B/. 75 (balboas; US$75) for a reentry permit. This was seven times the amount paid by other immigrants.[52] The reentry clause of the policy targeted migrants who maintained connections to their place of birth while also having established families and sources of revenue in Panama. This was the case for many Afro-Caribbeans who, because of the proximity of various Caribbean islands, made such trips. The new reentry fee followed up on a decree issued by the Ministry of Foreign Affairs a year earlier affirming that the executive could at any time, for racial or economic reasons, deny reentry permits to any "elements belonging to restricted races." Given that by 1934 the government had collected more than twenty thousand balboas/dollars on reentry permits alone, policed inclusion proved more profitable than full exclusion.[53]

Highlighting legislation that both banned and profited from "prohibited immigrants," the *Tribune* noted how calls for repatriation united officials and ordinary citizens throughout the republic. Following the 1929 US stock market crash and ongoing global depression, Canal Zone officials began labor force reductions that disproportionally cut Afro-Caribbean workers and impoverished the families they supported.[54] What to do about these "unemployed Afro-Caribbeans" in turn became a hot topic of public discussion among those voicing concerns over the country's imperiled economy. By focusing on the unemployed, these critics avoided addressing Panama's near-total economic dependence on the United States, as evidenced by the lack of an independent Panamanian currency and the reliance on the canal annuity from Washington (both subject to dollar fluctuations) to finance public sector jobs.[55] Instead, as noted by the *Tribune*, starting in July 1931 petitions by concerned Panamanian citizens demanding the removal of unemployed Afro-Caribbeans made their way to the office of the president. In these petitions, the paper reported, joblessness was but one rationale cited for the expulsion of this group. Other justifications offered included the inferiority of "West Indians of the negro race" and the regional exclusion of this group from countries such as Honduras, Cuba, and "even the United States."[56] Although the petitioners erred in including the United States in this list (immigration bans in the United States at this time targeted Asians), those writing resorted to an accepted hemispheric discourse of race-based exclusion.[57]

By exposing these petitions to its readers, the *Tribune* translated documents and popular talking points not readily available to them, hoping to harness community engagement against these new discriminatory policies. For the most part, Afro-Caribbean Panamanians reading other local papers could count on maybe one or two editorials covering these policies, with no directions on what, if any, options existed to fight against them. The *Tribune* provided this unique service to the community that its inaugural issue had promised.

Young's response to these petitions provided a perfect example of this mandate in action. As he noted, speaking on behalf of the entire community: "We believe that if ever there was a time when the West Indian community should gird its loins, and when our leaders should quit themselves like men, that time is NOW. It is not necessary for us to dolefully point out what the dangers are. This must be known to every man and woman, nay, to every child. These are times that try men's souls, and this moment is one for ACTION."[58] Young's comments extolled community action, emphasizing a masculinist response to communal threats. Men needed to unite and protect their community from outside dangers. One wonders whether women in the community, like Smart Chubb, Jump, or Denniston, would have agreed with this estimation. If given the opportunity, how would they have framed this call to action? Would they have agreed that attacks on the community indeed signified the need for stronger male leadership? Smart Chubb, as a feminist, would caution Young against assuming that men held the sole answers for how to best protect the community. Jump, as an educator, would question the limiting ethos of Young's pronouncement. Denniston might warn against an old-guard form of politics that rejected a multipronged approach to protecting the community.

Young himself began to express dismay at the effectiveness of his advocacy:

If there is any member of our group, among our intellectuals, our preachers or the humblest worker who is of the opinion that elevated arguments in the press, that an appeal to reason, or to the exalted sentiments of humanity and justice will avail against the expressed determination of a vociferous group of Panamanians to effect the wholesale repatriation of the West Indian community, they are sadly mistaken.... We have peaceably, sometimes laughingly, accepted humiliation and scorn. We have ignored jibes and ridicule, but no people however indifferent, however tolerant can wake up day after day to face an unceasing current of opprobrium which has now developed into a tidal wave of hatred and abuse.[59]

In this editorial, far from projecting a masculinist, confident paternalism that characterized some of his earlier editorial pieces, Young seemed defeated. Not even the press, he suggested, could effectively thwart the wholesale hatred and abuse directed at his community. What factors explained such a drastic shift in attitude? Why, in Young's estimation, were appeals to reason and peace now ineffective?

One clue as to the shift in Young's tone included the rise of militant nationalist groups calling for the expulsion of all Afro-Caribbeans from the republic. One such group was Panamá Para los Panameños (Panama for the Panamanians), or the PPP. By 1933 the PPP claimed a membership base of between 350 and 600 people and used *El Panamá América* (the Spanish organ of the *Panama American*) to urge others to join the cause. As with its coverage of the 1931 "citizen's petitions," the *Tribune* provided readers with an overview of the PPP's platform. The PPP, according to its manifesto, looked for members between the ages of eighteen and thirty-five and sought to bring together "whites, blacks, communists, Panchistas [supporters of Francisco Arias Paredes and the Liberal Renovation Party], Chiaristas [supporters of Adolfo Chiari and the Liberal Party], Harmodistas [supporters of Harmodio Arias and the National Revolutionary Party], [and] members of the police and fire brigade departments."[60] Nicolás Ardito Barletta, former Panama City police chief, was the group's leader. The group invoked Hitler and his ousting of Jews from Germany, as well as the leaders of Acción Comunal (Community Action), who in January 1931 led the first coup in Panama's history, as inspiration for their campaign. The PPP affirmed it would not allow any movement of Afro-Caribbeans, unemployed or employed, from between the Canal Zone and the republic and would, if necessary, use force to protect the nation's borders.[61] The PPP, through these sentiments, held much in common with parallel movements in countries like Italy, Argentina, Spain, Germany, Cuba, and the Dominican Republic, which pointed to specific groups as "enemies of the nation" and called on legislation and violent action to defend the country against "internal enemies" and "suspect foreigners."[62]

As noted by the *Tribune*, *El Panamá América* became an organ for the PPP and a platform for anti–West Indian sentiment by upper-class white and mestizo Panamanians. Evidence included a letter to the editor signed by eight young men from prominent families, E. Candanedo C., Ricardo Fábrega, L. C. Jimenez, Felipe E. Motta, Emilio Linares Jr., A. F. Alba, Daniel Salcedo G., and C. A. Arango L., which presented the repatriation of Afro-Caribbeans as a matter of national security and popular desire.

> The Panamanian public has demonstrated always its repugnance for codling with chombos which circumstances have forced upon us and now, in view of the incalculable evil that in every phase of life this race has caused us, the people should be given their desire in compelling the West Indians, within the shortest possible time to leave the country.... The West Indian problem will cease to be a problem from the moment the Panamanian authorities have sufficient courage to demand their repatriation from those who brought them here, giving deaf ears to the pleading of foreign commercial houses established here which are the only ones up to now who have benefited by the presence here of Jamaicans; but those benefits are detrimental to the future of the Latin race in Panama, detrimental to the language and at the cost of the misery of the Panamanian people. It is urgent, therefore, that force be adopted.[63]

With this statement these writers combined racism, xenophobia, and violence in their call for retaking the nation. This focus on West Indians as incompatible elements to the Panamanian essence held proponents prior to and after the consolidation of the republic. Pejorative terms like *chombo*, intended to alienate and vilify Afro-Caribbeans, formed part of the Panamanian lexicon in the late nineteenth century and early twentieth century and was invoked by these writers precisely because of its hateful bigotry. The PPP not only embraced this exclusionist discourse of incompatibility and racial danger but called for violence to end the threat. Patriotism, in this equation, corresponded with the forcible removal of Afro-Caribbeans. Young's disheartened editorial came amid this growing climate of racial intolerance and calls to violence.

As prophesized in Young's editorial, a consensus to repatriate Afro-Caribbeans had materialized. This consensus came not just from angry citizens but from three national governments: Panama, the United States, and Great Britain. In July 1933, in response to PPP protests at the presidential palace, President Harmodio Arias declared that his government would repatriate all unemployed foreigners, albeit in an orderly manner.[64] In a letter published in the *Tribune*, President Arias's office urged West Indian organizations and leaders to have their constituents request repatriation through Canal Zone authorities. This repatriation, Arias' office insisted, would "be far more advantageous ... than the repatriation or deportation which ultimately will be ordered by the Republic of Panama."[65] Given that Canal Zone officials controlled immigration and residency in this area, Arias could not deport those living in the zone. His threat still applied to Afro-Caribbeans who lived in the republic, the majority of the community.

The publication of this letter followed another that same month addressed to Sidney Young from the governor of the Canal Zone, Julian Schley, which rebuffed Young's suggestion that some of the open land in the zone be opened for "colonization or development" by unemployed Afro-Caribbean workers. The governor also called on the Afro-Caribbean community to "MAKE CERTAIN THAT EVERYTHING POSSIBLE IS BEING DONE TO HELP THEMSELVES."[66] Young chose to capitalize that part of the letter to highlight the enormity of its message. According to the US government, Afro-Caribbeans who lived in the republic and not the zone were on their own. Repatriation for eligible former workers, at the behest of the Panamanian government, represented the extent of zone interest and involvement in the matter.

British officials also joined the call for repatriation and increasingly pressed their Caribbean colonial subjects residing in Panama to "self-repatriate." A week before publishing the Young-Schley exchange, the *Tribune* circulated an official statement by Sir Josiah Crosby, the minister of the British legation in Panama, in which he called on legitimate subjects (those born in the British Caribbean or the children of recognized, married colonial subjects) to return to their island homes. He encouraged those eligible for Panama Canal–financed repatriation to pursue this approach. Crosby, the *Tribune* noted, made this statement as he began a five-month vacation to England. British colonial subjects would have to fend for themselves.[67]

During a visit to the White House one year and three months after the circulation of these published letters, the first by a Panamanian head of state, President Arias received assurances from President Franklin Roosevelt that funds would be set aside by the US Congress for repatriation costs.[68] Following the visit, Panamanian officials, at the behest of US diplomats, explored the possibility of using government funds to increase the repatriation pool. Given the economic strains facing the republic, combined with repatriation painted as a "US problem," such a step never took place.[69] This discussion, when examined alongside the efforts of Arias, Roosevelt, Schley, and Crosby, pointed to the extent that repatriation had by the mid-1930s become a transnational and cross-imperial rallying cry.

Repatriation and "Native Identities"

The readers and writers to the *Tribune* refused to concede to the normalizing of hate speech and calls for repatriation. The paper continued its function as central organ of the community while remaining open to dissent and contradictory voices. *Tribune* contributors like E. A. Lewis pointed to the rise in intolerance as an opportunity to use communal and individual approaches in combating this danger. For Lewis, the discourse appearing in Spanish-language news outlets was "extermination in the guise of repatriation of all West Indians on the isthmus." This, Lewis affirmed, could be prevented if Afro-Caribbeans came together as "a united front." "Unity," he extolled, "which is the primal factor of every success shall decide the ultimate fate of West Indians in Panama. It is now time that we should all stop arguing from which Island in the Caribbean we came, and other nonsensical topics which has the effect of retarding, instead of promoting our economic and moral respect."[70] As individuals with deep roots on the isthmus, Afro-Caribbeans could wage a legitimate fight against nativist newspapers and militant xenophobic organizations.

Yet while calling on Afro-Caribbeans to come together as one, Lewis encouraged those born outside Panama to consider returning to their places of birth. "If you are unemployed and without any future prospect in this country, rather than remain here to be ridiculed and abused by Panamanians; it is advisable that you return home."[71] Lewis prefaced this advice by reminding *Tribune* readers that this was now official British policy toward its colonial subjects on the isthmus. The wording of this advice pointed to Lewis's concern that unemployed Afro-Caribbeans faced greater hostility and violence than those with stable employment in the community.

Some readers, like Jamaican-born William Thompson, admitted that they were planning on returning to their island of birth, on their own terms, even as this meant leaving behind property. Thompson's principal concern regarding his return pertained to the preparation of the colonial government. As he asked Young, and by extension all those reading the paper, "Can you say whether the Jamaica Government is making any preparation, such as providing houses to receive the homeless until such time as they can better their position, or is it that we must be landed in the streets, only to know we have left the Isthmus? I am pining for home, sweet homeland."[72] Thompson's question and closing refrain spoke to the worry, resignation, and hope that others like him shared regarding returning to Jamaica and other islands of the Caribbean. Would those repatriated, he asked, move from one zone of poverty to another, or could they in time hope to improve their socioeconomic standing in their places of birth? "Colón men" of the early twentieth century, whom Rhonda Frederick and Olive Senior have documented, became the envy of those back on their island homes because of the money they amassed from the canal construction and then sent home. Repatriated men like Thompson had no such capital to take home with them. Instead they would be selling at a steep discount, or leaving behind, houses, fruit gardens, furniture, tools, and the bulk of their possessions, while facing an uncertain future.[73]

For other *Tribune* readers, like C. A. Dixon and C. Greenidge, the repatriation debate could not be neatly divided into unemployed versus employed, willing versus unwilling to be repatriated, or isthmian-born versus Caribbean-born. According to Dixon, the root of the problem rested in the impossibility of African descendants finding a home in the Western world. To Young's disillusion with the political climate, Dixon added a condemnation of the entire Western world: "Can't we see that there is nothing like hope for us in this western world. Well then, since we realize that we are not loved by the people of the western world and without love there is no existence, why can't we concentrate our minds upon the land of Africa and found a government there to take care of her children at home and abroad, where we would be no more subjects, no more aliens, no more chombos. Where we would not be driven from Republic to Republic."[74] Based on this call to a return to Africa, Dixon clearly adhered to the Garveyite movement's presentation of the African continent as the ancestral home of all Black people. Branches of the UNIA had formed part of the Panamanian landscape since the late 1910s. Not all members or sympathizers with the UNIA agreed with the back to Africa component of the movement. When *Tribune* readers and writers addressed the idea of "return," they often invoked a return to the Anglophone Caribbean—not Africa.[75] Concerns over the future of the movement particularly after Garvey's fraud conviction also factored in a disconnect between local and international branches of the movement. By the late 1920s, as noted by Hector Connor, former UNIA local president and *Tribune* contributor, some UNIA branches had severed ties with the international movement and instead focused on financing local projects. This did not mean a rejection of Garveyism, especially its core tenets like Black pride, ingenuity, and advancement. Instead it marked the evolution of a movement that went beyond Marcus Garvey or the return to Africa and instead centered on Black people finding protection in the spaces they called home.[76] Dixon's contribution held that neither the Anglophone Caribbean nor any of the American republics would provide a haven for Afro-Caribbeans. Those in Panama, then, had to refashion their perspectives on home and belonging.

For C. Greenidge, the president of a UNIA local branch in Panama City, the issue was less about finding an ancestral homeland and more about dismissing the employed versus unemployed divide that typified much of the repatriation debate. According to Greenidge, those employed who felt secure were "simply misrepresenting themselves; for the object of the natives is not so much the unemployed, as it is the jobs and positions that West Indians hold in this country, and all West Indians should be wise enough as to know this, for the people would be very proud to know that all West Indians were thrown out of all employments in this country."[77] Of note in Greenidge's letter is his reference to the dichotomy of "those native to Panama vs. the West Indians." Putting this division in such stark terms, Greenidge perhaps hoped, would bring Afro-Caribbeans together, yet it left unaddressed the question of what made someone "native" to the isthmus. Would Afro-Caribbeans' children born on the isthmus ever be natives? Did their place of birth or long-term residency not signify anything in these discussions? And could one be both a native of Panama and a member of the Caribbean diaspora? Based on the work and writing of people like Young, Smart Chubb, Jump, Denniston, and the scores of others invested in educating, advocating for, and upholding the Afro-Caribbean community, being both natives and members of a diaspora was imperative. Panama was home, but being in conversation with a wider world, whether through newspapers, travel, or popular culture, animated calls for race pride and community progress.

The official start of repatriation, with expanded efforts begun by Canal Zone officials a year earlier, temporarily cast aside these questions among Afro-Caribbeans. Starting in July 1934 with an expanded budget of $150,000, zone officials increased repatriation efforts with the goal of coordinating return trips and providing cash relief for roughly one thousand Afro-Caribbean families. Only those who had worked on the canal or in the Canal Zone area for three or more years were eligible for repatriation. Solo repatriates also qualified for twenty-five dollars in cash. Married former employees were eligible for fifty dollars with an additional ten dollars for each child, with a limit of one hundred dollars in repatriation compensation for any one family. Only those with the status of British colonial subjects, moreover, had access to repatriation funds. Not surprisingly, of those who eventually petitioned for repatriation, a significant portion were older re-tired men like the aforementioned William Thompson. Given that pensions (called annuities by canal officials) would not be available to retired Afro-Caribbean workers until 1937, securing repatriation dollars proved crucial.[78] Access to these funds by retirees and their dependents was not guaranteed. As reported to the *Tribune* in September 1937, able-bodied men, as well as the widows and children of former employees, faced difficulties securing any financing from the Canal Zone government. Among eligible applicants who successfully completed the process, very few received the full cash relief amount. Leaving the isthmus was not as easy as some in the press or national government suggested.[79]

Concern about what those repatriated would find on their islands of birth also proved an issue for those considering returning. Reading that in Barbados returnees experienced hunger and destitution likely gave pause to those eligible for repatriation. As reported in the *Barbados Advocate* and reprinted in the *Tribune*, twenty-one such returnees, ranging in age from seven to seventy-four years old, were "care-worn, toil-worn, penniless, home-less and in a few cases, in a state of decrepitude. Depression and want had done their work." One man, reflecting on his thirty-two years of working on the canal and living in Panama, had the following to say: "My best days were spent there and now I have nothing."[80] This was indeed a bitter end to decades spent working, loving, and living in the Panamanian isthmus. In all, between July 1934 and June 1936, only 954 people (454 employees and 500 family members) opted for repatriation back to the Anglophone Caribbean. This total represented less than half of the one thousand families zone officials had estimated would opt for repatriation. It also represented a minuscule portion of the total Afro-Caribbean population in Panama.[81]

Some who chose repatriation, particularly younger individuals, also used the very bureaucracy of the Panamanian immigration system to return to Panama. Joseph Jeremiah Dennis and his wife accepted repatriation offered by the canal government back to Jamaica, but prior to leaving Dennis pur-chased a reentry permit, a solo permit, it appears. Dennis took advantage of the lack of communication between zone officials and the Panamanian government to ensure that his departure from the isthmus would not be permanent.[82] How many others did the same is unclear. Preventing future cases of repatriated individuals returning to Panama would nonetheless remain an ongoing discussion between Panamanian and US officials.[83]

While government officials continued to discuss best practices for continued repatriation, including the apparent reluctance by most Afro-Caribbeans to accept the repatriation offer, militant pro-repatriation groups like the PPP reduced their calls for action by the mid-1930s. This did not mean that they disappeared. As I note in chapter 2, groups sharing such sentiments surfaced in the 1940s and commanded even more power. The departure of some Afro-Caribbeans temporarily appeased those who equated the reclaiming of the nation with the physical removal of non-Spanish-speaking Black people. Given that the number of those repatriated paled in comparison with the tens of thousands who remained in Panama and that some even managed to return, in practice repatriation could not have succeeded in the removal of all Afro-Caribbeans and their descendants from the isthmus. Repatriation was but one of several unfolding manifestations, however, that sought to define the cultural and racial makeup of the nation. Afro-Caribbean Panamanians, through their day-to-day lives reflected in the pages of the *Tribune*, had a very different interpretation of what it meant to call Panama home. The debate between their version of Panama and one that insisted on a xenophobic and homogenous republic would loom large for generations.

Writing for the Race and Reflecting on National Realities

When the *Tribune* made its debut in late 1928, no guarantees existed that the paper would run more than a single issue. Indeed, other English-language dailies, with more reliable equipment and mass-production capabilities, vied for a similar readership. Some of these dailies even included West Indian sections, which had grown successful through the undercompensated work of Afro-Caribbean Panamanians. What room existed, then, for a paper like the *Tribune*? What distinct contribution could the newsweekly bring to the table? And how would this contribution allow it to compete with better-funded more-established newspapers?

The answer to these questions rested in the total control that Afro-Caribbean Panamanians had of the content and in the exercise of editorial freedom. The *Tribune* from its foundation relied on an Afro-Caribbean base of writers, and the content of the paper incorporated news of a hemispheric and global Black diaspora alongside ongoing Panamanian realities. No single section of a paper could have sufficiently offered this coverage. More important, a committed chief editor at the *Tribune* knew why these connected histories mattered. Because of its unique readership base, the paper likewise became a forum where members of the community shared their ideas, hopes, and fears. The paper also revealed fissures that existed within this community. These included responses to issues such as repatriation, gender hierarchies, educational advancement, language practices, and the meaning of home and belonging. In all, the newsweekly revealed a complex community.

By the early 1930s, the *Tribune* also held status as the only major paper owned and operated by Afro-Caribbean Panamanians. The *Workman*, an early competitor, closed its doors shortly after the *Tribune's* first anniversary. The *Workman's* departure meant that the *Tribune* represented the survival of a still evolving Afro-Caribbean press in Panama. The *Tribune* team used this message in its capital-raising efforts throughout the 1930s, registered as a corporation, and thereafter began to sell company shares to supplement readers' subscriptions.[84] This mixture of revenue sources allowed the newsweekly to procure its own printing plant and the necessary machinery by July 1936.[85]

For its columnist Jack Jamieson, the *Tribune's* new independence ensured its continuance as "the champion and defender of Race people" and cemented its place "among the better weeklies of Central and South America because of a determined policy to cover the news intelligently and lucidly."[86] The *Tribune* team held hope for the paper's future tackling the issues of the day affecting Black people in Panama, while also paying attention to the hemispheric implications of their work. The *Tribune's* responsibility would only increase and become subject to greater scrutiny due to its new spatial and economic independence.

This question of responsibility also tied the paper to communal discussions about the future of race and language politics on the isthmus. While English remained the principal language of the newsweekly, starting in November 1936, the *Tribune* added a small Spanish edition. Writing about this development, Young affirmed that the Spanish edition fulfilled a growing need in the community. The Spanish edition provided Afro-Caribbeans born on the isthmus with "a new organ devoted to their cause."[87] This edition marked a conjunction of diasporic and ancestral frameworks and addressed the growing demands for bilingual spaces in the republic. Spanish-speaking neighbors could now learn more easily about Afro-Caribbean concerns. Notably, the edition came five years after journalist Amy Denniston had argued, unsuccessfully, for a multilingual vision of community making among her people.

Spanish editions of English-language newsweeklies nonetheless failed to satisfy those who viewed Afro-Caribbeans as perpetual outsiders. For some, the very idea of birth-based citizenship had to be radically reframed to counter the reality of an Afro-Caribbean isthmus. In response to this discourse Afro-Caribbean Panamanians developed two competing but related strategies: an open embrace of assimilationist discourse with the goal of confirming their citizenship and a continued diasporic framework that recognized shared histories and possible alliances with other Afro-descendants in the Americas.

2

Activist Formations

Fighting for Citizenship Rights and Forging Afro-Diasporic Alliances, 1940–1950

On September 9, 1941, Esmé Parchment wrote to President Arnulfo Arias asking that he recognize her Panamanian citizenship. Her petition, she explained, came in response to the "new Constitution," which stipulated that as someone with "parents classified as belonging to a restricted race," she needed "to solicit the recognition of her Panamanian nationality." Parchment, as her letter further highlighted, was born and raised in Panama and was a graduate of one of the country's largest teacher training schools. As she clarified in her letter, earlier in the year she had received a teaching position in the province of Darién but had recused herself because of her lack of citizenship certification. "I knew," she affirmed, "that without this recognition my employment would not be secure." Parchment wrote to President Arias only after having obtained an offer of employment as a teacher in the Canal Zone colored schools (czcs) and with the hope that, although her petition arrived after the allocated three-month deadline for such requests, President Arias, as chief executive, could belatedly recognize her citizenship.[1]

This chapter begins with Parchment's letter because it offers a concrete example of how increasingly established generations of Afro-Caribbean Panamanians navigated the issue of political belonging that had engulfed the pages of the *Panama Tribune* since its inception and that stoked the emergence of militant antiforeigner groups and intense repatriation campaigns throughout the 1930s. In particular, Parchment's letter illuminates how Afro-Caribbean Panamanians attempted to use their knowledge of the workings of nationalism and political protocol, as well as the space of the US-controlled Panama Canal Zone, to advocate for their citizenship rights. Parchment felt secure enough to write this letter, notwithstanding the lateness of her petition, because of her ability to support herself as a teacher in a space that other Afro-Caribbean Panamanians, including her father and siblings, also viewed as their home. This chapter explores how within the republic and in the US-controlled Canal Zone, Afro-Caribbean Panamanians relied on both nationalist and diasporic approaches to counter discriminatory policies that threatened their very right to the isthmus. The chapter also assesses the limits both approaches faced by the end of the 1940s.

Birth-Based Citizenship as a "Privilege"

During Arnulfo Arias's inaugural address as the twenty-first president of Panama, he warned his listeners that Panama faced a "grave ethnic problem." This problem, he declared, had roots in the opening of the Panama Canal and the migrant stream that thwarted the republic's full potential. As a counter to this reality, Arias offered a *panameñista* doctrine. This doctrine called for a full appreciation of the history and geography of the country, an upholding of those who farmed the land, and a prideful acceptance of "Panamá para los panameños," or "Panama for the Panamanians." Another crucial component of this doctrine called for the continued ethnic improvement of the nation. This could be achieved by only recruiting "desirable immigrants who sincerely sought to contribute to the development and progress of the country." It likewise required remaining vigilant against migration by less desirable groups, particularly antillanos, or Afro-Caribbeans, as well as Asians. His administration, Arias promised, would protect the ethnic integrity of the nation and, via a new constitution, uphold the interests of Panamanians over those of foreigners.[2]

Arias's intonation of "Panamá para los panameños" was not a new philosophical or political approach. As noted in the previous chapter, a group by that very name had been at the forefront of attempts to repatriate Afro-Caribbean migrants in the 1930s. Arias had helped form another hypernationalist group of the time, Acción Comunal, that promoted a similar message. Two things made Arias's use of this framing, in the early 1940s, distinctive. The first was the power that his position as president of the republic lent him. His racism did not emanate from disgruntled individuals or an independent group. His views were the official policy of the nation, and they coalesced with eugenicist and xenophobic platforms, including forced sterilization, which Arias had promoted as chief of the Department of

Health and Sanitation during the mid-1930s. Unlike most of his supporters, Arias had spent time in Italy and Germany during the consolidation of both the fascist state under Benito Mussolini and the Nazi regime under Adolf Hitler. He spoke with admiration of the need to reclaim the nation from internal enemies along fascist lines. Closer to home, Arias also had the example of Rafael Trujillo, who in 1937 ordered the massacre of twenty thousand Haitian migrants and their descendants, a group presented by Trujillo and the political elite as the true impediment to the growth of the Dominican Republic as an Iberian nation.[3] Second, unlike his predecessors, Arias focused on the offspring of "undesirable immigrants" as the true impediments to national progress. Previous hypernationalist campaigns also conflated migrants and their children; the 1928 Legislative Decree adding a petition process to birth-based citizenship recognition for those with foreign parents attested to this fact. Arias and his administration purported to go a step further. Rather than address the descendants of foreigners in general, they would, through a new constitution, denationalize those whose parents formed part of the "prohibited immigrant category."

Arias had presented reforming the country's constitution as one of the center pieces of his presidential campaign. In discussing this reform, however, he never mentioned changing citizenship rights. Most National Assembly deputies would not know of this provision until the reform was being debated in the assembly. A little over a month before taking office, Arias convened a special meeting of the assembly where he handpicked a five-man commission to review and update a reform project draft already in his possession. Based on this draft and following brief debate, the commission agreed to a constitutional clause denying birth-based citizenship to the children of "prohibited immigrants."[4]

On October 17, 1940, following a personal appearance by President Arias at the National Assembly, the constitutional reform project, including the denationalization clause, was made public. News outlets noted the momentous nature of the reform process, with one daily, *La Tribuna*, extolling the virtues of the new "Constitución Panameñista." Pedro Pezet, the president of *La Tribuna*, was also first alternate to the presidency and the president of the National Assembly. He had worked previously with Arnulfo Arias through Acción Comunal. Not surprisingly, his newspaper forcefully championed the reform efforts.[5] Only one newspaper, the *Panama Tribune*, denounced the proposed changes to citizenship recognition from its first public unveiling. Writing about Article 12 of the constitution, which denied automatic birth-based citizenship to those with "prohibited immigrant" parents,

Sidney Young asked: "What is to be the future of this group of young people? How is it possible to maintain an appreciable number of the population devoid of all national status, to be veritable men without a country, without creating a far worse problem than that which existed before?"[6]

Young called on the National Assembly to carefully consider what such a drastic change would mean not only for those affected but for the future of the nation. "It would be a very sad thing," he warned, "if this nation were to embark on a course which, except for its adaptation by a few misguided totalitarian countries, has been universally regarded as going backward."[7] This reference to "misguided totalitarian countries" alluded to Italy and Germany, although Young opted not to name them. This discretion connected to a shared understanding that Arias and members of his party, which he also did not directly name, admired totalitarianism and that an explicit condemnation by an Afro-Caribbean Panamanian newspaper might only lead to additional racial harassment. After all, only days before the 1940 presidential elections, Arias and his supporters had successfully pressured the only other candidate for the presidency to withdraw from the election, making Arias the uncontested winner.[8]

Young and the *Tribune* team were not alone in expressing their alarm at the prospect of tens of thousands of denationalized Afro-Caribbean Panamanians. The broadest example of this urgency came in the form of a petition submitted to the National Assembly in late October. In this petition, more than five hundred Afro-Caribbean Panamanian signers warned of the immense injustice that would befall not only the petitioners but thousands like them if the proposed nationality law took effect. They reminded the assembly deputies that all had spent the entirety of their lives in Panama, had registered for and voted in presidential and assembly elections, and had always "felt proud that Destiny allowed [them] to be born [in the republic]." The nationality law, however, especially if applied retroactively, had the potential of denationalizing tens of thousands of those whose parents formed part of the "prohibited immigrant" groups, even if their birth preceded the law's implementation. The petitioners therefore asked the deputies to consider carefully the proposed law and make the necessary changes to prevent unjust denationalizations.[9]

Of note in the petition is that its authors did not seek to attack the very idea of "prohibited immigrants." They apparently accepted that this aspect of citizenship and naturalization law would, for that moment, go unchanged. Instead they focused on protecting those who already had the opportunity to exercise "their rights and privileges as citizens," pointing to the grave danger of losing thousands of committed citizens as a result of unfair application of the law. Also significant about the petition is that many of the signees would go on to play prominent roles in ensuing debates about citizenship and the future of Afro-Caribbean Panamanian activism within and outside the isthmus. Elected officials responded with ridicule and distractions rather than serious engagement with the signers' concerns.[10]

The assembly further targeted Afro-Caribbean descendants despite adding a transitory article to "soften" the nationality law. In the October 17 draft of the constitution, those with one "prohibited immigrant" parent and one Panamanian-born parent remained eligible for citizenship. Following debate, this eligibility was revoked if the "prohibited immigrant" parent "belonged to the black race whose original language is not Spanish." Afro-Caribbean Panamanians were thus punished for pointing out the inequity of the law. As for the transitory Article 13, it delayed all denationalizations for three months after the ratification of the constitution and allowed for those disqualified to directly petition President Arias for their citizenship. The commission had proposed a six-month petition period but were outvoted by the assembly. Petitions were judged on the basis of each applicant proving that they were raised in Panama and that their principal language was Spanish. The inclusion of this article attempted to downplay the racism that undergirded the law by suggesting that those who truly sought citizenship could promptly and without difficulty submit their applications.[11]

Remarking on the passing of the revamped nationality law, the *Tribune* made note of the five deputies who voted against the measure: Alfredo Alemán (Panamá), Juan A. Galindo (Colón), Pablo Othon (Darién), José M. Varela (Herrera), and Simón Vega (Bocas del Toro). Othon held the distinction of being the only member of the assembly of Chinese ancestry. Collectively he and his dissenting peers denounced the racist nature of the law and questioned the idea of revoking anyone's citizenship rights, especially retroactively. They likewise noted the economic contributions made by so-called prohibited immigrants, the fact that some of the very officials voting on the measure owed their positions to the groups they now sought to bar, and the resentment and hatred that would follow denationalization.[12]

On November 22, 1940, a little after a month of discussion, the National Assembly voted in favor of the full proposed constitution, including the "softened" nationality law. Two days before this vote, the assembly also agreed to review a change in electoral law to allow for a plebiscite to determine when the new constitution would go into effect. Municipalities from all over the country sent letters to the assembly in support of the plebiscite. Arnulfo

Arias had proposed the plebiscite and securing municipal support during his pre-inauguration meeting with the National Assembly. Four days later the assembly passed Law 9, which introduced plebiscites into the nation's electoral process. Shortly thereafter, the Ministry of Government and Justice passed two executive decrees calling for the plebiscite to be held on December 15, which would allow the populace to decide whether the constitutional changes would take effect on January 2, 1941. This date was chosen to honor the tenth anniversary of the political coup led by Acción Comunal. A vote in favor of the measure would allow the assembly and Arias to skirt the requirement of waiting for the next elected assembly to ratify any constitutional changes.[13]

Ninety-eight percent of voters backed an early implementation of the new constitution. What explained this result? Critics of the reform and the speed of the process noted that most citizens approached the plebiscite with the understanding that the measure would pass, with or without their votes. Anyone employed by the government, they insisted, voted "yes" to keep their jobs. This did not stop at least one election official from refusing to participate in the process.[14] Given established patterns of election fraud, illicitly inflated numbers in favor of the plebiscite may also explain this very high percentage victory. Those advocating for the constitutional reform, including President Arias, took to the airwaves, public meetings, and newspapers to proclaim all the progressive aspects of the new constitution. These included welfare protection for all children (regardless of "legitimacy"), social assistance, habeas corpus, and state recognition of workers' rights. These campaigners brushed aside any criticisms of features of the reform that proved problematic, such as denationalization, presenting it as a necessary step toward improving the nation.[15] "Progress," in this way, was forged on the backs of those stripped of their citizenship. By using labels such as "prohibited" and "undesirable," epithets in circulation since the early twentieth century, political leaders acculturated their citizenry into accepting denationalization as inevitable.

We, Too, Are Panamanians

What of those most affected by the provisions of the new law? How did they respond to the new regulations pertaining to citizenship acquisition? Some actually went through the formal process of petitioning President Arias for their citizenship. This process, as outlined by Law 8 of 1941, required providing proof of birth in Panama, sworn testimonies by three witnesses attesting to the applicant having been born and raised in the republic, and fluency in Spanish.[16] Months after submitting their petitions, however, many still had no updates on their cases. Some would not hear back on their applications until three years later.[17] Part of this delay rested on an additional round of investigations that Arias often required for such petitions. Investigators from the Ministry of Agriculture and Commerce interviewed applicants, their families, and their neighbors to assess the validity of their applications. One such report, provided to Arias on August 20, 1941, included "observations" on thirty-one applicants. These investigations focused on where applicants worked or went to school, the ancestry of their parents, and their marital status. Only after reviewing these reports would Arias make a decision on citizenship recognition.[18]

Esmé Parchment, with whom I began this chapter, also petitioned Arias directly, although she did so outside the formal application process. Still her petition shared one key similarity with other applicants investigated in the August 1941 report—she was educated (although her teaching credentials placed her in a category all her own) and had gainful employment in the Canal Zone, where the president had no power. Her letter nonetheless acknowledged the shadow that the nationality law cast over her life. She had turned down a teaching position in Darién out of fear of being dismissed because of her citizenship status and wrote to Arias only after having secured a position in the Canal Zone.

Parchment was the youngest of three children born in the zone and the only one of her siblings educated at the secondary and teacher training level in Panama City. Her brother and older sister attended high school in Jamaica and eventually taught in the Canal Zone colored schools system. Her father, born in Jamaica, was a respected veteran teacher in this same system.[19] Not surprisingly, Parchment looked to the zone and the CZCS for gainful employment and support. Unlike her siblings and her father, though, Parchment was twenty years old when the 1941 Constitution was enacted. She did not possess a national identity card, without which daily life in the republic would be quite difficult. Just as she was about to begin her adult life, the new law challenged her rights to the isthmus. Through her letter, which showcased her educational credentials and her Spanish-language skills, Parchment hoped to prove that she had all the required qualities for Panamanian citizenship.

An additional item also made Parchment's letter to Arias unique. She acknowledged that dubious legal advice explained why she had submitted her application late. A "well known attorney," she explained had "informed her that she did not have any rights to [Panamanian citizenship] because she was born in the Canal Zone."[20] Such an interpretation relegated Parchment to perpetual statelessness. In writing to Arias, then, she not only presented the case for her citizenship recognition but also revealed that others like her faced the double challenge of misinformation and lack of political capital. By writing directly to the president, she sought to build some political capital for herself. Parchment did not attain her citizenship recognition through this letter, although she would before the end of the decade. In July 1946 Parchment traveled to the United States, and by 1954 she called New York City home. Both outcomes would not have been possible without first securing a passport to travel outside Panama. Her 1941 letter showcased her deep desire to prove that she was worthy of citizenship and spoke to the degree in which she viewed education, literacy, and patriotism as something that should earn her full citizenship without reservation.[21]

For others, such as Colón attorney Pedro N. Rhodes, challenging the legality of the nationality law and related immigration laws best affirmed his worthiness as a citizen. Rhodes was born in Colón in 1894, received his elementary education there, and traveled to the Anglophone Caribbean for his secondary education. On his return, he trained as a lawyer through correspondence courses and secured the tutoring services of well-known attorney Alejandro Rodriguez Camarena. By 1919 he served on the Colón Municipal Council. Six years later he applied for and obtained his license to practice law, making him one of only thirty-eight people in all of Colón, and 0.05 percent of the country's entire population, to have such a license.[22] Through his advocacy work on behalf of Afro-Caribbeans facing discrimination due to changes in naturalization and citizenship laws in the 1930s, Rhodes also received national attention and the support of Socialist Party leader Demetrio Porras. As a National Assembly deputy in 1934, Porras nominated Rhodes as second vice president of the republic, a symbolic gesture but one that hinted that Afro-Caribbean Panamanians had some allies.[23] Unfortunately, Porras was in the minority, as the passage of the nationality law made clear.

By 1941, Rhodes emerged at the forefront of those petitioning the assembly regarding the nationality law. Although this petition proved unsuccessful, Rhodes remained determined to fight against this law. He began by challenging the legality of Article 13 of the 1941 Constitution and Executive Decree No. 59 of January 1942. This decree declared that those individuals who had not submitted their citizenship recognition petitions by the three-month deadline would need to obtain identity cards as foreigners with the designation of *nacionalidad no comprobada*, or nationality undetermined. It also specified that individuals who already had Panamanian cédulas but had not submitted to the petition process would need to return said cédulas and receive new cards identifying them as foreigners of undetermined nationality. As Rhodes argued, this designation was "repugnant, detestable and void of all juridical meaning."[24] Even more alarming was that due to the unjust retroactivity policy, more than fifty thousand persons born in Panama since 1903 now faced the prospect of being labeled foreigners in their own place of birth.

In presenting this challenge Rhodes obtained the support of acting attorney general Felipe Juan Escobar. Escobar was the first person of African descent to hold this position. The Afro-Caribbean community followed his career closely. This shared pride in Escobar's accomplishments ran counter to attempts to pit Black people on the isthmus against one another on the basis of supposed cultural and physical incompatibility, which sometimes proved effective. At this early 1940s moment, this was not the case. Securing Escobar's support was quite significant because he had served as an outside expert for the commission behind the 1941 Constitution.[25] In his brief to the court, which the *Tribune* published in full for its readers, Escobar not only supported Rhodes's challenge of Article 13 and Decree 59 but also commented on the far-reaching implication of denationalization on the basis of race. This change, he declared, went against citizenship practices in all other American republics and relied on the false notion of the racial homogeneity of the Panamanian people, creating "a group of social pariahs" rejected by their own government. To resolve this injustice Escobar called on the Supreme Court to recognize the citizenship of all those who prior to 1941 enjoyed Panamanian status and to stop the practice of issuing identity cards with the label "nationality undetermined." Such a label went against all modern constitutional laws and denied these individuals access to their rightful nationality.[26]

Rhodes's appeal to the Supreme Court, notwithstanding Escobar's support, was denied. Denationalization and all provisions of the 1941 Constitution and related decrees remained in effect.[27] According to the records of the Ministry of Government and Justice, throughout 1942 hundreds of Afro-Caribbean Panamanians were issued identity cards as "foreigners" and "foreigners of undetermined nationality." Adding to this indignity was the parenthetical identifier of (born in Panama) also printed on these cards. One, thus, could be born in Panama yet remain a perpetual foreigner. The problematic nature of this policy was not lost on officials tasked with its execution. In an October 1942 report to the Ministry of Government and Justice, Manuel M. Grimaldo F., in his capacity as general registrar, expressed deep reluctance at having to issue foreign identity cards to individuals born in Panama. He cited cases of individuals seeking to register the birth of their children who now had to register themselves as foreigners notwithstanding already appearing in the civil registry as Panamanians. Grimaldo, following up on similar arguments posed by Rhodes and Escobar, cited various laws that in his opinion superseded Article 13, including Article 103, which upheld the practice of nonretroactivity in the implementation of laws. As he noted in his report, it still rested on the Supreme Court and the National Assembly to offer public officials like himself much-needed clarity on the future of citizenship laws in the country.[28]

Rather than waiting on justices or deputies to find enlightenment regarding the citizenship crisis, Rhodes and other Afro-Caribbean Panamanians called for a full-scale review of the 1941 Constitution. In January 1944, he and other interested men in the community created the Comité Pro-Reforma Constitucional (Committee for the Reform of the Constitution), with the aim of targeting all constitutional amendments that sought to deny or curtail the citizenship rights of Afro-Caribbean Panamanians.[29] As noted by Oscar Cragwell, a journalist for the *Panama Tribune* and another signee to the 1940 petition, the Comité Pro-Reforma proved especially significant because it indicated a move away from "the policy of permitting others to fight our battles, something we have been permitting for too long." Cragwell referred to the lack of political action and capital, which in his estimation made the Afro-Caribbean community vulnerable. The committee moved Afro-Caribbean Panamanians away from the role of bystanders and toward that of political agents. Only this level of engagement, Cragwell averred, would prevent something akin to "the shocking debacle of 1941 which made us men without a country." Men like Rhodes, he sustained, were poised to vindicate their community's goals.[30]

Cragwell was correct in noting the political vulnerability of Afro-Caribbeans in the mid-1940s. While the first years of the decade saw the rise of a Popular Front movement represented by leftist groups like the Socialist Party, the Partido del Pueblo (the People's Party), the Federación de Estudiantes Panameños (the Federation of Panamanian Students), the Juventud Antifascista Panameña (Antifascist Panamanian Youth), and the Frente Patriótico de la Juventud (Youth Patriotic Front), none denounced the denationalization feature of the 1941 Constitution. All expressed concern over the country verging toward fascism and growing dependence on the United States, concerns shared by other Popular Front movements throughout Latin America, but few challenged the racism and xenophobia that allowed for the nationality law and similarly discriminatory statutes to prevail.[31] Some Afro-Caribbeans did join some of these organizations. Floyd Britton was among the leaders of the Federación de Estudiantes Panameños and played a pivotal role during protests against the Canal Zone in the late 1950s and 1960s. Yet the collective consensus in these organizations was to avoid addressing xenophobia in the hopes of creating alliances that could cross class, ethnic, racial, and gender identities while not challenging an apparent consensus on conditioning citizenship access.[32]

Instability within the national government nevertheless brought Rhodes, the Comité, and his supporters closer to their aim of constitutional reform. In early June 1944, President Ricardo Adolfo de la Guardia, under pressure of a political coup, appointed a codification committee to rewrite the national constitution. De la Guardia had held the Panamanian presidency since October 1941, following the removal of Arnulfo Arias from office. As minister of government and justice under Arias, de la Guardia formed a coalition of similar-minded politicians seeking the president's ouster on the grounds that Arias sought to give himself dictatorial powers (the 1941 Constitution expanded the power of the presidency, including an extension of the presidential term from four to six years). De la Guardia did not oppose all aspects of the new constitution. During the assembly debates he championed the nationality law and its explicit denationalization of Afro-Caribbeans. Arias's unauthorized departure from the country, something prohibited in the new constitution, provided his opponents with the needed rationale to depose him.[33] By 1944 with the possibility of adding two more years to his presidency per the terms of the 1941 Constitution, de la Guardia faced growing opposition from the National Assembly regarding the legitimacy of his administration. With the codification committee, de la Guardia hoped to pitch constitutional reform as an immediate political agenda. The committee in turn promised to give detailed attention to the denationalization issue, a gesture that met with approval among Afro-Caribbean Panamanian advocates.[34]

Reflecting on de la Guardia's creation of the codification committee, Sidney Young expressed both hope and caution. As he told his readers, the committee would at last address Panama's shameful distinction as "the only nation among those professing the ideals of democracy that has deprived persons in its sovereign territory of a national status and designated them as of 'undetermined nationality:' veritable pariahs in the land of their birth."

He made note to his readers that the members of the committee, headed by attorney and former president Ricardo J. Alfaro, had invited organizations, institutions, and individual citizens to share their opinions on the reform effort. As Young insisted: "Common-sense indicate[d] that those most directly affected should be the ones to make their voices heard." Afro-Caribbean Panamanians had much to say regarding the disempowering and unjust effects of the nationality law.[35]

The Liga Cívica Nacional (LCN), or National Civic League, embraced the call for Afro-Caribbean self-advocacy in the constitutional reform debates. Business leaders, journalists, and entrepreneurs created the LCN in July 1944. The governing board of the organization also included signees of the 1940 petition, including Hugo C. Bycroft (president) and George Westerman (treasurer). Born after the 1903 founding of the republic, a new generation composed the bulk of the leadership and membership of the LCN and championed the slogan "unity and fraternity among all Panamanians without distinctions of race, origin or color." This slogan contrasted with the exclusionist mandates of the nationality law, although it too created a distinction between native-born and naturalized Panamanian citizens. Membership to the organization was open only to those born in Panama. This birth criterion excluded older longtime influential members of the community, such as Jamaican-born Sidney Young and other *Tribune* writers, and embraced a new wave of "native isthmian" leadership strategy. All members had to pay one balboa (US$1) as part of their membership dues. Based on the available records of the organization, no women were members, though women such as Nella Gunning provided their services as translators and donated generously to the organization.[36]

The LCN pushed forth an agenda that focused on nationalism, assimilation, and homogeneity, ideologies that had previously been used against Afro-Caribbean Panamanians but that the LCN now sought to repackage. As explained in the organization's mission statement, the organization sought to "foster a true national sentiment among all Panamanians, and to promote the existence of perfect solidarity among all elements of the Panamanian Republic." Another core goal included "assimilating all of its members to the culture, customs, and language of the nation, with the ultimate goal of making a wholly united and homogenous nation." These dual goals explicitly upheld Afro-Caribbeans as Panamanians, while also acknowledging the importance of greater assimilation efforts to promote a unified nation. In other words, the LCN proudly presented itself as a Panamanian organization that sought only to strengthen national unity.[37]

Regarding its challenges to the nationality law, on July 19, 1944, the LCN submitted a ten-page petition, signed by one thousand supporters, to the codification committee appointed by President de la Guardia. Westerman served as the chair of the committee, which put together the petition and coordinated signatures throughout the republic.[38] Westerman's involvement spoke to his rise as a respected journalist on the isthmus, and one who could, unlike Young and the older cadre of journalists, speak of himself as a Panamanian by birth. Born in Colón in 1910, Westerman received his elementary education in the Canal Zone colored schools and then secured tutors in Panama City. As a teenager, Westerman worked in the zone as a messenger, an office assistant, and a clerk-typist, before he became a sports columnists and regular contributor to the English-language press. Westerman also made connections with some of Panama's commercial elite through his work as a secretary for the Cerveceria Panamá (Panama Beer Company) and the Panama Light Company. One of his former bosses, Ernesto de la Guardia Jr., would become president of the republic.[39]

For the wording of the actual petition, Westerman and the LCN reached out to none other than Pedro N. Rhodes, who through his earlier work and creation of the Comité Pro-Reforma had a wealth of knowledge about citizenship and naturalization laws. The organization also recruited Jorge Illueca, a white Panamanian and Harvard-educated attorney, who shared in the LCN's desire to challenge the nationality law. The 1944 petition, not unlike that submitted four years earlier, focused on the dangers of statelessness, with data collected following the 1941 Constitution's enactment. In between the first and second petition, denationalization had grown from a theoretical possibility to a nightmarish reality. As noted in the 1944 petition, those affected by the nationality law included people "born in the Republic of Panama of West Indian parentage or of the 'Negro Race,'" "descendants of Panamanian mothers and Negro fathers," "descendants of Panamanian fathers and Negro mothers," "those who went to study abroad and [were] abandoned, without a country," "the parents of children whose only crime [was] that of being born [their] children," and all others who after 1941 became people of "unproven nationality." This list demonstrated that belonging to the "Negro Race" formed the core of denationalization, and that application of the nationality law had a dangerous multigenerational effect.[40]

The petitioners accordingly asked the codification committee to return to the birth-based and naturalization criteria for citizenship outlined in the 1904 Constitution, and for the extension of eligibility to all those born in Panama after January 2, 1941, whose parents formed part of the "prohibited immigrant" group. These changes, they argued, would cohesively and in a just manner bring together the principles of jus soli (birth based) and jus sanguinis (lineage based) to citizenship and naturalization. To defend their stance, the petitioners cited the work of two legal scholars who formed part of the codification committee, Ricardo J. Alfaro and José D. Moscote. They likewise strategically placed the citizenship question in the context of the ensuing world war. Panama, they affirmed, "could live up to the true democracy for which the allied forces, of all colors, races and creeds fight so resolutely today on all the fronts of the world." The nationality law, they insisted, while a very local matter had enormous consequences for the future of democracy.[41]

In response to coup plans by assembly deputies frustrated at the speed of the codification process, as well as to the growing popularity of opposition parties like the Partido Nacional Renovador (National Renovation Party), on December 29, 1944, President de la Guardia suspended the 1941 Constitution. He also announced Constituent Assembly elections for May 1945. The members of this assembly would review the work of the codification committee, vote on a new constitution, and also elect the next president of the republic. Until the promulgation of this new magna carta, all laws connected to the 1941 Constitution would be on hold, including the nationality law. A wide array of political parties supported a popular electoral process to create the 1945 Constituent Assembly. This directly countered the commission-via-the-executive that created the 1941 Constitution. As the leader of the reform effort, de la Guardia calculated that his political allies would secure the largest number of delegate seats.[42]

During these maneuverings in political strategy, members of the Afro-Caribbean community focused on the Constituent Assembly elections. By early April, three Afro-Caribbean Panamanians, Pedro N. Rhodes, Maximo Masters, and Henry Spencer, had secured political nominations from the Renovador Party.[43] The party had made explicit efforts to recruit Afro-Caribbeans and vocally denounced discrimination against this group. This marked a shift in the party, created in 1932 by Francisco Arias Paredes, a participant in the Acción Comunal coup, who by the mid-1940s spoke of the need for workers, peasants, Afro-Caribbeans, and women to unite against the oligarchy and demand state-led social and economic reforms. In addition to running for political seats, Afro-Caribbeans like Oscar Cragwell launched and edited a new section of the *Tribune*, the Political Page, sponsored partly by the Renovador Party, which called on the whole community to vote, regardless of party allegiances.[44] As the assembly elections would be the country's first truly universal election, recently enfranchised women received continuous reminders in this section to vote.[45]

Even with expanded suffrage, Afro-Caribbean Panamanian assembly nominees faced tremendous odds. First, they called on the very people who had suffered from unjust applications of the law to come out and vote. Second, some in the community had not secured their nationality cards since the 1941 Constitution had passed. Third, whether anyone outside their community would vote for them remained unclear. Last, of the three Afro-Caribbean Panamanian nominees, only one, Rhodes, was a first-round pick for the party. Renovador Party voters in Colón would need to choose between him and Gil Blas Tejeira, a well-known white journalist cited by the *Tribune* as a "supporter of the West Indian cause."[46] In the end no Afro-Caribbean Panamanians were elected to the Constituent Assembly. The community once more had to rely on outsiders, albeit some sympathetic ones, to speak on their behalf.

On February 26, 1946, the Constituent Assembly ratified a new constitution. To the delight of supporters of the Comité Pro-Reforma, the LCN, and Rhodes and the other Renovador Party nominees, the language of "prohibited immigrant" and direct attacks against Afro-Caribbean Panamanians did not appear anywhere in the constitution. A reframed version of the nationality law was also passed, although not without complications. Starting with the study and revision phase of the process, a clear divide emerged between those who sought to eliminate any qualifying criteria connected to birth-based citizenship (the minority opinion) and those who held that some citizens, specifically Afro-Caribbean Panamanians, had failed to assimilate into the nation (the majority opinion). Of the fifty-one deputies who voted on the law, only thirty approved recognizing birth-based citizenship and only if it included qualifying criteria. Those born in Panama of foreign-born parents would, on reaching legal age, provide an affidavit "opt[ing] for Panamanian nationality and irrevocably renounce the nationality of their parents." They also had to provide proof that they were "incorporated spiritually and materially to national life." While no longer made immediately stateless due to "prohibited immigrant" parents, Afro-Caribbean Panamanians remained "potential citizens" requiring proper vetting prior to gaining their full citizenship rights.[47]

The constitutional reform effort highlighted a direct attempt by Afro-Caribbean Panamanians to cement their presence on the isthmus via the legislative process. For those who affirmed that Afro-Caribbean Panamanians needed a stronger political presence and greater recognition within the nation, this was only the beginning. Yet, for others, what unfolded during the reform efforts indicated that the republic alone could not satisfy the various claims that Afro-Caribbeans sought to make on the isthmus. The Canal Zone soon emerged as a space in which to conceptualize activist struggles that included and went beyond securing still contested citizenship rights.

Educators as Advocates

By the early 1940s, Afro-Caribbean Panamanian teachers, trained in and outside Panama, formed a growing majority within the CZCS system. Prior to this period, teachers born and trained in the Anglophone Caribbean had filled these posts.[48] Unlike some of their predecessors, these 1940s teachers had known only the zone and the republic as home and were of legal age during the intense debates about citizenship eligibility, repatriation, and denationalization unfolding since the late 1920s. Furthermore, these younger educators, some inspired by mentorship received from senior colleagues, fully embraced their roles as advocates and leaders within the CZCS and the Canal Zone as a whole.

One such leader was Leonor Jump. Jump, whose support for higher education received attention in chapter 1, had by the 1940s steadily advanced within the CZCS. At a time when the number of men teaching still outpaced that of women, Jump had not only secured teaching positions outside the domestic arts posts typically reserved for women, but also was the principal of the only teacher training school open to people of color in the zone.[49] The La Boca Normal School became operational in 1935, graduating thirty-seven new teachers in December 1938. Jump was not part of this first class, having traveled to New York as a visiting student to Columbia's Teacher's College. Two years later she began teaching at the La Boca Junior High School. Jump later applied and was accepted to teach the second class of the Normal School, in March 1941. Two years later she was appointed principal of the Normal School.[50]

During her time at the Normal School, Jump promoted ideas that distinguished her from some of her older CZCS colleagues. In her first year at the Normal School, Jump created the Círculo Español (Spanish Circle) club. The task of this club was to "further develop and improve relations between Panamanians of West Indian ancestry and [their] Latin compatriots" through visits, cultural programs, and lectures by "eminent individuals in Panamanian society." Through such programs, the group hoped to learn more about their national culture and to also make clear their overall

FIGURE 2.1 Leonor Jump with Club de Español in La Boca Junior High School, 1940. From *La Bocan* (Panama City: Star and Herald, 1940), 26. University of Florida, Digital Panama Canal Collection.

"interest in all things Panamanian." The Círculo Español grew out of the success of a similar group Jump created while teaching at the La Boca Junior High School. The latter group's yearbook picture (figure. 2.1) featured twenty-three members, seventeen young women and six young men, attired with dresses and suits, hair pulled back and styled or closely cropped. Most are not smiling and instead replicate Jump's steady gaze. The photo is meant to exude dignity and pride. Jump took a similar mantra with her to the Normal School's Círculo Español. Due to her educational training in the Canal Zone and Panamá, including coursework leading to a pharmacology degree from the Universidad de Panamá, Jump had the connections and language skills needed to serve as the creator and faculty adviser for the group.[51]

The timing of the group's creation coincided with the drastic citizenship law changes noted earlier. By August 1941, the date of the Círculo's creation, the new constitution was in full effect. Some students who formed part of the recently admitted 1941 class probably went through the petitioning process and awaited a response from President Arias. Others might have opted to forego petitioning, either because they were not yet seeking employment, did not understand the process, or sought to see how the new law would unfold. According to the constitution, even Jump technically had to petition for recognition of her citizenship, although since she already possessed a cédula and a passport, she likely ignored this process. With the club, Jump (figure 2.2) provided students at the Normal School with the opportunity

FIGURE 2.2 Leonor Jump, 1944. From *The Thinker* (La Boca, Canal Zone: La Boca Normal Training School 1944), 8. University of Florida, Digital Panama Canal Collection.

to appreciate that their rights on and claims to the isthmus extended beyond the zone and included the republic. As more informed citizens they would also be better equipped for the political realities that awaited them after graduation.

In addition to serving as a key adviser and organizer of the Círculo Español, Jump also helped establish the first school-community library for students in the Canal Zone. Since the inauguration of the CZCS system, students had made use of secondhand textbooks discarded from whites-only schools. For reading outside the classroom, newspapers, small libraries in clubhouses (each town had one such clubhouse), and select household libraries were the only options. To address the lack of a library dedicated to student needs, in August 1942 Jump created a library committee with the task of raising funds for a student public library in La Boca, the largest of the zone colored towns. Jump served as its chair, with fellow teachers Robert H. Beecher and Edward A. Gaskin, as well as journalist George Westerman, rounding out the remainder of the group. All committee members shared as

FIGURE 2.3 Saturday Morning Story Hour, La Boca Library, 1950. The books and autographed photographs collected by the library committee are evident in this image. From RG 185, Photographs Related to the Operation and Development of the Panama Canal Zone, c. 1938–c. 1960, NARA, College Park, Maryland.

commonalities their birth on the isthmus and their status as alumni of the CZCS. Westerman also donated dozens of autographed photographs of prominent African Americans, in addition to numerous books from his own collection. As a result of its endeavors, the committee raised more than six hundred dollars and collected almost one thousand books from individuals and groups within and outside Panama. To ensure that the library operated efficiently, and to bestow a sense of ownership, Jump had Normal School students create a card catalog. Through events like the Saturday Morning Story Hour (figure 2.3), the youngest members of the community also had opportunities to claim this space as their own.[52]

The changes that Jump implemented within and outside her classroom paralleled growing confidence and energy among her peers. One key example of this growth included the creation of the Canal Zone Colored Teachers Association (CZCTA) in December 1941.[53] This association, unlike earlier groups such as the Panama Canal West Indian Employees Association (PCWIEA), had significant representation from isthmian-born

Afro-Caribbeans educated in the zone, who had worked in the CZCS system since the 1930s. The PCWIEA had emerged in 1924 as an alternative to labor union organizing following the 1920 Canal Zone labor strike. Since its inception, and up to the early 1940s, men born and raised in the Anglophone Caribbean led the PCWIEA on behalf of these workers and their families.[54] The CZCTA invited participation from all teachers, regardless of their place of birth, and had a young base of leaders and supporters for whom the zone was both workplace and home.

As a group, the CZCTA successfully fought for higher salaries and access to university courses through a University of Nebraska extension program in the zone. The association also had zone officials agree to place those with degrees from US universities on the US citizen payroll. Overall, the CZCTA made excellent strides obtaining higher salaries and greater educational opportunities for its members.[55] Securing greater opportunities for CZCS students proved more of a challenge. One of the first student needs taken up by the group included the creation of a high school within the CZCS system. Prior to 1940 education for students of color ended in the eighth grade. In the mid-1940s a ninth grade was added. The CZCTA called for secondary schools and professional training for students in the CZCS. In advocating for these measures, the association drew on years of campaigning led by more senior teachers, in addition to respected journalists in the community, such as Sidney Young, Albert E. Bell, and increasingly George Westerman. Members of the CZCTA also added their own specific experiences as CZCS alums. The first two presidents of the CZCTA, Aston M. Parchment (Esmé Parchment's older brother; figure 2.4) and Edward A. Gaskin (figure 2.5), had completed elementary and junior high school training in the zone. Gaskin would go on to form part of the first Normal School class, while Parchment received his secondary training in Jamaica. Both men were appointed as teachers in the CZCS system and in late 1941 created the CZCTA.[56] Jump did not serve as an officer of the union but was signatory to all association letters sent to US officials in and outside the Canal Zone. She would also be the only woman within the CZCTA's inner circle.[57]

Connecting Jump, Parchment, and Gaskin to their emergence as leaders in the CZCS was the support they received from senior teachers as well as select administrators. Jump's father, William Jump, was a respected teacher in the system, an active member and leader in various La Boca cultural and social spaces, an occasional contributor to the *Panama Tribune*, and by the mid-1940s, among those urging fellow Afro-Caribbean Panamanians to vote in the Constituent Assembly elections. Parchment's father, John A.

FIGURE 2.4 Aston Parchment, 1944. From *The Thinker* (La Boca, Canal Zone: La Boca Normal Training School 1944), 9. University of Florida, Digital Panama Canal Collection.

FIGURE 2.5 Edward Gaskin, 1954. From "Your Town: La Boca," *Panama Canal Review*, June 4, 1954, 9.

Parchment, had more than twenty-five years of teaching experience in the zone and served as an elementary school principal there as well. Unlike Jump and Parchment, who had familial connections to the zone schools, Gaskin, whose father worked in canal maintenance, obtained much of his educational mentorship from one key teacher, Alfred E. Osborne. Osborne formed part of a very small group of Afro-Caribbeans (he was born in Antigua and educated in the Canal Zone and in the United States) living and working in the zone who had secured US citizenship. He was also by 1940 the only administrator of African descent in the entire zone school system. He served as supervisor of instruction for CZCS. Osborne's father had been a teacher in the zone since 1912, which by the early 1940s made him one of the most senior instructors in the system. Support from the Osbornes strengthened Gaskin's educational and leadership potential. Jump, Parchment, and Gaskin all brought with them a long history of making the most of the Canal Zone's opportunities even within its segregated system. As such, they represented the embodiment of incremental progress for Afro-Caribbean Panamanians within this space.[58]

Partly because of this lived reality, the CZCTA's leadership base embarked on a wide range of initiatives to convince other members of their community to unite for greater improvements, such as high school education and professional training. Among these activities were community-wide parent-teacher meetings and direct appeals to zone officials.[59] Because of their established presence in the zone, the teacher core leadership also directed their concerns to the US-based officials who ultimately controlled policy decisions within their system. One example included their October 1943 letter to the US commissioner of education, John W. Studebaker. Their letter presented secondary education and professional training as advances that would benefit the zone by providing "more intelligent and skillful workers" while also giving workers the needed tools for "more meaningful" lives within and outside the enclave. Their proposal therefore aimed to promote happier workers and prosperous communities, to the benefit of zone officials and Afro-Caribbeans alike.[60]

In advocating for higher education, the CZCTA also addressed issues of citizenship. The first line of their letter described the young people they advocated for as having "no nationality status." Indeed, under the 1941 Constitution none of these young people, as children of "prohibited immigrants," were eligible for Panamanian citizenship. US citizenship was likewise out of the question given that lineage-based citizenship, which privileged those born on the US mainland and their offspring, represented the zone norm. In early February 1942, the Canal Zone also implemented a new policy whereby those born in the zone or the republic and unable to obtain Panamanian cédulas would be categorized as "West Indian" for the purposes of citizenship. Given that West Indian was not an official citizenship anywhere in the world, this merely reenforced their status as stateless strangers.[61] Through their letter, though, the association presented access to secondary education for occupational and professional training as needed security during a time of great citizenship instability.[62]

CZCTA leadership also connected their petition to the politics of race and democracy in the ongoing global war, an approach also taken by the 1944 petitioners noted earlier in the chapter. "The great military conflict that is shaking the foundation of our present civilization indicates clearly the need for a more effective training program in the social sciences if the postwar world is to be permanently shaped according to democratic patterns. Furthermore, the cosmopolitan nature of the Isthmus of Panama makes it imperative that our school provide the kind of training that will develop appreciations for all races and understandings of the conditions that are essential to harmonious living."[63] World War II, therefore, had as much to do with stopping the racist ideologies shaping undemocratic ideas and policies as it did with weaponry and training. Racist thinking in this conflict provided a justification for the annihilation of entire groups of people. While no such violence erupted on the isthmus, the potential for such destructive practices formed part of the questioning as to where such ignorance and prejudice might lead. This was especially true where racial difference became shorthand for justified discrimination. Understandably the letter did not address the threat posed to democracy by US-sanctioned segregation in the zone, under which all teachers had to work. Still this 1943 letter sought to emphasize the value of educational opportunities that focused on racial diversity and democratic ambitions.

Besides promoting democratic understanding, the CZCTA called for the introduction or expansion of core subjects within their schools. Two included Negro history and Spanish. Regarding Negro history, the association expressed concern about their students having limited "self-respect and race pride."[64] They proposed year-round courses, open to all class levels, on the history and achievements of people of African descent. As for Spanish classes, CZCS students had access to this subject only from the seventh to ninth grades, which for many, particularly those living in the zone, would be their only opportunity to work on Spanish grammar, syntax, and speech. This placed the students wishing to transfer to high school or college in the republic at a disadvantage, since Spanish would be the principal language of instruction there. This did not mean that select graduates could not pursue this approach. The leadership of the CZCTA represented some firsthand examples. Without more comprehensive Spanish-language work, however, making this transition would continue to be an exception and not a valid possibility.[65]

In the letter to Commissioner Studebaker, the CZCTA also highlighted the best practices to ensure successful high school and professional programs in the zone. Among the most important of these was recruiting teachers from the isthmus, particularly those already familiar with the zone. Senior teachers, the CZCTA noted, had taken the initiative to enroll in night classes at the Universidad de Panamá, to take all available training sessions provided in the zone, and to use their own money to "purchase professional literature." Recent graduates from the La Boca Normal School likewise represented a talented pool of prospective candidates. As the CZCTA insisted, no teachers from outside the isthmus would be as "conversant with the peculiar problems and cherished aspirations of the colored residents of the Canal Zone."[66]

The work of the CZCTA and other advocates in the zone and the republic resulted in the observance of Negro History Week in all elementary schools in the CZCS system. Black history courses did not form part of the regular curriculum, but for a week students were encouraged to talk about Black achievements and progress in their classrooms.[67] In early 1946, zone officials announced plans to open two occupational high schools. Unfortunately, two key parts of the CZCTA's recommendations did not appear in the proposed schools. First, Spanish would not be offered in the high schools. Instead the focus would be on job training for "existing opportunities in the Canal Zone," without any focus on skills that would be useful beyond the enclave.[68] In a *Panama Tribune* piece, George Westerman spoke of the danger of not expanding Spanish classes in the CZCS, noting how this placed Afro-Caribbean students at a disadvantage when it came to petitioning for citizenship. As outlined in the 1946 Constitution, all applicants would need to prove "spiritual and material" incorporation into the nation. Without Spanish classes, where students learned more about the language, history, and geography of their country of birth, he argued, acquiring citizenship would prove incredibly difficult.[69]

The second facet of the CZCTA's proposal ignored by zone officials was staffing decisions for the new high schools. Although alums of the CZCS would serve as teachers in these new schools, the supervisors and principals would be white male US citizens.[70] Afro-Caribbean Panamanian teachers were trusted enough to teach but not to lead in the development or oversight of ninth through twelfth grade teaching. By 1946, Jump, as principal of the La Boca Normal School, remained the only CZCTA member and Afro-Caribbean Panamanian with a postelementary leadership position in the CZCS. The result of the CZCTA petitioning revealed that the group needed a stronger representational body to advocate more fully for communities of color in the zone.

Educators as Labor Union Activists

Armed with their experience in the CZCTA, various educators decided to take part in unionizing efforts across the zone. Twice between 1939 and 1945, the PCWIEA had unsuccessfully petitioned the American Federation of Labor (AFL), the dominant labor union in the zone, for a union charter. The entrenched racism of the Metal Trades Council and the Central Labor Union, two branches of the AFL representing white US workers, repeatedly blocked these efforts. The emergence of a new Afro-Caribbean Panamanian-led group, the Canal Zone Workers Union (CZWU), in 1944 promised to bring together the interests of both the PCWIEA and the CZCTA.[71] The membership of the CZWU included disgruntled former members of the PCWIEA and key leaders in the CZCTA, among them Aston Parchment and Edward Gaskin. A frustration with the "West Indians only" membership policy of the PCWIEA and disappointment with the limited achievements made by the PCWIEA and, to an extent, the CZCTA drew this membership base together. The CZWU called on all non-US zone workers to come together and approach an international labor organization as the best means of gaining improved working conditions and higher salaries for its members. In 1945 the CZCWU reached out to the Congress of Industrial Organizations (CIO). The PCWIEA also petitioned the CIO that same year.[72]

For both unions, an alliance with the CIO made strategic sense given its international reputation, credibility in the United States, and willingness to represent workers of color. News of the CIO and its inroads in recruiting Black workers were repeatedly featured in the pages of the *Panama Tribune*.[73] In July 1946 the CIO, under the leadership of Philip Murray, responded to both the CZWU and PCWIEA and designated the United Public Workers of America (UPWA) as the CIO branch responsible for organizing non-US citizens in the zone. The official name of the union would be Local 713 UPWA-CIO. Of the CIO branches of that time, the UPWA was recognized as unapologetically progressive for recruiting across race and gender lines. It also boasted Black leadership among its top elected officials. Ewart Guinier, the international secretary-treasurer of the UPWA, the second highest-ranking official in the union, was a New Yorker of Afro-Caribbean Panamanian ancestry.[74]

A month after the chartering of Local 713, Canal Zone officials recognized the new union. Such recognition was not guaranteed, but this change on the eve of the Cold War was likely propelled by fears that a non-US-affiliated and possibly communist-oriented union might make inroads in the zone. Officials worried about the Mexico-based Confederación de Trabajadores Latino Americanos (CTLA)/Confederation of Latin American Workers and its Marxist leader, Vicente Lombardo Toledano. As a union incorporated in the United States, the CIO could, if necessary, be brought before the US Congressional Committee on Un-American Activities.[75]

Local 713 organizers did not pay much attention to such constraints, instead focusing on recruiting non-US workers and union leaders across ethnic, racial, and national lines. The union's US international representatives appointed as their field representative Pascual Ampudia. Ampudia's bilingual skills and status as a Black man not subject to the country's citizenship petition process (he did not have parents belonging to a "prohibited immigrant race") no doubt figured into his choice as an intermediary between the US-based union body and the majority Black workforce. Francisco Araúz served as local union president. Araúz was also not subject to the citizenship petition process. Ampudia and Araúz, moreover, formed part of a small but growing number of non-Afro-Caribbean Panamanians who had joined the zone workforce by the 1920s.[76]

Afro-Caribbeans and their isthmian-born descendants still made up the majority of the non-US zone workforce in the 1940s. This numerical majority was likewise evident in the bulk of union leadership positions beyond the presidency. Edward Gaskin, for example, was elected as union vice president, with the position of treasurer held by Afro-Caribbean Panamanian Teodoro Nolan and that of secretary by Jamaican-born and longtime Panamanian resident Cespedes Burke. Various chapters of the union existed in the zone, and Afro-Caribbean Panamanians, most born or raised in this territory, were elected as chapter leaders. Together all elected officials, in addition to the field representative, composed the union's executive board.[77]

Local 713's focus on a popular-based and transnational approach was evident in the rallies held by the union. In addition to the presence of the union's white US international representatives, Gaskin, Burke, Araúz, and Parchment appeared in all its recruitment rallies. Furthermore, though the assistance of the New York City–based UPWA offices, the union secured the participation of African American performer Paul Robeson at four sold-out fundraising rallies. During his performances Robeson directly critiqued the discriminatory policies of US zone officials. As a sign of solidarity with the mostly Black workforce, he refused to perform in whites-only zone towns, choosing instead venues in Panamá and Colón.[78]

By mid-1947, spurred by rallies and fund-raising concerts, Local 713 had secured fifteen thousand members, more than half of all eligible workers. Some of the key union demands included the elimination of the gold and silver payroll system (whereby white US citizens, or "gold" roll employees, received higher wages than non-US "silver" roll employees), the creation of a single job classification structure, a decent minimum wage including annual increases, and maternity leave. The union also wanted access to civil service jobs, improved sick and rest leave, a retirement and pension plan, and the creation of a joint union-management committee on housing reform.[79]

As part of the CIO, Local 713 had a direct connection to the United States and labor politics therein. The New York office of the UPWA created the Citizens Committee to End Silver-Gold Jim Crow in Panama and counted on African American activists Max Yergan and W. E. B. Du Bois among its members.[80] The union also published a pamphlet titled *Jim Crow Discrimination against U.S. Employees in the Canal Zone*, reprinting pictures of the substandard and segregated facilities afforded to non-US workers and their families in the zone (figure 2.6). The pamphlet provided comparison tables on the unequal wages earned by US citizens and "silver" workers for the same jobs. Jim Crow practices in the zone, the UPWA pamphlet warned, could jeopardize the international reputation of the United States.[81]

Accusations of communistic philosophies ultimately posed a challenge to Local 713's agenda. Starting in late 1947, CIO officials in the United States accused the national union, including UPWA president Abram Flaxer, of communist affiliations. Some of these accusations made their way to the US Congress and depicted the two UPWA representatives in the Canal Zone, Max Brodsky (international representative) and Joseph Sachs (regional director), both from the United States, as communist sympathizers. Brodsky and Sachs denounced these allegations as attempts to detract from the work and successes of the union.[82] By early 1948, however, some union members began to question their stance. Among those calling for a firmer anticommunist stand from the union were teachers. They sought to make clear that as employees of the US government and in accordance with US president Truman's executive order barring Communist Party members or

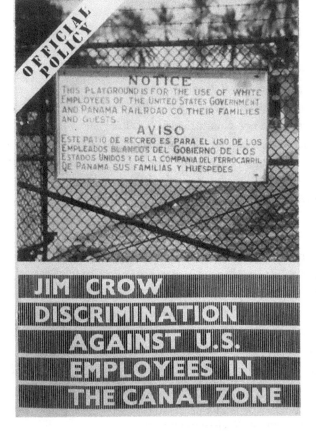

FIGURE 2.6
United Public
Workers of
America, *Jim
Crow Discrimina-
tion against U.S.
Employees in the
Canal Zone*, 1948,
Ewart Guinier
Papers, 9/9, Schom-
burg Center for
Research in Black
Culture, New York
Public Library.

sympathizers from federal employment, their union should oppose communism. They called for a resolution bearing this message but failed to secure
membership support. The majority of the membership did not want the
union to become embroiled in the communism versus anticommunism
debate. In March 1948, the Local 713 executive board told the membership
that the union would focus on labor matters alone and limit the attention
given to ideological and political ideas during union meetings.[83]

A handful of activists outside the union, primarily journalists, unsatisfied
with this result, began to push for an anticommunist pledge from Local 713.
Most adamant among them was George Westerman. Westerman remained
active in the Liga Cívica Nacional and was by 1947 also an associate editor
for the *Panama Tribune*. Westerman's first critique of Local 713 involved
Joseph Sachs's confrontation with the district attorney of the Canal Zone.

Sachs, in February 1948, demanded that DA Daniel E. McGrath "put up or shut up" regarding accusations of budgetary mishandling by Local 713 officials. For Westerman, this conduct was unbecoming of an international officer and jeopardized the overall cause of the membership. Allegations that Sachs and Brodsky had communist ties spurred Westerman to call on non-US zone employees to disassociate from the "communist-tainted" UPWA. Sachs expressed surprise that Westerman had chosen to denounce both him and the union as communist, given Westerman's support of the union prior to 1948.[84]

The ensuing debates between Westerman and Local 713 supporters revealed differences along class, ideological, and racial lines among advocates claiming to represent the same group: non-US workers in the zone. In one camp stood Westerman and his collaborators, including Sidney Young and teachers in Local 713. Young, Westerman, and CZCS teachers formed part of a burgeoning Afro-Caribbean leadership base that had years of experience navigating politics within the zone, whether as students, residents, or employees. In the other camp were Brodsky, Sachs, and their supporters, who included most officials on the Local 713 executive board, which represented various sectors of the zone employment base. For these officials, the accomplishments of Local 713 stood as evidence of the commitment of the UPWA and of Brodsky's and Sachs's support for key worker concerns. Pascual Ampudia traveled to New York in September 1948, as the elected president of the union, to express his frustration to W. E. B. Du Bois and others regarding the unfair label of *communist* being deployed against him and the union by white zone officials. As framed by Ampudia, accusations of communism simply sought to mask continued discrimination in the zone.[85] Indeed, Ampudia's assessment directly coincided with the strategies of US southern segregationists who labeled attempts at integration and unionization as communist-led campaigns. The Canal Zone was not the US South, and most zone officials were not white southerners, yet as Ampudia's observations suggested, connecting these two spaces were communist fears used to crush racial and economic justice.[86]

The national leadership of the UPWA and those opposed to Local 713 international representatives proved reluctant to see a connection between entrenched discrimination and accusations of communism. A month after Ampudia's New York visit, Abram Flaxer agreed to settle the civil libel suit against Sachs and the union. This followed Sachs's sentencing for criminal libel by a Canal Zone judge.[87] Reflecting on Flaxer's decision, Westerman reiterated that the *Panama Tribune* supported the continued affiliation of non-US zone workers to the CIO and welcomed "a strong, vigorous CIO

Union, whose white American representatives will confine themselves to industrial trade unionism."[88] The problem for Westerman was not anticommunist racists, as suggested by Ampudia, but rather domineering white men from the United States who he believed did not understand conditions in the Canal Zone. This September editorial was not the first time Westerman had referenced the whiteness of the Local 713 US representatives. He had done so eight months earlier, seeking to assure the union membership that Sachs and Brodsky were not the only "decent, sympathetic and courageous white American labor leaders belonging to the CIO" who were willing to work with non-US workers of color in the zone.[89] Following the UPWA court losses, Westerman no longer portrayed Sachs and Brodsky as decent, sympathetic, or courageous and instead suggested that there was a need to carefully monitor white American labor representatives who failed to condemn communism.

Westerman further alluded to race-based monitoring in one of his last editorials on the Local 713 debate. Sachs and Brodsky, he asserted, "were sent to serve the local membership; to suggest, recommend and guide, not to dominate the rank and file followers nor to become union masters."[90] Westerman, ever strategic with his use of words, knew the implications of terms such as "dominate" and "masters." What would it mean to have a white leadership, possibly communistic, dominating Black workers like overseers? In choosing to take such an avowedly anticommunist line, Westerman placed himself in opposition to unionist platforms that refused to demonize communism, the stance of most Local 713 members. Unlike these members, he saw no qualm in declaring communism the true enemy, thus inadvertently joining zone officials worried about the growth of a racially inclusive and progressive labor organization.

Why then did Westerman take this stance and why did many teachers join him? The designation of Canal Zone employees as "US government workers" appears to have been part of the consideration. In their estimation, the threat of being labeled communist risked the potential of upsetting zone officials who held the power to disband the union. As noted earlier, most Local 713 members were willing to take this risk, particularly given the progressive work undertaken by the union. Westerman and his allies were not. Instead, they focused on securing the trust and attention of not only zone authorities but also more moderate CIO officials initiating their own anticommunist purge in the United States. Westerman placed his own track record as a respected journalist and civic leader against the record of Local 713 with the confidence that US officials, in the zone and Washington, would ultimately back an anticommunism advocate. After all, the United States, the most powerful nation in the world, led the global anticommunism crusade of that period and had thousands of troops in the Canal Zone ready to enforce it.

The decision by Westerman and his allies to deploy an anticommunist discourse also revolved around "respectability politics" that called on members of an upwardly mobile working class to view their future success as anathema to "communist disarray." Understood in this manner, protesting against racism and discrimination in the workforce could continue, but only if carried out by specific race-conscious leaders who recognized communism as dangerous to class mobility. Westerman, as an emblem of a "self-made man" who went from being a messenger to the associate editor of a newsweekly, presented himself as the obvious leader in such an effort. Other Black activists, including politicians from the United States who shared Westerman's anticommunist sensibility regarding class mobility, would intervene in this debate over who should speak for Afro-Caribbean Panamanians employed in the Canal Zone.

Anticommunist Race Men and Proper Representation

On October 5, 1949, US Congressman Adam Clayton Powell Jr., the first elected Black congressman from the state of New York, declared his intention to investigate "labor management relations and fair employment practices in the Panama Canal Zone."[91] Powell chaired the House Subcommittee on Education and Labor, which explained his interest in zone labor affairs. Powell also formed part of what Martha Biondi has identified as Cold War liberalism, or anticommunist Americanism, among Black politicians beginning in the late 1940s. Embracing this ethos meant both critiquing communism in the United States while also pointing to racial segregation as communistic and anti-American.[92] The Canal Zone offered the perfect environment to put the latter judgment into practice.

As committee chair, Powell asked Westerman to provide him with a report on employment practices that affected non-US workers of color in the zone. Powell may have read some of Westerman's work in the *Panama Tribune*, which circulated in New York, or been familiar with Westerman's 1948 *Common Ground* essay, "Gold vs. Silver Workers in the Canal Zone," which documented race-based discrimination in pay, retirement, schooling, and housing.[93] Furthermore, through his campaign against Local 713 leaders in the *Tribune*, Westerman made known his firm condemnation of communists and their allegedly negative influences over a mostly Black zone workforce.

In his report to Powell, Westerman offered a mix of labor history, foreign relations, anticommunism, and concrete reform proposals. The report acknowledged some improvements in zone labor affairs starting in the late 1940s but emphasized continued discrepancies in wages, pensions, and other benefits between non-US and US workers.[94] Westerman also criticized the Local 713's US representatives and their continued supporters. He nonetheless expressed hope that through new leadership the CIO could "restore [its] prestige... in Latin America."[95] Westerman expertly employed a diplomatic tone, which found little fault in the US or Panamanian governments, while carefully critiquing zone policies.

Powell received Westerman's report during a two-week December visit to Panama.[96] Powell's trip, ironically, coincided with Arnulfo Arias's second term as Panamanian president and his first win under his newly formed Panameñista Party. During his second brief presidency, Arias created a secret police that harassed his critics, labeling most of them as communists.[97] This focus on anticommunism would grow in future Panamanian administrations. Powell did not meet with Arias during his visit, but he was asked to speak before the National Assembly, the very body whose members had only a couple of years earlier engaged in impassioned debates about the problem of English-speaking Blacks in the republic. As a US congressman concerned about the future of Canal Zone workers, Powell secured interviews with top Panamanian and zone officials, in addition to union leaders and Afro-Caribbean Panamanian activists.[98]

About a month after Powell's visit, the CIO expelled the UPWA and denounced several of its leaders as communists.[99] Westerman's report and Powell's trip did not directly affect CIO policy but succeeded in underscoring that a US political base, with support from Panamanian allies, now paid close attention to zone labor matters. Representatives of the CIO national office visited the zone to discuss Local 713's future. Edward Gaskin and George Westerman, two very vocal critics of the local, were among those consulted for their perspectives.[100]

Although expelling the UPWA enhanced the CIO's credibility in the early Cold War United States, the expulsion left non-US zone workers without an official union. Shortly after the expulsion, zone officials demanded that Local 713 members break all associations with the national branch.[101] Union officials attempted to bypass this demand by declaring their local independent from the UPWA. Following a unanimous vote by all Local 713 chapter leaders in mid-March, the union's executive board called for continued affiliation with the CIO. In this way, the union would still have access to the thousands of dollars in dues contributed by its members during their four-year affiliation with the UPWA. Other former members and officials of the local, including teachers in the CZCS and the *Tribune* editorial board, offered an alternate approach. They called on the CIO to create a new union local. A leadership impasse followed as to who should represent the interests of the zone's non-US workforce.[102]

In addressing this deadlock, CIO and Afro-Caribbean Panamanian community leaders converged to form a Black-centered unionist platform. It remained to be seen whether this would be enough to assuage those who felt betrayed by Local 713's disbandment. In April 1950 the CIO fulfilled its end of the bargain by appointing Edward (Ed) K. Welsh, an African American organizer from New York, as the US international representative for the newly launched Local 900 of the Government and Civic Employees Organizing Committee (GCEOC). The GCEOC was the CIO's response to the disbandment of the UPWA and looked to tap into places like New York and the Canal Zone, which had been fruitful for UPWA recruitment in the past. Having Welsh as the international representative marked the first time that an African American would directly represent the interests of Afro-Caribbean Panamanians before the CIO and zone officials. Tied with Powell's continued interest in the zone area, defenders of Local 900 could boast that Afro-Caribbean Panamanians employed in the zone had strong African American allies with no taint of communism.[103]

As for leadership within Local 900, Edward Gaskin was elected as the new union's president. In 1948 he resigned from Local 713 but maintained his leadership as president of the Teacher's Association. He had by this time formed an alliance with George Westerman and the public intellectual base he represented. With his election Gaskin became the first Afro-Caribbean Panamanian born in the Canal Zone to serve as the president of a zone labor union. His connections to several generations of non-US zone workers and residents facilitated his election, as did his role as an educator and principal of the La Boca Elementary School (the largest school in the CZCS system).[104]

Outside the zone, Westerman continued to advocate on labor policies, discrimination, and citizenship. Through these efforts he raised the question of whether a distinctly nationalist approach linked to international unionism could best reform the inequality faced by Afro-Caribbeans in the zone.

Westerman proposed that while international forums could help educate a global audience, real change could come only by pursuing citizenship rights with national obligations in Panama.

Westerman's participation in a UNESCO-sponsored conference of sociologists and political scientists, followed by a visit to Washington, DC, highlighted this approach. He attended the September 1950 conference, which focused on the role of "minority issues" in international affairs, as the director of research of the Liga Cívica. During his presentation he described discrimination in Panama as rooted in the discriminatory policies of the US-controlled Canal Zone and the intolerance of a small group of powerful Panamanian legislators.[105] While in DC, Westerman met with representatives of the Department of Defense and highlighted four areas in which zone discrimination was most obvious—wages, housing, retirement options, and civil service appointments. He emphasized that Panamanians were not provided with the same treatment and opportunities as their US peers in all four of these categories. Such a policy, he insisted, failed to acknowledge how the Panamanian government had throughout the years cooperated with the United States.[106] By addressing the zone labor question in strictly nationalist terms, Westerman suggested that the status of "Panamanian zone worker" held greater power and potential than that of "non-US zone worker."

This focus on nationalism did not mean that Westerman saw no value in diasporic or internationalist approaches that connected him with an African American leadership base. His Black internationalism went against nationalist and anticommunist mandates in Panama and the zone, which increasingly critiqued cross-border solidarities. Yet, in his diasporic and internationalist work, Westerman connected with a specific type of leadership base. As he noted in a speech in Colón less than a month after his travels, while in the United States, he met with not only US officials but also African American activists and intellectuals. These included Thurgood Marshall, Walter White, Roy Wilkins, and James Ivy. All these men were, like Westerman, known for their criticisms of more "radical" elements of activist struggles. They each wanted equality in labor, law, education, and citizenship but viewed affiliation with communists and leftist groups as detrimental to full inclusion as citizens. Instead they called on those in their community to fight for their rights in a controlled, strategic, and peaceful manner by changing the system from within.[107]

Inspired by his conversations with these men, Westerman asked his Colón audience to "go forward as Negroes" and join the "millions of black peoples in other parts of the world who are asserting themselves for freedom and equality." One key means of attaining this goal, he affirmed, was by simultaneously protesting discrimination in the Canal Zone and the Panamanian republic.[108] Injustices throughout the isthmus affected all Afro-Caribbean Panamanians. Although not referenced in his speech, the denial of birth-based citizenship marked a clear example of systemic injustice. No one in this late 1940s moment proposed tackling this issue. Debates about communism permeated all aspect of activist work in this period, robbing most groups of the ability to challenge governments and to address systemic racism and xenophobia. Instead, advocates were left to strategize on the best means to organize in the context of a US-led and hemispheric-embraced hysteria over the threat of communism. Lost in this grand strategizing were the needs of a complex community that sought alternatives, not added boundaries, to their survival as Black people in a white supremacist world.

Citizenship and Activism at Midcentury

At the start of the 1940s, the idea that men like Westerman would speak before international audiences and that an Afro-Caribbean Panamanian would hold the presidency of a Canal Zone union might have appeared impossible. Yet, by 1950 it was a reality. The decade had begun with a call to strip all Afro-Caribbean descendants of their citizenship and led to a compromise at middecade that allowed them to apply for that same citizenship. This compromise came after petition campaigns, after men like Pedro N. Rhodes sought election into the Constituent Assembly, and with bitter debates in the National Assembly about whether Afro-Caribbean Panamanians could ever be trusted as full citizens.

While these struggles concerning denationalization and potential citizenship played out in the republic, Afro-Caribbean Panamanians in the zone also fought for empowerment within this space. There they contended with being othered, in terms of race and nationality, although this did not prevent educators like Leonor Jump and Edward Gaskin, along with the CZCTA, from charting new possibilities within this discriminatory system. From supervising Spanish-language clubs to writing US education officials to promote greater opportunities for students of color, Afro-Caribbean Panamanians strived to make the zone a space of progress and advancement. Ironically, because it operated outside the Panamanian government's control, the segregated Canal Zone could serve as a refuge at times for Afro-Caribbean community building in a space protected from the bigoted dictates of the republic, though not those of the enclave.

A vested interest in securing effective advocacy networks linked Afro-Caribbean activists within and outside the zone. In the zone this was manifested by joining the membership and leadership ranks of the cross-ethnic and transnational UPWA-CIO, while outside this space, policing the politics of white US union representatives dominated the attention of men like George Westerman. The tensions between these two alternatives—supporting the UPWA or focusing on anticommunism and moderation—resulted in deep divisions among Afro-Caribbean Panamanians in the zone, with moderates like Westerman and Gaskin ultimately emerging as winners in a movement where the trust and respect of workers still needed to be reearned.

Moving into the 1950s, an additional challenge arose in balancing the potentials of Afro-Caribbean Panamanians as advocates in debates over the Panama Canal with the continued positioning of Afro-Caribbeans as questionable citizens. In rejecting this label, leaders took an even firmer anticommunist stand while still condemning the racial injustices in the zone and Panama. Whether these efforts would be enough and what this would mean for those still viewed as incompatible because of their place of birth, language practices, skin color, religious traditions, and connections to the Canal Zone remained looming questions.

3

Todo por la Patria

Diplomacy, Anticommunism, and the Rhetoric of Assimilation, 1950–1954

On August 16, 1953, *La Nación* published a public letter to President José Remón Cantera signed by two hundred Afro-Caribbean Panamanians. The letter thanked Remón for awarding George Westerman the Vasco Núñez de Balboa medal, the nation's highest civilian honor and the first awarded to an Afro-Caribbean Panamanian. The award, the signees declared, affirmed Remón's commitment to "decisively and honestly incorporate all of the sons of the Patria without distinctions of color, religion or political ideologies." They expressed pride that the honor recognized the patriotism of those "from humble classes" who with "faith in the ultimate justice of government" fought daily for greater improvements in the nation.[1] To the casual observer, this award and the public thank-you marked a possible improvement in racial and ethnic relations in Panama. As this chapter highlights, however, discussions surrounding the Balboa honor formed part of an evolving and still contentious conversation about what role, if any, Afro-Caribbean Panamanians could have in speaking for and representing Panama in the modern world.

By the early 1950s, George Westerman and Edward Gaskin had emerged as internationally recognized advocates for their community and, increasingly if not officially, for the Panamanian nation. Westerman continued making appearances around the world as a journalist and public intellectual, and Gaskin remained president of the CIO's Local 900. Together they formed a united front in connecting national politics to labor issues. The presidential candidacy of José Remón afforded a unique opportunity to advance the cause of Afro-Caribbean Panamanians and other non-US workers in the Canal Zone. The attention paid to the Remón administration by Westerman and Gaskin illuminated debates on the potentials and tensions of Black diaspora links regarding a "patriotic" vision of the Panamanian nation.

Advocating for Panama from Chicago

On October 16, 1952, Westerman delivered a speech titled "Sore Spots in United States–Panama Relations" before the eighth annual meeting of the Inter American Press Association. In the past, Westerman had addressed audiences in Europe and even met with officials in the US Department of Defense, but his Chicago speech marked the first time he offered his views to fellow journalists throughout the Americas. This meeting also marked one of the few moments of hemispheric conversations between Panama and its Latin American neighbors not initiated by Panamanians. Part of this imbalance was due to the view of Panama as a "questionable" nation still dependent on US empire and not fully sovereign.

In Chicago, Westerman had the opportunity to engage other journalists in the hemisphere as equals, even as he formed part of a very small group of fellow Black journalists. Chicago's Roosevelt University sponsored Westerman, and the International House of the University of Chicago was the setting for his speech. He addressed his audience as a newspaper editor and proud Panamanian, and he commented with candor on the injustices of US-Panamanian relations.[2]

Westerman's speech excelled at connecting labor inequality in the zone to broader questions on the rights due the Panamanian nation. At least half of the non-US employees of the Panama Canal were Panamanian, and two-thirds of them resided in the republic. Thus, the welfare of these workers and their families fell under the purview of the Panamanian nation. By affirming the Panamanian citizenship of zone workers, Westerman brushed past the citizenship petition process that still formed a reality for Afro-Caribbean Panamanians with foreign-born parents, choosing instead to emphasize a unified Panamanian citizenry. As for workers without Panamanian or US citizenship, Westerman reminded those present that the United States offered these workers a pitiful retirement plan. He also spoke of the burden Panama shouldered supporting these ex-workers.[3] With this language, Westerman largely repeated the official line of the government toward unemployed Afro-Caribbean migrants and their negative impact on the economy.

This approach by Westerman highlighted the extent to which a native born versus migrant divide among Afro-Caribbean Panamanians still held sway in the 1950s. Repatriation no longer emerged as an option and was replaced by the need to allocate financial responsibility. As Westerman clarified in his speech, while the Panamanian government would take care of all those within its borders, Panama's primary commitment had to be to Panamanian workers.

In closing his speech, Westerman suggested that the inequities faced by Panamanian workers in the zone rested on the unwillingness of the United States to acknowledge Panama as an equal partner in the canal: "If any country in the Western Hemisphere deserves help and cooperation from the big sister of the North, that country is the Republic of Panama, whose inhabitants have shown a determined loyalty to the United States in times of emergency, and whose citizens are known for their belief in democracy and freedom."[4] With this statement Westerman challenged the United States to view itself as a sister, not a brother or father, to the republics of Latin America. As elder sister, the United States held an influential role but had no rights or privileges over its younger and loyal siblings. Strikingly, the ease with which Westerman spoke of the elder sister and younger siblings contrasted with the total exclusion of women as political agents in the Inter-American Press Association and the governments of Panama, the United States, and other parts of the Americas. This use of women as symbols at the exclusion of actual women was of course not new. In the late 1920s, Westerman's colleague at the *Tribune*, Amy Denniston, and prominent Afro-Caribbean feminist Linda Smart Chubb had noted this problem. More than twenty years later, neither Westerman nor his fellow conferees addressed this disparity.[5]

In addition to speaking of a hemispheric alliance led by a symbolic elder sister, Westerman used his speech to remind his audience of Panama's continued military importance to the United States and the ongoing battle against communism. By 1952 the United States was fighting China and North Korea and was also policing communist activity throughout the Americas. National anticommunism efforts were also fully underway in Mexico, Bolivia, Peru, and Argentina having started in the 1930s and extending into the 1950s.[6] The United States monitored these efforts, but Central America, and the Panama Canal in particular, grew in importance. By the early 1950s US strategists strove to demarcate a stronghold of anti-communist governance in the region. For this very reason, Westerman offered assurance that democracy, not communism, continued to reign supreme in

Panama. A democratic Panama, he insisted, was already playing a key role in uniting the hemisphere.

By invoking an anticommunist and democratic Panama, Westerman aptly used an anticommunist vocabulary that by the early 1950s had particular reference points throughout the hemisphere. The use of anticommunist rhetoric, as opposed to a fixed ideology, made this approach very malleable. Anyone could invoke anticommunism, dictators, and even marginalized groups with the guarantee that such a stance would garner US and regional support. Hence, it is not surprising that at a hemispheric event, Westerman invoked the dangers of communism and showcased his country, even with its history of rejecting Afro-Caribbean descendants like him, as a shield for the defense of democracy in the Americas.

Westerman's Chicago speech received considerable attention from the Panamanian media and government. Panamanian dailies reprinted parts of it and congratulated Westerman on the veracity of his statements.[7] Media acclaim for his address continued to grow following the National Assembly's unanimous decision, spearheaded by Pablo Othon, to include it in the *Registro Nacional*.[8] Writing to John Gibbs St. Clair Drake of Roosevelt University on November 2, 1952, Westerman expressed his pleasure with the acclaim afforded his Chicago speech. St. Clair Drake had sponsored Westerman's appearance as part of the Labor Division of Roosevelt College. This support made sense given that St. Clair Drake's research and background held several parallels to Westerman's own scholarly and activist profile. St. Clair Drake's 1945 study, *Black Metropolis*, offered a model for investigating Black urban communities. Afro-Caribbean Panamanians by and large lived urban lives and, like Black Chicagoans, had to contend with formal and informal discrimination. St. Clair Drake, like Westerman, was of Afro-Caribbean descent and part of a first generation born outside the Anglophone Caribbean.[9] Both men represented a Black male diasporic intellectual leadership base that, while independent of governmental sponsorship, still focused on the promises and potentials of state-specific nationalism.

Along with thanking St. Clair Drake for his support, Westerman reported on the numerous articles and radio broadcasts discussing his speech, which he declared "has touched off an explosion back here." Westerman noted the resolution by the National Assembly as the ultimate testament to its impact. The October 30 resolution marked the first time Panamanian officials introduced into the national record a protest against both "treaty violations and practices of discrimination in the Canal Zone." As Westerman explained to St. Clair Drake, zone discrimination toward Panamanians had been taking place for decades, but previous administrations had shied away from opposing it. Panamanian officials had used forums like the International Labor Organization to demand greater access to Canal Zone jobs, but racial discrimination as experienced by Afro-Caribbeans never emerged in these discussions.[10] The reason for this absence, Westerman confided, was the reluctance among officials to label Panamanians "colored." By discussing racial discrimination, the National Assembly broke this silence around race. Westerman concluded that in any forthcoming treaty discussions, discrimination against the mostly Black zone workforce would finally receive the attention it deserved.[11]

Affirmations by President Remón that zone discrimination had to end no doubt reassured Westerman regarding his comments to St. Clair Drake.[12] Speaking to the press two months after his inauguration, Remón reaffirmed this stance and declared that "racial discrimination in the Panama Canal Zone must end." He also demanded that Panamanians in the zone be afforded the same treatment given to US workers. Failure to provide such treatment, Remón concluded, "would make a farce of democracy."[13] In using these words, Remón validated Westerman's belief that his administration would bring change not only to economic and political affairs but also to Afro-Caribbean Panamanians and other citizens facing discrimination.

Westerman heavily campaigned for Remón's election. This was a first for him as he previously focused on political advocacy through the Liga Cívica Nacional, international forums, and the pages of the *Tribune*, only rarely promoting a specific candidate. During the 1948 presidential election, Sidney Young and Westerman had agreed that the *Tribune* would run ads for all presidential hopefuls but not endorse any candidate. Arnulfo Arias's second turn at the presidency in 1949 tested this approach.[14] After less than a year in office, Arias proposed replacing the 1946 Constitution with the one enacted in 1941. In 1951 the National Assembly deposed Arias after a coup, but his year and a half in power reminded Westerman and other Afro-Caribbean Panamanians that presidential policies could destroy their citizenship rights.[15]

Remón's nontraditional political advancement also gained him the support of Westerman and other Afro-Caribbeans during the presidential campaign.[16] Remón's political profile was unique in many aspects. He was, like most past presidents, white and had studied abroad, but he had been educated in public schools, and his study abroad focused on military training, not university degrees in letters, medicine, or law. Remón created a political space for himself outside traditional electoral politics by advancing through the ranks of the national police and eventually serving as the chief of this institution from 1947 to 1952. During this time, he earned the reputation of being a fair man who promoted officers without distinctions of race or class. This propelled his popularity among working-class Black and mestizo populations, whom he heavily recruited into the force. Remón embraced this role as a "fair Jefe" and into his presidency responded to letters from concerned citizens expressing distress at the treatment of Black police officers. As chief of the national police, Remón wielded significant political power and was directly involved in overthrowing three presidential administrations between 1949 and 1951. Remón militarized the police into the National Guard, which provided him with unprecedented influence and ushered in the militarization of politics in Panama.[17]

As a presidential candidate he sought to downplay claims of praetorianism and instead centered his campaign on rehabilitating the nation's economy through free elections and good relations with the United States. His principal opponent, Roberto Francisco Chiari, reminded voters of Remón's authoritarian style, which included his removal of former presidents. Remón countered by accusing Chiari of communist sympathies. Chiari did not identify as a communist and in fact did not form part of any of the groups that by 1952 aligned with communist or socialist philosophies. Some of these groups included the Partido del Pueblo (the People's Party), the Federación de Estudiantes Panameños (Federation of Panamanian Students), and the Federación Sindical de Trabajadores de Panamá (Federation of Panamanian Workers). All these organizations had come under intense attack under the second Arias administration. As chief of the national police, Remón had also compiled reports on "communist" activities in Panama. Outspoken university students particularly earned his attention and ire. Faced with accusations of communism and the powerful Remón as his opponent, Chiari lost the election.[18]

Regarding Remón's relationships with Black Panamanians, particularly Afro-Caribbean Panamanians, as a part owner of *La Nación*/the *Nation*, a bilingual daily, Remón had hired three Afro-Caribbean Panamanians for the English edition of the paper (one as a main editor and two as writers).[19] The *Nation* and the presence of Afro-Caribbeans therein garnered him support from this community. Westerman and other Afro-Caribbean leaders were thus excited when two months after assuming the presidency, Remón explicitly addressed the issue of racial discrimination in the Canal Zone.

An Ode to Democracy

For labor union leaders such as Edward Gaskin, the sudden awareness shown by the Panamanian National Assembly and Remón of "colored" Panamanians in the zone and of racial discrimination in this space offered no immediate guarantee of a change in zone policy toward the mostly Black canal workforce. Gaskin instead continued to believe that direct negotiations between labor leaders and top zone officials offered the best solution for the problems of his constituency. As president of the new Local 900, Gaskin in 1950 presented zone officials with numerous reports detailing the need for higher wages, equal pay for equal work, and greater job opportunities. These had been championed by Local 713 representatives, and they continued to be popular among non-US zone workers. In addition to writing these reports, in 1951 Gaskin spent four months in the United States studying labor-management relations under the sponsorship of the US State Department and had an opportunity to testify before the Senate on labor conditions in the zone. These were both firsts that had not taken place under Local 713 and spoke to the importance of being part of an international labor union recognized by the United States. It still did not fully explain why anticommunism rhetoric had overtaken discussions about Local 713 or the infighting that had ensued, but it did allude to the promises of cordial relations between a strong local labor union and zone officials.[20]

The inauguration of a new Canal Zone governor in June 1952 renewed Gaskin's commitment to working with US officials, within and outside the zone, on behalf of his union base. On assuming the zone governorship, US Army general John S. Seybold expressed his interest in addressing the concerns of non-US workers as part of a wider effort to ensure friendly relations between Panama and the zone.[21] When approached by Local 900, however, Seybold, like his predecessors, rejected the union's demands. In response to the first petition submitted by the union, Seybold defended the continued use of a dual wage system whereby US citizens received higher salaries than all other workers. "Most of the local rate workers in the Canal Zone," he declared, "do not have either the fundamental abilities or habits required for the higher aptitude positions and jobs carried out by the employees brought from the United States." Seybold clarified that he did not mean this as a critique of local-rate workers but rather as a recognition of the limited economic development of Panama. He used the language of "local-rate workers" versus "silver workers" due to the success of Local 713's campaign to remove this label from the zone lexicon. The name change, however, came without any adjustments in the zone pay structure, which continued to privilege white US citizens. As a supposed concession to local-rate workers, Seybold affirmed that the administration would pay them wages on par with those in Panama.[22]

As for Gaskin's response to Seybold, a February 1953 report from the zone's Internal Security Branch (ISB) emphasized his disappointment, anger, and frustration. Since its inception in 1952, the ISB kept a close eye on Gaskin and Local 900 activities. The ISB was created in response to post–World War II fears of communist infiltration in the Canal Zone. Non-US employees, zone officials believed, were easy targets for communist propaganda.[23] According to a conversation between Robert C. Walker (ISB chief) and Gaskin, Governor Seybold's letter dashed aspirations for labor improvements and wage increases among local raters. Gaskin expressed confusion at Seybold's letter since, back in August, Seybold had promised a fair and objective assessment of the problems of non-US workers. Hostile advice from other zone officials, Gaskin surmised, had clouded Governor Seybold's judgment. Walker closed his report by concluding that the Gaskin he had met was "one eating humble pie." Still, he cautioned zone authorities against making any moves that might assist Gaskin in maintaining his leadership.[24]

Gaskin did not, as Walker assumed, turn to zone administrators for assistance. On the contrary, he took to the Panamanian airwaves through radio station HGQ in Colón. As Local 900 president, Gaskin had limited contact with the national media. Instead, as with most other labor union presidents, he had spent most of his political energies within the zone. Zone officials preferred this model because it kept zone workers isolated and fully dependent on them. Seybold's February letter caused Gaskin to reevaluate this model. In doing so, he not only broke the tradition of not mixing zone union politics with political happenings in the republic, he also brought the struggles of Local 900 to the attention of tens of thousands of fellow citizens. All residents of Colón and many zone workers, along with residents of Panamá, had access to the HGQ broadcast. A radio broadcast, unlike a newspaper article, reached a wider audience, avoided misreporting or omissions, and tapped listeners on an emotional level. With a radio outlet in the republic, Gaskin projected Local 900 as a union no longer isolated or solely dependent on zone-exclusive negotiations.

In his address, Gaskin made clear that Local 900 had sought "no favors" from the zone government and had instead assumed an "attempt would be made to meet most of [their] justified demands—especially the far-reaching ones having to do with the very crux of the wage philosophy or structure."[25] Governor Seybold's defense of the dual wage system, Gaskin declared, not only disparaged experienced local-rate workers, but also presented a warped understanding of justice. To support this statement, Gaskin used the example of "the native worker with 30 or 40 years of experience who is passed over in promotion by a US worker with only six months of training on the job." As for the Panamanian economy, Gaskin noted that its Canal Zone counterpart kept the earning power within the republic at low levels. Due to this policy, workers lacked adequate pay within and outside the zone.[26]

Gaskin's radio address also linked the zone's unfair labor practices to the threat of communism. Westerman had been vocal on this issue in the past, but Gaskin now offered an insider's perspective as someone who worked in the zone and represented its workers. His assessments connected communism and poverty, although he offered a much more forceful call for democracy as the ultimate weapon against communism. Gaskin thus avowed the staunch anticommunism of his constituents and reminded listeners of the "communist dinosaur who feeds on the vegetation of poverty, hunger, and frustration" throughout the hemisphere. A "total defeat" of communists, Gaskin contended, would require more than "mere financial pledges of support for democracy and empty boasts of how much we hate their guts." Rather, in Panama, Gaskin argued, the United States had the opportunity to show the entire hemisphere "its moral stature as the leader of the world's democracy."[27] In this way, democracy signified prosperity, whereas poverty represented the failure of democratic leaders to use the power of capital and justice to defeat communist discontent.

Gaskin continued to speak of the threat of communism in several parts of his speech and ended with something approaching an ode to democracy: "We are not asking for charity, loans, alms, or for anything to which we are not justly entitled; all we seek is a decent day's pay for a decent day's work... in order to demonstrate to our people and our common enemies that it is possible to overcome poverty, hunger, frustration, and oppression, within the framework of our democratic way of life."[28] Zone workers denied US-rate pay had for decades performed to the best of their abilities, often under prejudicial circumstances. All they now asked of Canal Zone officials was a pay scale that acknowledged this reality. Ignoring this request and permitting continued injustice only cleared the path for those seeking to destroy democracy everywhere. Gaskin's speech proved powerful because of the passionate way he spoke for his constituents while also imploring action from the United States.

Workers' Rights and Treaty Revision Rumors

President Remón's March 15, 1953, national speech injected unprecedented urgency into the Canal Zone question and rekindled some of the sentiments of Gaskin's March 1 radio broadcast. In an address to the largest political party, the Coalición Patriótica Nacional (National Patriotic Coalition), a newly formed multiparty arrangement, Remón declared his intention to visit US President Dwight Eisenhower and demand a "just" revision of the original Panama Canal Treaty. "The Treaty of 1903," Remón asserted, "was signed by a traitor who had no connections to [the Panamanian] nation." Remón expressed his desire to have Panama's youth aware of this reality and know that "leaders of the nation, like those in the Coalición Patriótica, defended their patrimony." His administration would ask for "neither millions, nor charity, but only justice." This justice would come in the form of a new canal treaty, which would grant greater financial benefits to the state and the improved treatment of Panamanian canal workers. As "one family," Remón declared, Panama would no doubt succeed in its negotiations with the United States.[29]

A push to revisit the 1903 accord was not distinctive to this early 1950s moment. Not long after the signing of the treaty, conflicts over its interpretation, specifically US control of ports and key waterways in Colón and Panamá, emerged. Treaty revision debates beginning in the 1920s and culminating in 1936 attempted to ameliorate some of these issues. The Hull-Alfaro Treaty limited further expansion of the zone into Colón and promised further efforts to include Panamanian businesses in the zone. It also included a separate note, which went unenforced, regarding "equal opportunity" in canal employment. None of these concessions questioned the hegemony of the United States over the zone or offered a fundamental restructuring of the Panama-US relationship. The rejection of the Filos-Hines Convention in 1947, which sought to extend US control of military bases outside the zone (a temporary measure taken during World War II), most directly indicated growing Panamanian desire to end business as usual. Mass popular protests, led by students, workers, and everyday citizens, explained this rejection. Remón as the chief of police had attacked and jailed a number of these protestors, yet in the early 1950s, he channeled their anti-imperialist spirit, as well as the work and words of Afro-Caribbean labor leaders, to buttress his own calls for a new and fair treaty between Panama and the United States.[30]

Gaskin must have been shocked and perhaps flattered to have words very similar to his repeated by Remón. At last, the most powerful man in the

nation had declared his commitment to a just resolution of the labor problems in the zone. Remón, like Westerman before him, relied on the discourse
of a unified Panamanian citizenry addressing the US government. This focus
on *Panamanian citizens* as opposed to zone workers marked a key difference
in Remón's and Gaskin's approaches. Obtaining the public support of the
president was nonetheless unprecedented. The previous chapter highlights
how Arnulfo Arias used his executive powers to police access to citizenship
rights. Unlike Arias, Remón spoke to the idea of a Panamanian family that
included the very populations Arias had strived to denationalize.

Notably, public commentary on Remón's speech failed to mention the
views of zone workers. *La Estrella de Panamá* published readers' letters
in support of Remón's treaty revision efforts. Most letters saluted Remón
as a true patriot and a defender of the next generation. The majority of
letter writers included local politicians, all men. Women heading benevolent associations also wrote to *La Estrella*. Teachers, women and
men alike, formed part of the campaign.[31] The Chamber of Commerce
and wealthy businessmen published full-page letters of support. The
Sindicato de Periodistas de Panamá (the Panamanian Newspaperman's
Association), in addition to submitting a resolution supporting Remón's
efforts, also created a special committee to develop propaganda in favor
of a treaty revision.[32]

Gaskin and Local 900 responded to Remón's speech by holding a union
rally in Colón on March 22. Organizers promoted the rally to publicize
the union's protest of Governor Seybold's letter outside the Canal Zone. The
union obtained the permission of the city's mayor and secured the participation of three top Colón officials. Local 900's decision to hold the rally
there made sense given the demographics and anticipated participation. As
noted earlier, much of the city's majority Afro-Caribbean adult population
either worked or had family employed in the zone. This event also marked
the first of the union's rallies outside the zone. The zone's ISB noted this
and sent agents to surveil the gathering.[33]

The ISB reported that the rally was well organized and modestly attended.
An eight-piece drum and bugle corps led the march, and participants held
up banners reading, "We Want Justice Not Charity," "Banish All Poverty
and Fear," "Teach Democracy but Practice It Too," "Live and Let Live,"
"CIO's Gain Is For All," and "37 Cents Per Hour = Starvation, We Demand
a High Minimum." The parade ended in Colón Park with a total of about
250 people gathered to hear a lineup of speakers that included Canal Zone
workers, CIO representatives, and Colón officials.

Gaskin addressed the rally first as a zone worker and as president of Local 900. He reminded those present that the most important recommendations presented to Governor Seybold had been rejected. This countered media reports that suggested satisfaction with zone salary policies.[34] Gaskin also called on nonmembers to join the union's cause. Marín Porras, representing the San Blas (Guna Yala) people who worked in the zone, also addressed the crowd. Porras encouraged all present, and especially his constituents, to support Local 900. Porras was the first person of Indigenous ancestry to address a CIO rally. His invitation marked an effort by Local 900 to expand its base to as many Panamanian zone workers and Colón residents as possible.[35]

Ed Welsh spoke as a CIO representative. His presence reminded the local of its connection to a US-based international organization. Welsh emphasized the importance of Local 900's CIO affiliation. As the US representative of the CIO, he declared, workers should view him as the man in charge of that organization's local affairs. This statement, while correct in terms of union bureaucracy, hinted at a growing tension between a onetime welcomed African American ally and those wishing to challenge the citizenship hierarchy in the Canal Zone. During his address, Welsh expressed his interest in accompanying President Remón to Washington for the purpose of advocating for a revised canal treaty. This comment, likely intended as enthusiasm for Remón's visit, evidenced some paternalism, assuming Remón required a middleman to advocate for his own citizens.[36]

The Colón officials present at the rally also spoke of Remón's proposed Washington visit but focused more on the connections between the welfare of Panamanian zone workers and that of the entire nation. José D. Bazán, mayor of Colón, assured zone workers of his personal cooperation in all future negotiations. The Canal Zone, he declared, formed part of the republic, and what happened to zone workers mattered to the Panamanian government. National Assembly deputies Ernesto Esteñoz and Henry Simons Quirós concurred. Esteñoz declared his certainty that discrimination in the zone was a key problem that motivated Remón in seeking a treaty revision. Simons Quirós, a onetime student in the United States, expressed his dismay that the United States would allow injustices and discrimination in the zone. Curiously, Simons Quirós made no note of the segregation and discrimination that formed part of most cities in the United States in this era. As a white man, Quirós had likely avoided race-based discrimination while in the States.[37]

Even as the Colón rally was underway, US surveillance and intelligence gathering on popular support for the treaty revision proceeded. Starting on

March 16, the US embassy and Canal Zone collected intelligence on Panamanian politicians, political groups, press, radio, and individuals of interest. Their purpose was to assess why Remón initiated a revision campaign, the level of support for the campaign, and the extent of any anti-American sentiment. Spying, as noted by scholars of US Cold War policy in Latin America, was often a prelude to funding coup efforts or sanctioning military intervention, all in the name of protecting the hemisphere from communism. In the case of Panama, treaty arrangements facilitated this interventionist agenda.[38] The first reports noted that anti-American groups backed Remón's campaign. They likewise suggested that Remón had launched a revision campaign only to secure a loan from the United States to avoid national bankruptcy.[39] The latter half of the espionage reports declared incongruously that Remón lacked political and popular support for his treaty efforts, revealing how incorrectly ISB officials assessed the political reality in Panama. One such flawed report commented on a former Panama City mayoral candidate who refused to endorse Remón on the grounds that he had erred in trying to "bully the United States." Additional reports concluded that Remón would not be able to maintain popular support since several politicians and persons of influence were openly criticizing his approach and directly suggesting alternative diplomatic strategies.[40]

A little over a week after his March 15 speech, and shortly after the Local 900 rally, Remón publicly clarified that cordial relations would continue between Panama and the United States and that his speech should not be viewed as an ultimatum. He planned to meet with Panamanian ex-presidents and other influential leaders to discuss the next steps in negotiations with the United States.[41] Panamanian dailies asked readers to entrust their patriotism to proper channels and to avoid spreading demagogical rumors. Editorials and letters in support of Remón and a treaty revision continued but warned against the public getting carried away and enemies of the republic taking advantage of their enthusiasm. Too much popular support, it now seemed, could undermine the very delicate nature of Remón's talks with Washington.[42]

By April 1953, the Remón administration had scaled back its pro-revision campaign. Instead, his cabinet put together a four-point aide memoire on relations between Panama and the United States. The four discussion points included Panama's share in the economic, industrial, and service dimensions of the Panama Canal; the annuity paid to Panama for the canal; commercial competition from the zone; and last, "principles of equality of opportunity and treatment" for Panamanian and US citizens working in the Canal Zone.

The aide-memoire closed with an assurance that the good friendship between Panama and the United States had not been affected and that President Remón hoped to strengthen this bond with his visit to the White House.[43]

The US State Department indeed felt that the Panama-US friendship had been compromised and rejected Remón's request for a visit to Washington.[44] Most Panamanian dailies avoided commenting on the rejection and instead focused on a compromise: sending a Panamanian delegation to Washington after the US government had an opportunity to review the aide memoire. Putting a good face on the US rebuff, *La Estrella de Panamá* phrased it best in claiming that President Remón had accomplished the mission of his intended trip without having to disrupt his presidential duties.[45]

In this uncertain political landscape, Gaskin took the necessary steps to ensure that the interests of Local 900 would not be forgotten by negotiators. On April 22 Gaskin met with Alejandro Remón, the president's brother and a member of the Foreign Affairs Committee of the National Assembly. At this meeting Gaskin obtained assurance that Local 900 would be the only agency to present its views on Canal Zone labor problems. He would provide the negotiation team with a report prior to its departure for Washington. Gaskin also informed the zone's ISB of his meeting with Alejandro Remón to allay any fears of double dealing. Chief Walker did not, as in earlier reports, offer an opinion on Gaskin's state of mind or what zone officials should expect, noting only Gaskin's seeming satisfaction at the role extended to Local 900 by national officials.[46] Gaskin had reason to celebrate the union's inclusion in the negotiation team's circle. He could now promise his constituents that their concerns and demands would receive the attention of both governments. Getting concessions from the zone government was no longer the only option.

In a meeting with US ambassador to Panama John C. Wiley, Ed Welsh expressed his worries about an alliance between Local 900 and the Remón administration. Such a partnership, he believed, would lead to the eventual weakening of the union and the end of an international US-based labor organization in the zone. Non-US workers, he worried, would henceforth look to the Panamanian government for answers and neglect the cause of the CIO.[47] Adding to Welsh's concerns, on June 13 President Remón confirmed in a press conference that the republic's foreign affairs minister, in preparation for the upcoming Washington talks, would consult with Local 900 representatives on zone labor concerns.[48] Such a declaration affirmed Gaskin's belief that approaching national government officials was a good move for the union. For Welsh, the declaration meant that CIO international representatives like himself, all US citizens, would lose stature among non-US workers. Gaskin and Welsh would never see eye to eye on Local 900's alliance with the Panamanian government. This, among other factors, would lead to Welsh's eventual departure from the zone and the end to direct African American participation in the Black male internationalist leadership of this space.[49]

Speaking for La Patria Openly and Unofficially

While Gaskin worked on securing the Remón administration's commitment to Local 900's agenda, Westerman supported the administration through the international and local attention garnered by his publications on US-Panamanian relations and treaty revision efforts. In February 1953, his "Sore Spots" Chicago speech was added to the US *Congressional Record*, with five thousand copies distributed throughout Congress. Adam Clayton Powell Jr., whose involvement with Westerman I discussed in the previous chapter, pushed for this printing, effectively linking the US civil rights movement with the struggles of Afro-Caribbean Panamanians. The appearance of this printing also directly coincided with the Afro-diasporic networks forged by Afro-Caribbean Panamanians since the 1920s and Westerman's ability to connect these networks to a nationalist platform.

In expressing his support of Westerman's speech, Powell emphasized that from a "straight common-sense point of view" the United States was not "playing smart [by] continually sowing the seeds of bad relations with our darker skinned neighbors on whose native land we happen to own a one-mile strip across the Isthmus."[50] Panamanian officials did not take kindly to Powell's reference to them as "darker neighbors" or to his description of the zone as an area owned, rather than leased, by the United States. The strip was also ten miles wide. Nevertheless, Powell's involvement marked the first open congressional support for the Panamanian cause.

As vice chair of the special propaganda committee created by the Panamanian Newspaperman's Association to support the treaty revision, Westerman also authored the pamphlet "Fifty Years of Treaty Negotiations Between Panama and the United States (1903–1953)." The Panama City government published the first edition, and the Newspaperman's Association published two others, one of which was bilingual (Spanish-English). All copies were handed out free of charge, although it is unclear who, other than government officials and journalists, received them.[51] Shortly after the publication, Remón announced his plans to decorate Westerman with the

Vasco Núñez de Balboa medal. Westerman's official decoration took place at the Panamanian embassy in Washington, DC, and Westerman used the occasion to stress his nation's excitement and optimism over ending Canal Zone discrimination and the overall progress of the treaty talks.[52] The Panamanian embassy transmitted Westerman's press release to more than four hundred news agencies in the United States.[53] Westerman, it appeared, had captured the full attention of the Remón administration.

In addition to writing "Fifty Years," Westerman in August 1953 traveled to a UNESCO-sponsored Second World Congress of Sociology in Belgium, stopping in New York City to advocate for the Panamanian negotiators. Addressing New Yorkers through the WOV radio station, Westerman asked the Panamanians living in the city to support the Remón administration's revision efforts.[54] Panamanians who lived in New York at the time, most of whom were of Afro-Caribbean descent, knew firsthand of the discrimination and segregation that was prevalent in the Canal Zone. They also faced their share of racial discrimination in New York housing, education, and even recreation. Leonor Jump was among these Afro-Caribbean Panamanians residing in New York, having moved there to continue her career in bilingual education. Whether Westerman and Jump crossed paths during his visit to New York is unclear, though they had strong shared interests and life experiences. What did calls for a just treaty mean for Afro-Caribbean Panamanians in New York, especially for those who had worked or lived in the Canal Zone? What might they have included as necessary elements of the treaty? Creating effective cross-national linkages possibly formed part of the diasporic strategy connecting Westerman and his New York listeners.

Westerman declared that any improvement of inter-American relations, a platform of the Eisenhower administration, would require a full treaty revision.[55] Westerman challenged the Eisenhower administration to follow through on its promise of hemispheric democracy. His background as an expert on the canal somewhat affiliated with the Panamanian government lent credibility to his statements. He could speak with more freedom than any government officials on an array of bilateral issues. His bilingual skills and familiarity with US media circuits (including those of US-based Afro-Caribbean Panamanians) made him an ideal, if unofficial, diplomat.

Panamanian officials were aware that Westerman's background and his awards and prestige helped make a case for Panama's supposed racial inclusiveness. His acceptance and success offered a contrast with continuing practices of segregation and discrimination in the United States, including in the nation's capital. As noted by Chris Myers Asch, early 1950s Washington, DC, "remained a Southern city whose white leaders defended racial restrictive covenants, upheld the dual school system, and supported Jim Crow practices."[56] The district in this way mirrored the realities in the Canal Zone. Westerman's presence in DC to accept the Balboa honor, in turn, offered the Remón administration an opportunity to present Panama as a hemispheric leader in race relations.

Pride in Westerman's awards and achievements as a representative of his nation inspired Afro-Caribbean Panamanians to write a public letter thanking Remón for honoring Westerman with the Vasco Núñez de Balboa medal. They viewed his success as evidence that even the humblest Panamanian could through hard work and dedication receive the respect of a Panamanian head of state. Westerman, after all, came from a working-class family and had not attained a formal secondary or university education, yet he had made a name for himself "as a journalist and sociologist." His decoration with the Balboa honor thus confirmed that all those interested in being of "use to the Nation" could do so through hard work and a commitment to contributing to the "cultural and economic development" of the country. The honor Westerman received also denoted Remón's commitment to fighting racial discrimination and Afro-Caribbeans' "absolute faith in [Remón's]" dedication to "solidifying democracy through an honest incorporation of all of the sons of our small Patria." Remón, the letter writers hoped, would effectively usher in a new political reality, after so many setbacks, where all Panamanians had the opportunity to serve and be recognized as full-fledged citizens. Two hundred signatures and a call for "Todo por la patria" closed the letter.[57]

By ending the letter with the Coalición Patriótica Nacional motto, the letter writers demonstrated a mastery of the patron-client form of politics. As a humble and an astute mass, they declared their gratefulness to Remón (the nation) and pledged their abiding commitment to obtaining further commendations from him. Remón, who also understood his role as patron, published his own public letter thanking the letter writers for their gratitude and affirming his lifelong disdain of racial discrimination.[58]

While hundreds of Afro-Caribbean Panamanians thanked Remón, Gaskin presented the Panamanian negotiating mission with a document titled "Summarized Statement on Socio-Economic Problems Affecting Panamanian Nationals Employed by the United States Government on the Panama Canal Zone." The eleven-page report resembled many of the briefs Gaskin had submitted to the zone government as Local 900 president, but unlike these reports, the August 1953 statement emphasized the citizenship rights of

Panamanian zone workers. In the past Gaskin had emphasized their rights, as laborers, regardless of citizenship. He now focused on their national affiliations. Gaskin made clear that what happened to zone workers deserved their government's attention. As stated in the opening paragraph: "As long as the Canal Zone remain[ed] the largest single employer of local employees, the conditions on the Canal Zone [would] forever loom as an important factor in the minds of politically alert Panamanians."[59]

Labor problems in the Canal Zone, Gaskin insisted, could not be allowed to fester. He presented the negotiating mission with fourteen important labor recommendations. Ten dealt with wages and job opportunities. Creating a single wage system topped the list. The other recommendations asked the mission to seek just retirement and disability relief laws, to disprove Governor Seybold's claim that Panamanians did not have the skills or work habits to fill higher skilled jobs, and to demand an end to segregation and discrimination in the zone. Gaskin ended his statement with a romantic appeal to the republic and to hemispheric democracy: "Here at this melting pot of the western hemisphere; at this crossroad of the Americas by land, air, and sea, the people of the hemisphere cannot help but be pleasantly and lastingly impressed, their faith strengthened, their hopes nurtured, their resolve redoubled in a wholehearted determination to keep and preserve this part of the world solidified behind the democratic forces. Our very survival—physically, morally, and spiritually—is vitally dependent on how well, how quickly, and how resolutely we go about the task of resolving these vexing problems."[60] Gaskin resorted to a vocabulary that he believed would get the attention of the Panamanian negotiators. He emphasized the loyal citizenship of most local-rate employees, the geographic importance of Panama, the republic's religiosity, and the hemispheric Cold War battle for democracy. Through his use of the "melting pot" descriptor, Gaskin advocated the notion, however problematic, of a country infused by racial diversity but grounded as one. Within this melting pot metaphor, African descendants could serve as the liquid material for diversity, only if subsumed into a racially neutral national identity. Gaskin knew Panama was far from racially inclusive, but he also understood the public discourse and silence regarding race in this political moment. Indeed, one of the reasons Afro-Caribbean descendants faced such open hostility was their supposed reintroduction of race into the national equation. The popularizing of this myth avoided confronting the long history of racial and ethnic discrimination that marked the nation's foundation going back to the early colonial period. With his report to the negotiators, Gaskin strategically accepted this evasion. Worker realities still formed part of Gaskin's overall discourse, but citizenship, particularly the promise of a racially harmonious Panamanian citizenship attuned to hemispheric geopolitics, trumped, even if momentarily, a race-conscious and labor-specific activist approach.

In deciding to emphasize citizenship, Gaskin broke with his practice of negotiating with zone officials as a first step. Instead he concluded that Panamanian citizenship could be brought to the table when traditional union organizing failed. Yet, Gaskin did not account for the consequences of relying on his national government to decide the fate of his constituency. Panamanian negotiators had no vested interest in improving the condition of Panamanian workers. Their priority remained, as it had since the 1920s, on a greater financial share of the canal operations and the zone economy. Apparent attention to working conditions nevertheless garnered greater international attention and served as a bargaining tool. In his decision to prioritize citizenship, Gaskin also underestimated the increased hostility he and his fellow zone workers would receive for their supposed lack of patriotic fervor and cultural adaptability. This hostility became most evident during accusations surrounding a farewell ceremony held in honor of the negotiating mission.

Ungracious English-Speaking "Criollos"

On August 27, 1953, more than fifty thousand people made their way to Plaza Cinco de Mayo for the farewell ceremony of the Washington-bound Panamanian negotiating team. The rally was the largest organized political gathering in the history of the republic and celebrated the start of formal treaty discussions with the United States. Despite the mass in attendance, select journalists and commentators concluded that Afro-Caribbean Panamanians were absent from the ceremony. Joaquín Beleño of *La Hora*, in particular, used an August 29 column to start a series of poisonous debates on whether Afro-Caribbean Panamanians (often called "criollos," or creoles, by their critics) even attended the farewell rally.[61] Beleño, a Black novelist and journalist highly critical of the US Canal Zone and the Afro-Caribbean presence in Panama, informed readers that he personally looked for "criollos" in the crowd and found none. This, he stated, proved one of his established theories: these "aliens" solely identified with English-language media and sought American, not Panamanian, citizenship. Beleño's decision to take this stance proved ironic since he had worked in the zone after high school while enrolled at the Universidad de Panamá and knew of the discrimination faced by all Black people in this space. In fact, his fictional depiction of this discrimination won him a literary prize in the late 1940s.[62] Yet, in 1953, when met with real-life Black men and women denouncing discrimination and inequity in the Canal Zone, Beleño opted to challenge their patriotism. For almost a month, journalists and subscribers wrote to *La Hora*, the *Nation*, and *La Nación* to comment on Beleño's observations

Beleño, it bears noting, formed part of a broader national audience that did not see Afro-Caribbeans as true Panamanians. For this reason, throughout the duration of the farewell ceremony debates, Beleño only referred to this group as "criollos." "Criollos," unlike him and his fellow compatriots, were disloyal aliens who despite their birth in Panama could never be trusted as true citizens. Beleño's rationale drew on the same discriminatory logic that had shaped debates about birth-based citizenship since the 1920s. Afro-Caribbean Panamanians, as descendants of a once "prohibited immigrant race," needed to constantly prove their right to Panamanian citizenship. Beleño also critiqued the ungratefulness of "criollos" and their inability to appreciate the rights and generosities bestowed on them by the republic. In outlining these benefits, Beleño used a very clear "us versus them" dichotomy. The "us" marked the generous and noble Panamanians like himself, who had tolerated too much of "their," the "criollos'," disloyalty and indifference.[63]

Beleño was particularly incensed that so many "true" Panamanians showed up at Plaza Cinco de Mayo to support negotiations to improve the working and social conditions of "criollos" in the Canal Zone. How unpatriotic could one be, he suggested, to not attend an event explicitly designed to help one's own group. Sarcastically, he declared that following the farewell ceremony debacle, "all of them [criollos] deserve[d] a Vasco Núñez de Balboa decoration in honor of their loyalty to the Fatherland." Coincidentally, Westerman, recipient of that award, did not attend the ceremony. He was in Belgium, as a Panamanian delegate at the UNESCO conference. Whether Beleño knew of this or not, he had no qualms in using Westerman to direct an insult at all Afro-Caribbean Panamanians.[64]

Editorials and letters denouncing Beleño's assertions dominated the first week of responses to his derogatory column. Most respondents self-identified as Afro-Caribbean Panamanians and sought to affirm their patriotism. They also critiqued Beleño's patriotism and journalistic integrity. Letters in support of Beleño's column also appeared and grew in frequency as the debate intensified. Beleño responded almost daily to his critics but remained firm in his stance regarding absentee and unpatriotic "criollos."

One of the first responses to Beleño's article came with a letter to the *La Hora* editor from Alonso E. McFarlane, a Panama City resident. McFarlane poked fun of Beleño's assertion that "criollos" should have formed a unified group at the farewell ceremony and cautioned Beleño against exacerbating the presence of racial discrimination among the citizenry. As for Beleño's reference to the Vasco Núñez de Balboa honor, McFarlane reduced this to jealousy. "If the Balboa honor granted to George Westerman (a Panamanian of Antillean parents) and a journalist of world fame has made [Beleño] envious, I suggest that he take as an example the work of Westerman and desist with ridiculous critiques." Westerman, McFarlane concluded, had made his mark around the world and had done so with utmost respect and pride for his country.[65]

A *Nation* editorial expanded on the idea of Beleño's lack of patriotism. The editorial denounced Beleño as a "demagogue" who dared to return the Panamanian nation to old disputes about "Latin vs. non-Latin" Panamanians (or Iberian Americans vs. Afro-Caribbeans) debates. The relationship between these two groups "had long since been settled by education and social intercourse." What was missing from the August rally, the editorial noted, was the use of English, not "criollos." The younger generations of Afro-Caribbean Panamanians were so incorporated into the nation that nothing distinguished them from "the Latin element." Thousands of "criollos" formed part of the tens of thousands present at the Plaza Cinco de Mayo on August 27. Any assertions otherwise occluded the truth and provided "fodder for anti-government propaganda."[66]

Beleño responded with a column titled "A Sieve of Inaccuracies." Beleño asked "los líderes y dirigentes," those leading and working for "criollos," to look for future opportunities to prove their loyalty to Panama. "El Pueblo [the People]," he declared, did not see a mass of "criollos" at the rally. "Criollos" were not a part of "the people," as presented by Beleño. By invoking "el pueblo," Beleño presented himself as the voice of this entity and true guardian of the nation.[67]

Beleño further argued that the choice remained between Panamanians accepting "criollos" as dubious citizens with foreign habits and idiosyncrasies, or "criollos" adopting the language and customs of true Panamanians. Returning to the August 27 demonstration, he noted that geographically speaking, "criollos" had ample access to attend and earn their citizenship. "The Plaza Cinco de Mayo," Beleño declared, "is at the border of a neighborhood with a majority criollo population. By logic alone their presence should have been noted." The neighborhood Beleño referenced was El

Chorrillo. A large Afro-Caribbean population did in fact live there, but Beleño's comment suggested something inherently recognizable about this group. Somehow, the men and women of this neighborhood should have stood out to observers.[68]

These allusions to physical and other distinctions between "criollos" and "true" Panamanians dated back to 1920s texts such as *El peligro antillano* that obsessed over distinguishing African descendants with "roots" in colonial-era Panama (called Afro-coloniales) from those who migrated from the Anglophone Caribbean (called Afro-antillanos). The former supposedly had more in common with their Spanish masters than Afro-antillanos. According to *El peligro*, Afro-antillanos (Afro-Caribbeans) shared physical, behavioral, and cultural traits with African Americans that made them a dangerous impediment to an Iberian or Hispanic tradition on the isthmus. Like their US counterparts, Afro-antillanos only showed "sincere loyalty to their oppressors" and in this paranoid fantasy would join forces with the British to conquer Central America or Latin America.[69] Those advancing the Afro-coloniales versus Afro-antillanos paradigm into the 1950s and beyond also spoke of Afro-coloniales as having fairer skin tones, refined facial features (with European characteristics), fidelity to Catholicism, and a mastery of the Spanish language. These characteristics and their supposed perfect integration into the nation made them ideal citizens. Afro-antillanos, in contrast, allegedly had flat noses, bad hair, spoke improper Spanish (if they spoke any Spanish at all), and practiced an alien religion, Protestantism, which tied them to US interlopers in the Canal Zone. All these features made them incompatible citizens.[70]

While not deploying all these prejudices, Beleño did resort to the incompatible citizens paradigm. He accused "criollos" of failing to thank President Remón for honoring a member of their community. Beleño apparently had not read the public thank you to Remón signed by two hundred Afro-Caribbean descendants. Instead, Beleño chastised "criollos" for their "ingratitude to a nation that treats them as equals, that calls and honors them, and treats them with considerations they w[ould] not receive in any other part of the world." Most countries, Beleño reminded his readers, shunned Afro-Caribbean migrants; accordingly, "criollos" should express gratitude for a nation like Panama that not only allowed their presence but also facilitated their integration.[71]

Jack Jamieson, a Jamaican-born Panamanian journalist writing for both the *Nation* and the *Panama Tribune*, denounced Beleño as part of the old guard that sought to return Panama to the racism and intolerance of former times and administrations. "At one time," Jamieson noted, "the West Indian immigrant had been the whipping boy, until death or repatriation cheated the demagogues of a juicy but sorry theme. Now the spotlight has been focused on the children of West Indians." This time around, Jamieson affirmed, the Criollo was working side by side with his "Latin compatriot to the honor of his country."[72] This was the case on August 27, when the "so-called criollos" made their presence known "not as a distinct element but as proud Panamanians among other Panamanians." The new generation had no intention of being apathetic and would, if necessary, "fight fire with fire—for country, for fatherland!" Jamieson did not expand on what he meant by "fire with fire" but ended with an ode to a nation of equals he sought to reaffirm and defend.[73]

Beleño responded to critics with reprints of letters in support of his assertions: "It cannot be denied that the children of the workers hired by the United States know how to fight; whether they are right or wrong. I am convinced that in the case of the Date with the Nation [the August 27 Ceremony], they are wrong. But I accept that they know how to defend themselves. The Panamanians who challenge them also know how to use their freedom of speech and can respond. Below I include some replies."[74] Beleño and his supporters tried to disconnect the descendants of Afro-Caribbean migrants from the Panamanian nation and credit their presence to the machinations of the United States. A framing of Afro-Caribbeans as invaders of the isthmus with US or British affinities had formed part of anti–West Indian lore since the late nineteenth century. Beleño updated this bigoted framing to encompass Afro-Caribbeans born on the isthmus, a group he described as accidental Panamanians, as disloyal and untrustworthy as their parents.

The letter writers supporting Beleño bemoaned the overall failure of "criollos" to properly assimilate into the nation and show patriotic fervor. For Manuel J. Berrocal, even if more "criollos" were attending Panamanian schools, they were still "going about in the streets speaking in a dialect that they've always considered their own language … without respect for the Castilian language which is used in schools, and is the national language."[75] For Berrocal, English usage lay at the heart of the problem. Juan B. Olivera, in turn, regretted that "criollos" chose the year of the nation's fiftieth anniversary to reveal their lack of patriotism.[76]

Such critics ignored that at the very moment they penned their comments against "criollos," Westerman, the most famous one in the nation, was speaking on behalf of la patria in Washington, to a large international audience. Yet, to focus on Westerman would discredit their assertions. He spoke Spanish, fully understood the patron-client relations that shaped day-to-day aspects of national political life, and financed his own trips to champion Panama. He embodied a patriotism few in the nation understood. He spoke English that he learned from his Afro-Caribbean parents, not in the foreign prep schools where the nation's elite learned it. Westerman, with his growing fame and political connections, could rise above these criticisms. For many in his community, eschewing these criticisms was difficult, if not impossible.

External and Communal Policing for La Patria

Three days after Westerman was officially decorated with the Vasco Núñez de Balboa honor in Washington, DC, Beleño published one of his last major statements on unpatriotic "criollos." His piece, "Clear Proof of Criollo Sectarianism," reproduced a letter to the editor printed in the *Nation*.[77] Both the letter and Beleño's introduction called for heightened vigilance toward Afro-Caribbean Panamanians.

Eduardo Archibold P., the letter writer who captured Beleño's attention, complained that Assemblyman Alfredo Cragwell, a self-identified Afro-Caribbean Panamanian elected to the National Assembly, had not publicly denied allegations of "criollo absenteeism" during the farewell ceremony. Regarding the topic of language usage, Archibold conceded that several Afro-Caribbean Panamanians continued to speak in English, but he averred that this had to change "at all cost, for our allegiance cannot be pledged to two flags, and least of all to a flag that divides the human race into categories of metallic value." He also insisted that most Afro-Caribbean Panamanians identified the republic as their home, regardless of their language use. Archibold concluded his letter by asking Colón officials to end offensive radio broadcasts against "criollos."[78]

For Beleño, Archibold's letter served as irrefutable proof that "criollos [we]re a minority sect directed by overseas lodges and labor unions, managed by the CIO in the United States, who [we]re ready to use all arms to combat our nationality." Archibold had not mentioned the CIO in his letter. His allusion to the unfair gold-silver payroll proved to Beleño that Archibold was a CIO emissary. If authorities acceded to Archibold's request that the Colón broadcasts end, Beleño proclaimed that such an act would mean "Panama had become a North American protectorate governed by a criollo." Beleño ended his comments by asking the forgiveness of his fellow citizens for reproducing Archibold's letter in its original English form.[79]

Despite Beleño's bigotry, most letter writers in the monthlong debate defended Afro-Caribbean Panamanians. Many expressed pride in belonging to the group. What about those who wrote to congratulate and support Beleño, though? Were they the exceptions? How many agreed with them? More importantly, what did it mean that both those opposed to and in agreement with Beleño expressed a similar desire for a "Spanish-only Latin Panama"? Apparently, Afro-Caribbean Panamanians had but to embrace this identity and all prejudices would disappear. The majority in the debate over the farewell ceremony promoted a homogeneous and confining vision of Panamanian identity.

This push for homogeneity intensified following a major national union rally that featured President Remón. The rally, coordinated by Local 900, took place six months after the farewell ceremony, with an eye to the continuing treaty discussions. An estimated ten thousand people attended.[80] In his address, Gaskin focused on the tireless work of union officials and organizers and affirmed that no one sought to "browbeat the United States" to secure a decent standard of living. Instead he emphasized that Local 900 wanted to "inspire faith in and love for democracy" by ensuring that workers and their families had security and stability.[81] With this focus on workers, their goals, their needs, and their anticommunism, Gaskin shifted attention from loftier diplomatic themes and noted the real men and women affected by unjust labor policies.

Remón, the star of the rally, kept his comments focused on the "groundbreaking" work that would result from the treaty negotiations. He likewise commented on the republic's continued campaigns against communism. He assured all those present that the welfare of Panamanian workers formed part of the proposals in Washington. The negotiation mission, Remón declared, "had special instructions to see to it that justice is done for Panamanian workers in the Canal Zone—that they be treated with the fairness due human beings." As head of an administration that decried discrimination of any kind, he proclaimed fairness for Panamanian zone workers a priority. "Equal pay for equal work," Remón declared, was "imperative" for the success of the talks. Remón also stated that Panamanians working in the Canal Zone shared his disdain of communism and would join the fight for democracy.[82] This adamant stance coincided with the intensification of diplomatic, covert, and military campaigns by the United States against the supposed communist government of Jacobo Arbenz in neighboring Guatemala.[83]

While the national media projected a positive review of the rally, as a "transcendental date in the history of the labor movement in Panama," the

Nation critiqued Gaskin's decision to deliver his speech in English.[84] The paper called it a "flagrant violation of protocol ... [and in] decidedly poor taste" that only served to "prove that children of West Indian parents born on the Canal Zone are desirous of imposing the American culture and customs upon Panama." By imposing a bilingual structure on a national event and using those "deficient in Panamanian traditions and national sentiments" to lead it, the editorial railed, Afro-Caribbean Panamanians effectively rejected full-fledged assimilation.[85]

This critique of Gaskin by the *Nation* held many parallels to the "criollo lack of assimilation" debate initiated by Beleño and others. Language usage (Spanish vs. English), place of residence (the republic vs. the Canal Zone), and cultural affinity (Panamanian vs. American) shaped all these criticisms. While *Nation* editorials first condemned Beleño back in September 1953, by January 1954 at least one *Nation* editor employed his tactics: obsession over Gaskin's language choice, while ignoring the actual substance of his speech.

The editorial referred to Gaskin as the president of Local 900 and the man who addressed a national audience "in the English language, instead of the language of the country to which he claims allegiance." The writer likewise made clear that "others in Local 900 could have measured up to the occasion in a way to leave no resentment or unfavorable criticism," though it offered no names.[86] Because of Gaskin's failure to showcase his commitment to the nation, the entire republic would continue to question the national allegiance of Afro-Caribbean Panamanians.

Why such a strong condemnation by the mostly pro-Remón *Nation*? The newspaper's lambasting of Gaskin quite possibly rested with its Afro-Caribbean leadership base. Leslie Williams, an Afro-Caribbean, served as the newspaper's English-language section editor. The newspaper placed a great deal of attention on Afro-Caribbean Panamanian affairs. Still, not unlike the *Tribune*'s policing of the Local 713 union, Williams and the *Nation* now sought to monitor the image projected by Local 900. According to the *Nation*, as a union that had amassed substantial national attention, the local needed to project an image of stalwart patriotism. Any other approach would lead to failure and invalidate the aspirations of tens of thousands of Afro-Caribbean Panamanians.

Ironically, the editorial critiquing Gaskin was in English. Could not the argument be made that the very existence of an English national daily went against national assimilationist goals? This debate, however, had less to do with language, and more with the ease through which commentators could marginalize and "other" an entire group—us versus them, the patriots versus the aliens, the thankful ones versus the ungrateful ones. Upholding these binaries was an acceptance that nationality rested on homogeneity, assimilation, exclusion, and a constant policing of ideological, cultural, racial, and physical borders.

This conflict over homogeneity and assimilation had its roots in the 1930s and continued to evolve into the early 1950s. As noted in the previous two chapters, Afro-Caribbean Panamanian journalists and teachers, such as Amy Denniston, Sidney Young, Leonor Jump, Aston Parchment, and Edward Gaskin, had promoted the use of Spanish in schooling and newspapers for decades. Yet, this push toward greater Spanish instruction and public use was never presented as a replacement for Afro-Caribbean culture or the English language. All those noted above remained very attuned to happenings in the Anglophone Caribbean and the United States and traveled to these areas for greater educational or advocacy opportunities. They held a vested interest in centering the isthmus as an Afro-diasporic base that drew on rich histories of migration and international exchange, while evolving into something unique. This potential and ability to combine linguistic, cultural, and pedagogical opportunities represented what they viewed as the isthmus's special and transcendent qualities.

Alongside those calling for a pluralistic view of the isthmus, however, were those who proposed total assimilation as the only viable option for panameñidad. The Liga Cívica Nacional's discourse in the mid-1940s mirrored many responses to Beleño's attacks in 1953. A decrease in English-language usage, a greater number of letters thanking government officials for being inclusive, and speaking for the nation (in Spanish) came to typify what would be required for a full acceptance of Afro-Caribbeans as true Panamanians. The response to the 1954 rally marked the growing hegemony of this thought frame, something Gaskin had not fully anticipated.

According to the *Tribune*, Gaskin provided a Spanish translation of his text to the press and handed out copies at the rally. Gaskin had also informed the Remón administration that he would deliver his speech in English.[87] More importantly, Local 900 had made President Remón the guest of honor. Was not this a sufficiently nationalist stance, to showcase the president before a crowd of thousands, with thousands more listening from home? How could it all be reduced to Gaskin's use of English? Why would English use undermine all other aspects of the rally? Would it have made a difference if Gaskin had addressed the crowd in Spanish, rolled his *rr*s with perfection, and topped it all with a solo performance of the national anthem?

The January rally marked the peak of Gaskin's and Local 900's influence within the Remón administration and the Panama-US treaty negotiations. But his activism would continue. Gaskin would share with Remón observations regarding race, equality, and justice that he could only have gathered as a zone resident. For the sake of the Panamanian nation, his homeland, he would half plead, half demand that Remón's government not forsake the Panamanians who had made the Canal Zone their home.

Full Citizenship as Assimilation?

By the mid-1950s the lives and careers of George Westerman and Edward Gaskin provided some parallels to key aspects of Afro-Caribbean realities on the isthmus. Westerman, who attained success first through print journalism and later as a public intellectual, personified incorporation at its best. Westerman's career spoke to an explicit shifting away from a general interest in documenting Canal Zone labor affairs to speaking as a Panamanian citizen championing the welfare of his fellow citizens and his country. Westerman's activism, as a result, became less about zone workers and more about national sovereignty in US-Panamanian relations. President Remón recognized and celebrated Westerman's transition, as did others who saw him as a role model to future generations.

Gaskin, through his activism, also shifted toward ardent nationalism like Westerman, but he remained reluctant to part ways with the potentials of locally grounded international unionism and a pluralistic understanding of citizenship, which included the use of the English language and the retention of Afro-Caribbean culture. Maintaining this perspective would only grow in difficulty, as assimilation and homogeneity in the form of a Spanish-only and anti-Black foreigner nation, continued to dominate both the popular and political imagination.

Strikingly, even as the results of their activism differed, both Westerman and Gaskin remained adamant anticommunists. This they insisted could prove the greatest tool in the arsenal of Afro-Caribbean activism. While anticommunism provided both men with an opportunity to push US officials on promises of democracy and to highlight Panama's importance as a key democratic force in the hemisphere, this ideology prevented a firm criticism of continued discrimination in Panama. This connection between anticommunism and nationalist mobilization shaped official discourses throughout the Americas. When discrimination did make national news, such as following Westerman's Chicago speech, it was to highlight discrimination faced by

Panamanians at the hands of zone officials—not racism in the republic. Indeed, even Gaskin in his report to the Panamanian negotiation team emphasized Panama as a melting pot where racial discrimination had disappeared as a problem.

Yet, condemnations of Afro-Caribbean Panamanians as outsiders—even as members of this group wrote letters; organized and attended rallies; promoted the nation overseas; embarked in labor organizing; and pledged their allegiance to the nation's president—suggested that race and inequality remained entrenched issues. The attacks on Afro-Caribbean Panamanians by Beleño and others drew from collective notions of them as perpetual outsiders. That Beleño, a Black man, could lead this campaign alluded to the effectiveness of this discourse. Afro-Caribbean descendants became the "other" against which everyone could measure their own citizenship. Given that the nationality law, which dubbed them "possible citizens," remained official policy, those critiquing Afro-Caribbean Panamanians, regardless of their own class, ethnic, or racial background, could point to this legislation as incontrovertible evidence of their superiority.

To Be Panamanian

The Canal Zone, Nationalist Sacrifices, and the Price of Citizenship, 1954–1961

On December 19, 1956, President Ernesto de la Guardia, speaking before the Panamanian Chamber of Commerce, urged those concerned about adverse effects of the newest treaty with the United States, the 1955 Remón-Eisenhower Treaty, to remember what it meant to be Panamanian. *Ser panameño*, to be Panamanian, he affirmed, was a status gained by birth, by making a livelihood in the republic, and by raising future generations of Panamanians. For Panamanians, he insisted, the statuses of "Canal Zone worker" or "Canal Zone resident" were "transient conditions." Indeed, even after losing the latter conditions, the status of Panamanian would always remain.[1] De la Guardia's speech, as this chapter highlights, formed part of a continued simultaneous struggle to include and exclude from the republic's body politic both the Canal Zone and the Afro-Caribbean Panamanians whose lives and labor had made the canal and zone area possible. Defining ser panameño at this juncture proved especially urgent given that the new treaty provided key concessions and granted the republic greater control over a group largely regarded as questionable or conditional citizens. Yet, this elite-driven nascent anti-imperialist moment came in the shadow of an activist movement led by Afro-Caribbean Panamanians that challenged the notion of conditional citizenship. Attempts to define ser panameño, as a discursive, physical, and geopolitical act, laid bare growing fissures regarding the terms of nationalist inclusion at a time when racism and struggles for economic sovereignty coalesced on the isthmus.

In the previous chapter I discussed the beginning of treaty discussions between Panama and the United States and the particular ways in which Afro-Caribbean Panamanians proved crucial in this initiative. I also noted how select Afro-Caribbean Panamanians found themselves lambasted by critics within and outside their respective communities, on the grounds of insufficient or improper participation. In this chapter I focus on contestations regarding access to citizenship, using as a backdrop attempts to redefine the Canal Zone space, the impact of the 1955 treaty, shake-ups to established labor union leadership, and the repeal of the nationality law. Connecting these moments were exclusionist assumptions regarding who could truly be Panamanian, and the sacrifices expected of Afro-Caribbean Panamanians, within and outside the Canal Zone, for full acceptance as citizens.

Expulsion and Conversion for a Better Panama

The introduction of two Canal Zone policies, school conversion and depopulation, in 1954 illuminated powerful ties between white Canal Zone officials and white and mestizo Panamanians invested in defining what de la Guardia described as ser panameño. Canal Zone Governor John Seybold implemented the aforementioned policies invoking, on one hand, budgetary needs of the zone, and on the other, a desire to assist Panama in the creation of "more wholesome" citizens. In their reactions to the depopulation and school conversion policies, officials and citizens, while expressing dismay at another power play by zone officials, also used the opportunity to instruct and critique "questionable citizens" on the ideal of being Panamanians. Delineating outsider and insider definitions ultimately connected these cross-national government officials and ordinary citizens alike.

Although Seybold announced his depopulation plan in March 1954, talk of removing a larger portion of non-US citizens from the zone first emerged in 1952.[2] The early 1950s coincided with increased fears that communism would spread to Central America and somehow infect canal workers. Zone officials viewed non-US workers and their families as susceptible to communist propaganda. Budget concerns also drove part of Seybold's interest in depopulation. Under growing pressure from the US Congress, Seybold had to justify the perceived pampering of white US citizens working in the Canal Zone. The zone, observers noted, operated like a socialist republic for whites, with free housing, schooling, and health care as well as generous salaries that included a "tropical" differential.[3] This criticism led to the end of federal subsidies to the Panama Canal Company and Canal Zone government, leaving canal tolls as the only income for the operating budget. Seybold responded with cutbacks in both the US-rate and local-rate workforce, while maintaining the benefits afforded to white US citizens.[4] Rather than curtail any of these benefits—understood by Zonians (white US citizens born or with a long residency in the zone) as rights—Seybold and his administration kept most by cutting back on the few housing and schooling benefits offered to non-US citizens. In this way, perceived communist threats and a need for cost-cutting measures merged in the targeting of non-US zone residents of color. Depopulation also aimed to make the zone more of an all-white space, a goal that linked the zone with suburbanization trends taking place throughout the United States. Black expulsion rather than white flight typified efforts within the zone.

The unfolding treaty talks between Panama and the United States also factored into Seybold's depopulation policy. One of the demands made by the Panamanian diplomats included the return of lands no longer in use by the United States. A phone conversation between Seybold and US assistant secretary of state for western hemisphere affairs John M. Cabot in December 1953 offered details on Seybold's perspective regarding this demand. According to Cabot: "The Governor said that he favored the return of the New Cristóbal area in Colón, in addition to the other lands currently under consideration.... The Governor desires that the transfer of the land in question carry with it the residences of a large number of local-rate labor in furtherance of his plan to have most local-rate labor reside in the Republic rather than in the Zone. Since local-rate labor is likely to oppose this plan, the Governor's purpose is to remove from US authorities as much as possible the onus of the transfer."[5] The Panamanian public would only learn of these depopulation plans when they appeared in English-language dailies.[6]

Seybold proved more forthcoming with his school conversion plans, at least with Panama's elites. He announced the forthcoming changes at the Panamanian Rotary Club.[7] The conversion, he explained, would finally address the failure of Canal Zone colored schools (renamed local-rate schools in the late 1940s) to prepare young men for their role as Panamanian citizens. "We must orient this student to his future—culturally and socially," he declared, "and it must be realized that his future is conjoined with his citizenship."[8] Both young men and women attended local-rate schools and had since the 1910s, but Seybold expressed concern only for male students.

In his remarks, Seybold avoided discussing the continued segregation in these schools, choosing instead to focus on the seemingly pluralistic descriptor of "Latin American" schools. The use of this term and its implied Pan–Latin American orientation proved ironic since US officials had no interest in any such engagement. *Latin American*, in this instance, filled the space of *other* or *foreigner*. This descriptor also capitalized on discourses of racial mixture and racelessness in Latin America, while nonetheless highlighting that the term itself could be used to categorize entire populations as nonwhite, including groups who in the Panamanian context enjoyed white privilege. Students in the newly renamed schools thus strategically became both foreign and generic nonwhite Latin Americans.

Seybold also stated that beginning in August 1954 the newly named Latin American schools would adhere to a Panamanian educational curriculum with the goal of a total conversion by the 1955–56 school year. To further streamline the process and keep costs down, classroom sizes would be reduced, and all nonresident students would go on a wait list. This conversion meant that at least two thousand students would no longer have access to schooling. All these changes, Seybold insisted, would in the end give the affected children an opportunity to "build a better world."[9]

Reactions to Seybold's proposals ranged in intensity but ultimately shared clear assumptions regarding whether those affected by them deserved to be part of the Panamanian nation. Hearing news of the intended relocation of hundreds of "local rate workers" and their families to New Cristóbal, a group of Colón professionals protested the decision. According to a letter signed by twenty-four New Cristóbal residents and sent to Governor Seybold, President Remón, and other top Panamanian and US diplomatic officials, the creation of a "barrio obrero" would destabilize the "customs" and "general tranquility" that shaped the lives of the "businessmen, professionals, and consular representatives" who called New Cristóbal home. The basis of their complaint was not racial discrimination, they insisted, but rather a desire to avoid inevitable clashes due to incompatible class and cultural backgrounds. With New Cristóbal redefined as a "working-class neighborhood," they complained, the economic and cultural potential of Colón, as a whole, would suffer.[10]

Colón had the nation's largest Afro-Caribbean descendant population by the 1920s. Still, a small but vocal base there used the airwaves and other platforms to critique the citizenship credentials of Afro-Caribbean zone workers. The residents of the New Cristóbal neighborhood formed an elite group seeking to maintain their status quo. Their privileges included municipal leadership levels and province-wide commercial and legislative power, unattainable for most Afro-Caribbeans.

Indicative of their status, these professionals also sent telegrams to Remón and Roberto Huertamatte, Panama's ambassador to the United States.[11] Huertamatte, following exchanges with Seybold and other US officials, concluded that "the transfer of jamaicanos to [New Cristóbal] could only be interpreted as the Panama Canal's desire to devalue land that they would soon have to return."[12] Huertamatte's commentary, more so than revealing a conspiracy on the part of US officials, highlighted how he and other Panamanian officials viewed Afro-Caribbean zone workers. In referring to the workers to be transferred as *jamaicanos*, or Jamaicans, Huertamatte reiterated false assumptions that Black workers on the canal were foreigners—not Panamanians. Many indeed had ancestors from the Caribbean (more from Barbados than Jamaica) and were proud of this, but none would have described themselves as solely Jamaican. The label *jamaicanos* ultimately meant to push these men and women outside the boundaries of Panamanian citizenship. Not unlike the "conditional citizen" criteria that formed part of the nationality law, those facing relocation were doubly excluded on the grounds of their ancestry and alleged incompatibility with nationalist principles. Their lives were deemed of less value than those of New Cristóbal professionals, hence the danger that their very presence would "devalue" the entire province. Many white US and Panamanian officials held similar opinions.

And what of those whose future "relocation" animated letters, telegrams, and diplomatic inquiries? What did they have to say about relocation? Not much documentation of their opinions exists, but Edward Gaskin, as president of Local 900, wrote to President Remón, alerting that depopulation would not only adversely affect workers and their families but by extension, the entire republic.[13] In framing his critiques, he avoided discussions of "human value" and "jamaicanos" and instead condemned the Canal Zone government for once more shirking its promises to the Panamanian nation. As Gaskin made clear, for zone administrators, "racial segregation, housing, schooling, slum clearance, equal pay for equal work [would all] be solved ... by the simple expedient of dumping all of the local rate employees into the Republic."[14] No longer interested in offering any solutions for these matters, depopulation become an expedient cure-all.

Gaskin also cautioned against the false claim that the republic was prepared for depopulation and outlined three conditions to ameliorate the negative effects of this policy. These included a "doubling or tripling of salaries" to absorb the higher cost of living in the republic, an agreement between the United States and Panama for the construction of low-cost housing, and a promise by the Panamanian government to begin plans for the educational, health, and welfare needs of the affected workers and their families.[15] These changes, he insisted, would benefit the entire nation and highlight the unity of the Panamanian people.

Yet, even with his carefully outlined proposal, Gaskin remained concerned about the extent to which workers and their families would continue to factor into the plans of policy makers. After all, a push to declare a win in gaining equity between the United States and Panama could involve a willingness to sacrifice those already viewed as questionable citizens. Writing again to Remón, Gaskin asked for clarification regarding Governor Seybold's claims that depopulation adhered to Panama's desire to have all its citizens live within its jurisdiction. Such a goal, Gaskin asserted, contradicted past conversations between the union and the Remón administration. Gaskin demanded "the exact position of the Panamanian government" on relocation. He softened his inquiry by describing himself and fellow union members as "devoted allies in the efforts at national progress" but warned against misinformation and betrayal.[16] Gaskin asked for inclusion, but in doing so, he revealed the growing distance between Remón's administration and the Local 900 leadership. Gaskin now understood that several decisions would be made without the input of the union or its soon-to-be-affected workers.

Protecting (White) Children and the Spanish Language

The school conversion decision best highlighted the lack of decision-making power among Afro-Caribbean zone workers, while also confirming ongoing preconceptions about what they did and did not deserve. During his first speech on the subject, Seybold mentioned having the support of many Afro-Caribbean Panamanians, including George Westerman.[17] Westerman, surprisingly, had very little to say about the forthcoming school conversion. Earlier in the year he had applauded the efforts to expand Spanish-language training to all grades in the local-rate schools, believing this would lead to fewer assimilation problems as Canal Zone–born youth sought citizenship.[18] Perhaps in recognition of this attitude, Seybold comfortably assumed that Westerman was an ally in the school conversion cause. But many Afro-Caribbeans in the zone expressed no such enthusiasm for the plan. In at least one town, teachers of the soon-to-be-renamed Latin American schools, as well as Local 900 officials and members, created a committee to study the conversion plans. Teachers, in particular, cautioned against the speed of the conversion.[19]

Gaskin, in his correspondence with Remón, also expressed outrage on behalf of students in the local-rate schools. These children, he insisted, were being pushed out in an attempt by zone officials to "get out of educating any of our citizens" and instead force the republic to overfill its already over-crowded schools.[20] Gaskin observed that school conversion maintained the same segregationist practices of earlier decades, couched in the language of "Latin American" and "US-rate" schools. He pointed to the planned closure of the La Boca Junior College (an expanded version of the normal school discussed in chapter 2), which predominantly served Afro-Caribbean Panama-nians, as one such example: "It is strangely significant that local rate children shall be denied Junior College education next year even though their parents live and work on the Zone; yet, offspring of white Panamanian well-to-do families who are non-employees and non-residents of the Zone continue to attend the U.S. rate schools. This might well be a sinister and subtle maneuver to continue the vicious practice of injecting the virus of racial intolerance into the body politic of the Panamanian nation and thus divide its citizenry against each other?"[21] Wealth and whiteness allowed for the advancement of elite Panamanians within the zone. Black students, in turn, faced unjust punishment for factors outside their control: the color of their skin, their lack of family wealth, the place they called home, and treaty negotiations in Washington. In exposing how race determined schooling in the zone, and by calling out complicit white Panamanians, Gaskin acknowledged the effects of racism throughout the isthmus. Canal Zone officials were the key perpetrators, but white Panamanians collaborated in their policies.

Gaskin touched on a topic here that few Panamanian elites or members of the middle class wanted to address—the presence of white and mestizo Panamanians in US-rate zone schools (formerly whites-only zone schools). Who were these Panamanians who sought out US-rate schools? Why had these students not been required to attend local-rate schools? Would they, at the start of the 1954 school year, be required to attend the Latin American schools with their darker fellow citizens?

Governor Seybold's administration offered some answers in early June. Effective for the 1954–55 school year, the 104 Panamanians enrolled in US-rate schools would have to transfer to Latin American schools. These students were eligible for the transfer because their parents both worked and lived in the Canal Zone.[22] While this statement cast some doubt on Gaskin's allegation that white Panamanians who did not reside in the zone attended US-rate schools, it did confirm that select Panamanians had, in the past, been allowed access to whites-only schools. In specifying that these students now had to attend the Latin American schools, Seybold's administration could also adhere to the *Brown v. Board of Education* US Supreme Court decision that called for an end to racial segregation in US schools. In this way, race would technically no longer factor into enrollment decisions in either US-rate or Latin American schools, with the focus shifting toward nationality and providing a culturally appropriate, nondiscriminatory experience for all students in the zone. Black students would nevertheless remain over-represented in Latin American schools as were white students in US-rate schools. This embodied de facto racial segregation with a linguistic twist.

Letters from parents of the soon-to-be-relocated Panamanian students to First Lady Cecilia Pimel de Remón and her husband confirmed that for these parents, their children could attain the best education only in the predominantly white US-rate schools. Twenty-four mothers described efforts to move their children to the Latin American schools as "a truly unjust form of discrimination" and implored the first family to save the "intellectual wellbeing of their children."[23] Cecilia Remón was a well-known philanthropist and communitarian whom the Panamanian zone mothers viewed as an ally. In a follow-up telegram to their letters, the mothers reminded President Remón that one of the students affected by the transfer was his godson, who, like the other students in question, had begun his educational career in the US-rate schools. The mothers beseeched Remón to use his power to prevent the transfers.[24]

Neither the president nor the First Lady responded personally to the petitioning mothers, but the Ministry of Foreign Affairs kept Remón informed of efforts to communicate with Governor Seybold on the issue. In November, Minister Guizado forwarded to Remón's office letters Guizado had exchanged with Seybold's executive secretary. These letters, in addition to revealing that the petitioners had successfully amassed the support of some top officials, highlighted how they articulated their demands to Seybold. The mothers emphasized that they wanted their children to learn English, not Spanish, since English was the dominant language in the zone. The Latin American schools would offer instruction only in Spanish. They also expressed worries about the quality of education in the new schools.[25]

Seybold assured the mothers that students in these schools would continue to receive an excellent education. By referring to this "continued excellence," Seybold relied on the preconversion history of the zone's segregated school system. As outlined in chapter 2, Afro-Caribbean Panamanian teachers, parents, and interested community members had fought hard for years to improve zone colored schools since the early 1930s. Seybold, in his efforts to appease the petitioning mothers, touted this excellence as a personal accomplishment of his administration and those of his predecessors. Seybold's response also reaffirmed the motivation that had shaped both his depopulation and school conversion policies. As he reminded the mothers, schooling in the zone was a right secured only for US citizens, confirming that the Canal Zone was a white US space.[26] This was a reality that even Panamanians who had been allowed access to this space because of their lighter skin or status as employees needed to recognize.

No further communications followed between the mothers and Panamanian and US officials. Some students transferred to the Latin American schools, while others enrolled in Panamanian public and private schools, but the correspondence underscored the power of white privilege in Panama and the Canal Zone. None of the parties involved questioned the existence of whites-only schools, now dubbed US-rate schools, and instead struggled to secure access to this whiteness (vis-à-vis the schools). In effect, a shared understanding of white privilege allowed everyone involved in this petitioning process to make claims to the zone in ways that avoided explicit racial discourse while fully embracing racial hierarchies.

The very nature of the conversion hardened these hierarchies and placed the burden for success or failure on Afro-Caribbean teachers and students. As part of the conversion plan, Afro-Caribbean teachers were given only six months to transition from English-only to Spanish-only instruction. Most of the teachers, particularly those teaching since the 1940s, were bilingual, but their lesson plans and books had all adhered to the English-language Canal Zone curriculum. Careful time and training was needed for the kind of transition envisioned in the conversion plan, but this was not the focus for zone officials. As noted earlier, as a result of the *Brown v. Board of Education* decision, schools could not remain racially segregated. Separating schools by language instruction kept the racial status quo, while forcing all the instructional challenges on Afro-Caribbean teachers and students. This segment of the zone school population was used to innovation and had made the most of an inequitable system, but the conversion plan asked for dramatic changes at warp speed, with little input from the most affected populations. Instead, as critics within and outside the zone predicted, any failings or limits in the plan served as further evidence that Afro-Caribbeans could never be trusted as true Panamanians.

As early as April 1954, critics of the conversion plan focused on the linguistic abilities and national affiliations of the teachers in the new school system. One critic warned that "foreign teachers" would be instructing students in the newly converted schools. The danger of such a practice, the writer warned, rested in the already large number of "unassimilated West Indians" in these schools. To fully assimilate these students, their teachers would re-

FIGURE 4.1 Robert Beecher, 1955. Beecher was in charge of the summer institute (May–July 1954) in La Boca. Canal Zone school officials, with guidance from educators and education officials from the republic, created the curriculum for the Latin American schools. No Afro-Caribbean educators were invited to participate in this process, but they were expected to learn and teach the new curriculum. Beecher and his colleague Owen B. Shirley in Rainbow City coordinated peer courses centered on the new curriculum. This photograph was taken shortly after Beecher was named principal of the La Boca High School. A year later he would migrate to New York. From *Panama Canal Review*, August 5, 1955, 12.

quire Spanish fluency "from birth" and have "a native intonation." Otherwise "the purity of the language would be corrupted," followed shortly by the corruption of the republic's essence.[27] This quest for Panamanian cultural purity established an unattainable ideal that subordinated Afro-Caribbean Panamanians and their language practices as debased. It also ignored teachers like Robert Beecher (figure 4.1), Basilio Cragwell (figure 4.2), and Evalina Pringle (figure 4.3), all born in Panama, who led and taught in summer institutes and workshops created after the conversion decision. They spoke Spanish "from birth," yet critics viewed their language skills with suspicion.

FIGURE 4.2 Teachers in summer institute, June 1954. *Left to right*: Clarence Skeete, Gloria Holmes, Basilio Cragwell (instructor), Carmen Butcher, and Daphne Watkins. Newspapers, newly assigned textbooks, writing assignments, and oral presentations all formed part of the summer institute. From *Panama Canal Review*, June 4, 1954, 2.

Following the rapid-speed conversion, teachers like Elsie Graham inaugurated the Latin American schools. Being bilingual facilitated the process for Graham and many of her peers, but the pressure was on her and her colleagues to dazzle critics. Figure 4.4 is a photograph taken during an open house where zone officials observed classrooms that had undergone conversion. The image captures Graham giving a lesson as her students try to contain their excitement and curiosity at being observed. The blackboard and the walls are decked with lesson plans and student artwork on topics ranging from colors and arithmetic to literature. Graham and her colleagues continued to provide their students with the same level of care and attention as in previous years but now faced additional scrutiny within and outside the school system.

Professors and deans from the Universidad de Panamá, all white or mestizo, warned that graduates of the Latin American Schools might have "dialects, mannerisms and political views" that conflicted with those of "true Panamanians."[28] In their commentaries, opinion writers and educators avoided any explicit mention of race, though their use of terms like *foreigner*, *West Indian*, *Spanish*, and *our history* codified undesired Blackness and a lack of authentic Panamanian essence. For them, denouncing Afro-Caribbean teachers was not racist but an act of patriotism. Within this rationale, ser

FIGURE 4.3 Teachers in summer institute, June 1954. *Left to right*: John Evans, Mabel McFaquhar, Evalina Pringle (instructor), Pearline Carter, Sylvia Doig, Ruby Thompson, and Verona Campbell. A number of the instructors in this session formed part of a third generation of zone teachers, having graduated from teaching schools in the late 1940s and early 1950s. Carter, a resident of Panama City and a 1947 graduate of the La Boca Normal School, was the youngest principal within the zone school system (she taught in and headed the Chagres School in Gatun). Everyone wishing to teach in the Latin American schools, notwithstanding seniority or leadership positions, had to attend the summer institute. From *Panama Canal Review*, June 4, 1954, 2.

panameño required denouncing suspicious outsiders who did not embrace cultural conformity or patriotic honor. Making these critiques via racially coded language turned bigotry into a nationalist performance.

The power of this oppressive patriotism even emerged in critiques by fellow Afro-Caribbean Panamanians. In September 1954, "E. A.—a Panamanian Parent of W.I. Origin" wrote to *La Nación* that the paper's editor, Leslie Williams, had been correct in his apprehension over the Spanish-language aptitude of Latin American school teachers. The zone government, this parent insisted, wanted students in the schools to have "a second rate education."[29] As noted in the previous chapter, *La Nación* had published scathing words against Gaskin's use of English during a national rally. Williams's concerns that teachers like Gaskin would be in charge of Spanish-language training in the Latin American schools was thus not particularly surprising. For E. A. and Williams, critiquing Afro-Caribbean teachers in the Canal Zone allowed

FIGURE 4.4 Paraiso Elementary, open house, third-grade classroom, October 1954. From RG 185, Photographs Related to the Operation and Development of the Panama Canal Zone, c. 1938–c. 1960, NARA, College Park, Maryland.

them to express genuine concerns about schooling there while joining the patriotic coalition championing ser panameño. A necessary sacrifice in this championing included calling out select Afro-Caribbean Panamanians as culturally and politically incapable of promoting national citizenship.

This confederation of critics decided the boundaries and requirements of ser panameño and revealed the power of racially coded language throughout the republic and the Canal Zone. Speaking about "true Panamanians" and what it meant to "be Panamanians" became easier with the foil of the perpetual outsider. This outsider, an outsider in both the Canal Zone and the republic, could never be innately Panamanian. Instead, on her or his person, the collective nation could assign blame for economic troubles and national disunity, while ignoring the inequities that caused them. Scapegoating the perpetual outsider distracted attention from privileged Panamanians enrolled in whites-only zone schools, from racism outside the Canal Zone, and from officials condemning fictive "jamaicanos" for invading and devaluing the republic.

Focus on the "other" also deflected criticism of US geopolitical and economic power in Panama. Rather than assessing the school conversion and depopulation plans as imperial policies that enhanced US goals at the expense of Afro-Caribbeans, Panamanian officials and select onlookers emphasized the harm these policies would inflict on the Panamanian nation. In this way, questionable citizens, and not US officials, became the chief obstacle to unifying the nation. Targeting these "aliens" allowed select Panamanians to make use of the zone for their own purposes without explicitly challenging US hegemony or looking in the mirror at their own racism.

A Fair Treaty for the Nation

Drawing more resources from the zone, via businesses and taxing Panamanian workers' income, emerged as a key state strategy to gain profit while proclaiming ser panameño. Such a scheme also paved the way for branding any zone workers critical of this policy as traitors to the nation. A focus on patriotic profiting from the zone, through and against questionable citizens, manifested itself during debates around the Remón-Eisenhower Treaty and its consequences. The end result of these disputes demonstrated the tensions between competing understandings of ser panameño and the unequal sacrifices it required.

The treaty and its accompanying memorandum included an increased annuity payment from canal operations, the return of land no longer in use by the US military (as well as some "returned" citizens), and the end of commissary privileges for Panamanian zone workers not residing in the enclave. State taxation of Panamanian zone workers' salaries, equal opportunity within an equal wage scale, and openings for Panamanian businesses to participate in the zone market were also agreed on in the accord.[30] Of these planned changes, the end of commissary privileges and the creation of an equal wage scale provoked intense debates about the republic's negotiating power and the costs of ser panameño.

Even prior to the treaty debates, addressing the concerns of Panamanian businessmen frustrated at the competition posed by Canal Zone commissaries formed a key component of the Panamanian state's desire to revise its relationship with the United States.[31] Remón's and Gaskin's "ni millones, ni limosnas, solo justicia" slogans galvanized the public, but Panama actually did want millions of more dollars from the treaty. The quest for justice, a kind with no specific price, proved more difficult to attain. In the main treaty talks, commissary privileges and curtailing US businesses in the zone ranked high on the list of priorities. As early as the 1930s, Panamanian businessmen complained about the unfair competition of zone commissaries, which provided zone workers with a wide array of basic goods and food staples at duty-free steep discounts. Contraband from the commissaries hampered competition, given that savvy zone workers created their own side businesses selling these goods. The zone government, under the auspices of the Buy American Act, refused to purchase goods from Panamanian industries, choosing instead to import from the United States products readily available on the isthmus.[32]

The 1955 treaty called for exemptions to the Buy American Act that would allow a greater allotment of Panamanian purchases, but the biggest treaty concession for local business concerns was the restriction of commissary privileges to zone residents.[33] By the mid-1950s more than thirty-five thousand Panamanian men, women, and children living in the republic had access to commissary privileges. A residency-based restriction would ensure that less than half of this population retained this privilege. Following the planned depopulation of La Boca and other such local-rate towns, this number would shrink even further. For Panamanian business owners, commissary restrictions represented a government-guaranteed profits bonanza.[34]

As Afro-Caribbean Panamanian workers and their families complained to their state representatives, commissary restrictions and other treaty features privileged the rights of businessowners while crushing the working class. Assemblyman Alfredo Cragwell, the first person of Afro-Caribbean ancestry elected to this body, served as a mediator between these communities and the government.[35] Cragwell attended a community meeting on these issues in February 1955, in the Río Abajo neighborhood of Panama City.[36] Cragwell, like many at the Río Abajo meeting, had family narratives that connected the Anglophone Caribbean, the republic, the Canal Zone, and the United States. Cragwell's father had migrated to Panama from Barbados in the early 1910s and taught for several years in the Canal Zone. He was also a respected reverend in Panama City. Cragwell's brother served as a section editor and chief political commentator for the *Panama Tribune* before migrating to New York to join four of their siblings.[37]

Cragwell's family enjoyed greater prosperity than most working-class Afro-Caribbean Panamanians, but they had elected him to the assembly. These constituents wanted answers about the new treaty. For those present at the meeting, commissary limitations and a prohibitively high cost of living loomed large. They demanded that Cragwell explain the benefits ordinary people would gain from the treaty and asked whether only merchants had been considered in the commissary decision. Most present understood the significant gains for the republic in the accords but worried about its overall effects on the "ordinary man."[38]

By invoking this "ordinary man," the residents of Río Abajo sought access to a more inclusive ser panameño that acknowledged and addressed their grievances. As they reminded Cragwell and other government officials, they stood on the front lines of the sacrifices expected by the nation to secure profits and business from the zone. Their loss of jobs, commissary privileges, and access to schooling, in addition to the taxes on their zone incomes, might factor greatly in the making of a new Panama, but such changes decimated their living standards. Left unanswered was whether this new nation would have any room for the men, women, and children of Río Abajo.[39]

While positing their concerns over the treaty, Río Abajo residents had to fear appearing disloyal. The assassination of President Remón in early January made such accusations more probable and even dangerous. Politicians and journalists alike presented the signing of the treaty as the best way to honor Remón's legacy. President Ricardo Arias, who succeeded Remón, even used his famous "ni millones, ni limosnas, solo justicia" speech as the quintessential expression of Remón's patriotism.[40] Too overt a critique of the treaty risked besmirching an alleged martyr. For this reason, engaging with government officials, even as they understood that the treaty placed an unfair burden on working-class families, proved a careful balancing act.

In addition to seeking out assembly representatives, those hurt by the commissary restrictions and other aspects of the treaty looked to the work of a brand-new Canal Zone union, Local 907. The local, representing Panamanian workers employed by the US Armed Forces within and outside the zone, was organized in September 1954. Local 907 focused on bridging the gap between an established Afro-Caribbean labor leadership and a growing mestizo Panamanian presence. It also split the labor movement and weakened Local 900's union dominance. This focus partly coalesced with proponents of ser panameño, who sought to avoid describing Panamanian zone workers as Afro-Caribbean Panamanians, even though the vast majority, including Local 907 members, identified as such. Instead, under the leadership of José de la Rosa Castillo, a mestizo Panamanian, the union presented itself as the true representative of the nation. Whether or not the union membership agreed with this, Castillo capitalized on this mantle by asking for more input in the 1955 treaty talks.[41]

By March 1955, as the National Assembly debated ratifying the accord, Local 907 coordinated public meetings that outlined "minimum aspirations" for an equitable ratification. These included assurances that the percentage of Panamanians working on the zone would not decline even if these reductions were presented as necessary for treaty implementation, and the application of the equal wage scale bill to compensate Panamanians who lost various privileges in the zone. The union also wanted wages for zone office employees, professionals, and technicians comparable to those made by their US peers in the United States, and the implementation of the US minimum wage in the zone. Recognition by Panamanian and US government officials that the cost of living in Panama was "equal and sometimes higher than in the United States" rounded out their concerns.[42] In asking for these assurances, Local 907 leadership revealed that they did not trust those involved in the treaty ratifications, in either Panama or the United States, to keep worker welfare a priority. By insisting on the equality of Panamanian and US workers, they deployed a key tenet of ser panameño—presenting Canal Zone workers as above all Panamanians, no racial descriptors necessary. Ensuring their just treatment safeguarded the interests of the entire nation.

Notwithstanding their advocacy work, no labor union representatives from either Local 900 or Local 907 formed part of the ratification debates in either nation. The National Assembly ratified the treaty in late March 1955. The US Senate followed four months later. Participation in the US Senate deliberations proved an unrequited aspiration. Greater enthusiasm existed for the National Assembly, given that this body represented all Panamanian citizens, including those working in the Canal Zone. But, like the Senate, the National Assembly excluded workers.

Commenting on the ratifications, Gaskin, in his annual Labor Day address, spoke of the political moment as one where "workers on the Isthmus—regardless of race, color, creed or national origin—fac[ed] the most ominous period of their existence."[43] Here he inverted the race-neutral emphasis of ser panameño rhetoric by insisting that the racially and ethnically diverse workers who made up the nation would all suffer under the new accord. Still, he insisted that what happened to zone workers had a wide-reaching impact on all workers in the republic.

Gaskin also addressed those excited by the assumed bonanza that would follow the end of commissary privileges and the taxation of Panamanian zone workers. The treaty, he noted, contained no guarantees of pay increases to compensate for taxation and lost privileges.[44] Without a salary increase, consumer demand would remain stagnant, and the nation's economy would suffer. Gaskin asked his audience to consider past lessons in the nation's history regarding unemployment and unrequited promises of improvement:

"For several years now there have been approximately 20,000 persons out of work in the dying city of Colón and approximately another 25,000 unemployed in the city of Panama. With all of the pious promises and pledges of official representatives and interested organizations and groups, virtually nothing has been done to alleviate the accompanying suffering and privation of this army of human beings."[45] No tangible solutions, Gaskin emphasized, had emerged for the forty-five thousand unemployed men and women in these cities, even as politicians and philanthropists spoke of hope and change. He called for "organized, persistent, unrelenting, [and] determined pressure" to ensure that promises of help materialized into "practical and demonstrable deeds."[46] Ser panameño, to Gaskin, involved citizens actively demanding concrete solutions from their government. Failure to perform this civic duty would result in the continued neglect of thousands, especially citizens in Colón and Río Abajo, areas with large Afro-Caribbean populations, viewed as marginal to the envisioned remaking of the nation.

While Gaskin called for greater civic engagement, Castillo wanted the international CIO to exert greater pressure on US officials to protect zone workers. This shift by Castillo pointed to his attempt at asserting an internationalist influence on ser panameño. For Afro-Caribbean Panamanians, this internationalism, grounded in a Black diasporic framework, involved connecting local campaigns within Panama to events and movements in other parts of the world. This was the local internationalism that fueled diasporic world making. Two such examples included the creation of a Black internationalist newspaper and the formation of international coalitions to address racial discrimination and labor inequities in the Canal Zone. Gaskin had also pursued internationalism in the past, although in doing so he had been labeled an emissary of foreign labor bosses.

Writing to James F. Carroll, the CIO's legal counsel, Castillo sought a detailed interpretation of the labor components in the treaty. Carroll found no US government changes, other than the elimination of the terms *local rate* and *US rate*, in its application of wages.[47] Workers recruited in Panama would receive payment comparable to that in the republic, and those recruited from the United States would receive wages based on US salaries. Carroll noted that the memorandum did offer some positive promises. One that could yield "relatively immediate gains" was the assurance that Panamanian workers would have access to all the training programs available in the zone.[48] With a greater group of trained Panamanians, more job opportunities should become available.

Though Carroll perhaps ended his letter on a positive note, his overall responses to Castillo's queries reiterated the points made by Gaskin in his Labor Day address. The treaty merely reframed one of the most entrenched policies of the zone, the labeling of all Panamanians as foreigners in a US-controlled space. As "foreigners" Panamanian citizens would never obtain equal pay or equal rights, without the advocacy of their government and labor representatives. In just questioning the treaty, Panamanians who worked in the zone yet lived in the republic risked alienation from their own nation. Even Castillo, a mestizo Panamanian, hazarded being labeled unpatriotic and ungrateful. Still, the discourse of questionable citizens most often targeted Afro-Caribbean Panamanians. The reliability of this targeting rendered the members of this group as outside the radius of national belonging. While technically Panamanian, their ability to ser panameño was suspect.

In the ratification debates the exclusion of Afro-Caribbean Panamanians was less apparent than, for example, in zone depopulation practices. Yet, the push to silence these men, women, and their families remained strong, particularly because they found ways to communicate to government and union officials their already precarious position within the republic's power structure. Ser panameño required upholding the nation above all else and casting aside any disunity. To this end careful monitoring of suspect citizens continued.

"Privileged Workers" and Bad Union Leadership

Edward Gaskin once more emerged as a key questionable citizen requiring policing. Despite past denunciations, Gaskin as Local 900 president could not remain silent about his continued concerns over the treaty. In January 1956 he issued a manifesto to *La Nación*, a paper that not so long ago had critiqued his leadership potential, on why the agreed-on wage structure was not only disappointing but a blatant disregard of the "hopes and aspirations of this substantial army of workers." The wage scale structure, Gaskin noted, still depended on "local salaries" based on wage standards within the republic, while US workers earned much higher salaries than Panamanian workers. Most distressing for Gaskin was the support given to this wage structure by "high and influential quarters in the Republic," who sought to avoid the creation of a "privileged labor class."[49]

Worries over a largely Black privileged labor class informed the struggles over the Canal Zone's presence on definitions of ser panameño. For Black workers of Caribbean ancestry to obtain US salaries would destabilize the entire class and racial hierarchy on which ser panameño was built. An

Afro-Caribbean Panamanian worker within this hierarchy must never have access to dollars, US culture, and travel on a par with the elite and upper middle class, be they white or mestizo. These members of the Panamanian body politic, after all, continuously used economic policies and legislative maneuvering to sustain their privileged status. In speaking out against the retention of the same old zone wage structure, Gaskin reminded his readers that a two-tiered system also operated in the republic as a whole. References to wage equality, rather than the pursuit of equity and true social justice, served as convenient political talking points for current and aspiring members of a Panamanian elite benefiting from the status quo.

For their pursuit of just wages, labor leaders faced not only external critics but internal bureaucratic reprimands. In February 1955, the US-based officials from the AFL-CIO (which had merged into one union in 1955) removed the governing Local 900 board. This move forced Gaskin's resignation and the replacement of his elected board with an organizing and administrative committee that would decide the future of the union. According to Milton Murray and Anthony J. Federoff, the two CIO officials leading the restructuring, financial inconsistencies, principally Local 900 operating beyond its means, had called for drastic action. Local 907 also came under the supervision of the national office, but its leadership board remained intact.[50]

For longtime critics of the union, Gaskin's resignation and the union's financial troubles demonstrated the hypocrisy of ineffective leaders professing to support the interest of their constituents and the nation. How could labor leaders back "official" or alternative visions of ser panameño if they could not successfully manage a labor union? Did the intervention by the US-based national office indicate that these leaders had no real power at either the national or the international level?[51]

As criticism of Local 900 grew, the former leadership found their past governance and reputations under attack. Rather than remain silent, some focused on the incompetence of the CIO national office. Erald L. Durant, recording and corresponding secretary for Local 900, found that in its tenure the union had collected more than $60,000 in dues but never had the national office represent its interests before the US Congress. As evidence of this neglect, Durant provided the *Star and Herald* with a copy of an October 1955 letter in which Local 900 asked for greater involvement and representation from the national office. No reply came.[52] After Gaskin's 1955 Labor Day address, his plea for help from the national offices received the same silence.

The collapse of Local 900's leadership prompted some commentators to cast it and Local 907 as unpatriotic organizations. In response to Local 907's continued calls for public conversations on the wage scale bill and commissary restrictions, the Panamanian Negotiating Mission asked the union to remember that a growth in sales within the republic would ultimately benefit thousands throughout the nation. By this logic, Panamanian zone workers, through their spending, would propel the nation forward.[53] "Panamanian workers," they emphasized, "should be especially careful in their choice of spokesmen, to prevent that they be represented by persons who appear to have an understanding with certain officials of the Zone and with certain Zone labor leaders who have striven and still strive to keep the provisions which favor Panama from being complied with."[54] In other words, union members had to be wary of leaders only interested in appeasing US government and labor officials. These leaders, according to this critique, rejected the ethos of ser panameño, opting for foreign approval at the expense of their fellow citizens. Like Beleño's warnings about "ungrateful criollos" and La Nación criticizing Gaskin's use of English, the negotiating mission asked zone workers to prove their allegiance by not engaging with foreign officials even as they talked to them every day. Instead the mission called on workers to submit to their duties as Panamanian citizens.

Demanding that workers and union leaders prove their patriotism remained an ongoing struggle for citizens viewed as accomplices to "foreign machinations and interests." Gaskin would remain outside the union movement for almost ten years, and on returning, he opted to work with another US-based international union representing Panamanian zone workers, a decision that further fueled critics concerned about improper allegiances.[55] Durant's exposé on the failures of the national CIO did not end accusations of his unpatriotic behavior. Others, like the Local 907 leadership, continued to offer critiques on the treaty while distancing themselves from the avalanche of accusations and condemnations aimed at former Local 900 officials.[56]

Within the unfolding treaty debates, very few acknowledged that Gaskin had been correct about the "new" salary scale. As confirmed by zone officials, the salaries offered to Panamanian and US workers would not be equal, and furthermore, the Panamanian mission had no grounds to assure Panamanian workers of a forthcoming salary increase. They received a small raise at the end of the ratification process that did not make up for what they had lost.[57] The elimination of commissary privileges and the closing of select commissaries proceeded as scheduled, while the national government failed to contain inflation caused by isthmian businesses inflating prices as predicted. Compounded with depopulation, these measures significantly lowered local-rate workers' living standards.[58]

Rather than address the reality that the republic made gains at the expense of the nation's Afro-Caribbean workers, "patriots" castigated labor leaders who, in their opinion, "directed themselves against the Government of the Republic, against the negotiators, the treaty signers, elected officials, and against almost the entire country." This attitude prevented adequate discussions of either commissary restrictions or concerns about ongoing pay inequities. To the critics, union leaders legitimately fighting for the rights of their constituents were "adversaries of the nation."[59] Despite such epithets, the rank-and-file workers understood that the treaty results were not a matter of international law and "patriotism" but a sellout of their interests for elite gains.

Insulting commentaries about workers' assumed "privileges" appeared absurd in comparison. Those affected by the commissary restrictions, according to their critics, were but a small sector of the country "who w[ould] suffer temporarily from the loss of their privileges," for the greater benefit of the overall Panamanian economy. Their sacrifice was both necessary and unavoidable. Panamanian zone workers unwilling to make these sacrifices were neither part of a privileged class nor allies of US imperialism as their critics claimed. They instead recognized that both their national government and the United States profited from their marginalization.[60] The issue was not whether the United States needed to pay higher salaries or consider the instability that would result from lost commissary privileges and added taxations, but rather how Afro-Caribbean zone workers should gracefully accept their losses. To be part of the nation, to ser panameños, they needed to eschew their individual interests for the patria. Failure to do so would only confirm their disinterest in joining the Panamanian family that had always opposed their membership.

Historical Revisionism and the Spirit of Patriotism

A similar message of "do it for the nation" shaped one of the earliest speeches made by President Ernesto de la Guardia. He assumed office in October 1956, at the height of debates over commissary restrictions. Speaking before the chamber of commerce thirteen days before the commissary restrictions went into effect, de la Guardia offered paternalistic reassurances that largely depended on Panamanian zone workers and their families patriotically sacrificing for the nation. In his words, "no one could be insensitive to the worries that in those days dampened the spirits of the Panamanian workers and employees of the Canal Zone. But the hope [wa]s that these very workers, inspired by a spirit of patriotism, w[ould] see the problem, above all, like

Panamanians." De la Guardia asserted that "the temporary difficulties" these workers would experience as a result of their loss of commissary privileges would in the end aid the overall economy. These workers, after all, would go from being "clients of the commissaries to clients of national commerce."[61]

As noted, de la Guardia tailored this speech for the businessmen present, not the Panamanian zone workers. His address formed part of his Conversaciones con el Pueblo Panameño (Conversations with the Panamanian people) series. He sought to expand his audience beyond the chamber to "el pueblo." As a result, in talking about Panamanian zone workers, de la Guardia emphasized their patriotic obligations, declaring that their status as Panamanians would always remain, even if they lost their "transient" titles as zone workers. They were "Panamanians by birth and residency," a status that "their children and grandchildren would surely inherit."[62] Yet, in reminding these workers of the conditions and components of ser panameño, de la Guardia contradicted the very idea of an inherent identity and suggested that being Panamanian required performing a particular behavior to validate that identity. By asking Panamanian zone workers to push aside their worries regarding commissary restrictions, de la Guardia reminded them that their national performance needed fine tuning. Birth, residency, and biology might form the core of "lo panameño," but patriotic thoughts and actions determined who had full access to this identity status.

De la Guardia's speech avoided making any racial or ethnic differentiation between Panamanian zone workers and the remainder of el pueblo. This distinguished him from other officials and commentators, who explicitly labeled these workers jamaicanos, "criollos," or foreigners. It instead aligned him with peers who chose to use panameño as an ahistorical and all-encompassing descriptive. Still, the tone of his invitation and the overall panameño label suggested a chasm between zone workers and the remainder of the country. The commissaries in this instance was the cause of the divide, but problematic policies and rhetoric including the end of automatic birth-based citizenship, language wars, pro-whitening immigration policies, and access to zone jobs had previously nourished these tensions.

In calling for zone workers to join el pueblo unreservedly, de la Guardia assumed that the republic had no debts to this community. Afro-Caribbean Panamanian workers had extensively championed the cause for labor reform and equality in the Canal Zone. They had approached government officials, broadcasted Labor Day addresses, traveled abroad representing Panama, and organized rallies. Yet, like Gaskin, they faced possible excommunication not only from the zone but also from the republic if they questioned de la

Guardia's invitation. Ser panameño, understood through this lens, depended on a careful performance of patriotic enthusiasm, voluntary sacrifices, and willful forgetting. Historical amnesia in this way absolved the nation of discriminatory and hurtful episodes from its recent past.

Writing in July 1957, after the commissary restrictions and before the passage of the long-awaited equal wage bill by the US Congress, George Westerman called on his readers to "be as proud of their nation as North Americans [were of their own]." Yet he qualified this pride by emphasizing that Panamanians had no plans to nationalize the canal or to supplant North American labor from this space.[63] The Egyptian nationalization of the Suez Canal a year earlier likely influenced Westerman's statement. His words assured all parties that no popular upheaval would occur in Panama to threaten continued US control of the canal. Decolonization in Panama would proceed along a diplomatic approach spearheaded by like-minded leaders invested in a more equitable canal treaty. As radical protests waged by students, workers, and civic groups by 1958 and well into the 1960s indicated, for younger generations, a focus on diplomatic channels and delayed equality would not be enough. Westerman and other leaders, however, as late as 1957, championed the Remón-Eisenhower Treaty as the best option available. It bears noting that Westerman's assessments coincided with his new role as Panama's ambassador to the United Nations, an appointment made by de la Guardia. Westerman's public enthusiasm for the road ahead rested in his new position as an official representative of the Panamanian state and his long history of moderation.

Compared to Westerman, President de la Guardia offered some initial caution. While using further speeches to urge his constituents to look past the nation's immediate economic troubles and envision a stronger economy, he recognized that the Canal Zone remained a significant employer in the country, the second largest after his government.[64] For this reason his administration made economic calculations based on both the commissary restrictions and a presumed generous salary increase that would morph into an equal wage scale for the zone. The wage bill that finally passed in 1958, while allowing Panamanian workers greater access to zone employment opportunities, continued the practice of basing Panamanian workers' salaries on wages paid in the republic. As a compromise the bill offered the possibility of reviewing wages periodically. This had not been the "equal pay for equal work" that Panamanian labor leaders and workers had championed. Even de la Guardia asked US president Dwight Eisenhower to intercede for a more equitable application of this law.[65]

Disappointment with the wage scale bill did not stop de la Guardia from reminding Panamanian zone workers of their duties to sacrifice for the nation. Speaking before the National Assembly at the start of his final year in office, he acknowledged treaty tensions and the frustration these provoked in many citizens. The continued uncertainty over equal opportunities and just salaries proved unfortunate, but he reminded his audience that "even with its limitations, the Treaty offers our country great advantages." Those still worried about commissary restrictions needed to patiently await these advantages. Those still "disgusted and resentful" about the commissary restrictions should remember that the "privileges that they had [in the zone] were paid during fifty years by the remainder of the Panamanian populace. This amounted to a sort of tribute paid by one nation to the wealthiest country in the world."[66] De la Guardia not only asked for a change in attitude from those losing commissary privileges but also rewrote the history of these privileges. According to him, the enemy was not the Canal Zone and Washington but Panamanians who failed to recognize their duties and past debts to a new and ever improving Panama. He was also careful not to criticize the oligarchy, of which he was a member, for benefiting the most from the treaty.

Ser Panameño and Citizenship Rights Come Full Circle?

The negotiation and implementation of the Remón-Eisenhower Treaty marked the supposed emergence of a new Panama that both relied on and decried the recognition of Afro-Caribbean Panamanians as full citizens. As the majority of the non-US workforce in the zone, they formed a strategic labor group to court and a useful collective to exploit against Washington. Their struggles and discrimination under the zone labor regime helped unify the republic's treaty stance. Thinking of these workers as full members of the nation, after generations of prejudice, proved more daunting. Instead, focusing on these particular Panamanians as US loyalists, treacherous toward their own government and incapable of patriotic self-sacrifice, remained politically advantageous. Their allegedly flawed patriotism gave license to the racist and xenophobic attitudes of officials and ordinary citizens. Indeed, it reinforced Minister Arosemena's depiction of zone workers as "jamaicanos" and justified the desire of white and mestizo Panamanians to educate their children alongside white US citizens and not Afro-Caribbean Panamanians. Such racism buttressed the claims of professionals in Colón who worried that zone workers would make their neighborhood "working class," and supported the negotiation mission and the press's questioning of the allegiances of zone labor leaders.

This new Panama chose silence on the subject of racism even as these very factors shaped how large swaths of the population experienced day-to-day life. It called for a collective amnesia and presumed that ser panameño could subsume all past transgressions and all future problems. Even as government officials, including the president of the republic, called on Afro-Caribbean Panamanian zone workers to forget the past and work toward a new Panama, a looming question regarding citizenship rights remained unaddressed. The nationality law discredited the notion that all could "be Panamanian" given that entire groups remained conditional citizens.

Those calling to amend the nationality law resorted to the discourses of raceless patriotism and equality deployed by proponents of the new treaty. Serving as a figurehead for the amendment campaign was onetime Colón City mayor and later assembly deputy for Colón, José Dominador Bazán. Bazán, as noted in chapter 3, had participated in at least one of the labor and treaty reform rallies coordinated by Local 900 in 1953. His bid for the National Assembly in 1956 had the backing of a cadre of Afro-Caribbean Panamanian activists in Colón, some of whom had made unsuccessful candidacy bids for the assembly.

As a representative of Colón, the Panamanian province with the largest population of Afro-Caribbean Panamanians in the nation and in local offices, Bazán strategically participated in the treaty and labor reform efforts and advocated for a change in the nationality law. While this law no longer deprived those with "prohibited immigrant" parents from citizenship, it did require that all those with foreign-born parents petition for their citizenship on their twenty-first birthday and prove their "spiritual and material incorporation" into the nation. This process remained rigorous, with applicants having to provide notarized evidence of their "incorporation" in the form of school records, proof of continuous residency, and witness testimonies. Longtime Colón municipal council representative Hector Connor spoke often of the "whim and caprice" that informed decisions regarding citizenship recognition. In September 1953 he called for the nationality law to be amended or eliminated on the grounds that giving officials the power to mitigate someone's citizenship represented an abuse of power.[67] Activist attorney Pedro N. Rhodes, who had campaigned against the nationality law, also petitioned government officials against the denial of citizenship to Afro-Caribbean Panamanians into the mid-1950s. Rhodes noted that a discriminatory interpretation of the 1946 Constitution had allowed officials to declare that everyone born prior to this constitution still had to petition for citizenship. Even when individuals sought to "follow the law," they had no guarantee that their citizenship rights would be respected. For Connor, Rhodes, and others, amending or eliminating this law would at last address the deep chasm in the body politic that disproportionally affected their community.[68]

Entrenched ideas of what it meant to be Panamanian and wield citizenship dominated depopulation, school conversion, and treaty implementation, posing powerful obstacles to amending the nationality law. Bigoted officials and intellectuals backed these impediments. Former president Ricardo J. Alfaro, who had helped draft the constitutional reform reviewed by the 1945–46 Constituent Assembly, declared that the citizenship petition process was intended as a safeguard against children born in Panama but raised abroad being able to vote in elections or run for the presidency. Alfaro offered no evidence of anyone attempting this either before or after the 1946 Constitution passed. Still, a focus on "false Panamanians" plotting a "West Indian take-over" had informed the national paranoia since the mid-1920s. Former president Harmodio Arias also expressed opposition to amending the nationality law. As noted in chapter 1, during his presidency and in conjunction with the US and British governments, Arias had called for the repatriation of unemployed Afro-Caribbeans for the best interest of the nation. The interests of the longtime residents being asked to repatriate were irrelevant to him. Twenty-five years later, Arias's position remained unchanged.[69]

Curiously, in one of his last acts as president, de la Guardia parted ways with his predecessors and supported amending the nationality law. This move reversed his own earlier position on the topic. While on a campaign visit to Colón, he rebuffed claims made by residents about the discriminatory nature of the law. It would take another Colón resident, José Dominador Bazán, a fellow white man, successful businessman, and member of the National Assembly, to give de la Guardia an opportunity to reassess this claim.[70]

Because the Bazán amendment, as it was called, would amend the constitution, it required approval by two national assemblies. Those still critical of the measure used the second review to express their disagreement. Cesar A. Quintero, a university professor, took on the responsibility of assessing the credibility of Afro-Caribbean Panamanians as citizens, something his colleagues had often done in the past. Quintero returned to arguments of Afro-Caribbean Panamanians as perpetual outsiders. He pointed to the possibility of someone born in Panama but raised elsewhere becoming president. Like Alfaro, he offered no evidence of this hypothesis. Quintero told the committee that West Indians remained loyal to the British government and thus refused to assimilate to the national culture. Like past hypernationalists and bigots, he claimed that Afro-Caribbeans could never truly be Panamanians.[71]

In the end the Bazán Amendment received a second vote of approval by the assembly, and in February 1961, President Roberto Chiari signed it into law.[72] The amendment came twenty years after the 1941 Constitution and thirty-three years after the first inclusion of qualifying criteria for birth-based citizenship. The passage of this law marked a milestone for Afro-Caribbean Panamanians, who employed petitions, newspapers, community meetings, and political office to tackle the discrimination facing their group. A *Tribune* article dubbed the amendment "one of the most significant events in the history of this country," which "paved the way for the complete unification of the Panamanian household ... regardless of parental origin or any other incidental distinction."[73] Given the extent to which "undesirable" heritage factored into the thoughts and initiatives of officials and intellectuals for much of the twentieth century, dubbing this heritage "incidental" proved a misnomer. Still, the end to conditional citizenship signaled a break in the discriminatory status quo.

For some, the amendment's passage came too late. While waiting on this legislative act, thousands, including those who went through the citizenship petition process, left Panama. Unlike Rhodes, Cragwell, Westerman, and Gaskin, who had remained on the isthmus following the passage of the 1941 and 1946 constitutions, those leaving in the 1940s and 1950s saw no room for their unique experiences and gifts within the republic. They remained unimpressed by the nationalist rhetoric that demanded a fixed notion of qualities and obligations for citizenship into the 1960s. Even the *Tribune* article celebrating the end to citizenship discrimination reminded all previously affected that it was now their responsibility to "justify the 'Bazán' Amendment" by "convincing" those who had opposed the measure of their "moral and spiritual read[iness] for full citizenship."[74] In this way, citizenship would still come at a price.

The men and women who left the isthmus before and after the 1961 amendment remained unwilling to pay this ever-shifting price. Many had grown frustrated by generations of discrimination. They embraced instead a diasporic practice of citizenship that formed part of the isthmian histories embraced by Afro-Caribbean Panamanians since the early twentieth century. This proved a viable alternative to restricted understandings of being Panamanian. In returning to this practice, they continued to cement their claims to Panama while seeking citizenship outside the republic to push the boundaries of nation-state-specific understandings of home and belonging.

5

Panama in New York

Las Servidoras and Engendering an Educated Black Diaspora, 1953–1970

On April 20, 1963, Las Servidoras, a Brooklyn-based scholarship-granting organization created by Afro-Caribbean Panamanian women who migrated to New York starting in the late 1940s, celebrated their tenth anniversary. As part of the celebration, the organization invited longtime educational leader and former teacher and principal in the Canal Zone colored schools Leonor Jump Watson as their guest speaker.[1] Jump Watson praised the organization for their "understanding of a noble concept of leadership—that of opportunity for service." She also congratulated the entire membership for using "their resources of intelligence, effort and magnanimity to help young men and women acquire higher education."[2] In addition to inviting Jump Watson as a speaker, the Las Servidoras membership used the occasion of their anniversary to become lifelong members of the NAACP (National Association for the Advancement of Colored People). The event, as a whole, spoke to the Black diasporic networks that throughout the twentieth century connected spaces like New York with the Panamanian isthmus.

Las Servidoras, this chapter highlights, through its organizational and memory-keeping work embarked on a project of defining Panama that countered the nation-state-specific, homogenously linguistic, and supposedly raceless articulations of ser panameño. This chapter, unlike previous parts of the book, makes a full geographic shift from Panama to the United States as a way to assess the potency of diasporic world making by Afro-Caribbean Panamanians outside the isthmus. The women and work of Las Servidoras,

I argue, served as reminders that claiming Panama, especially when under-stood as a diasporic process, was about not just geography but the idea of a continuous becoming and a purposeful claiming. Being outside the isthmus, with both inherited and bourgeoning questions about citizenship and be-longing, fostered a unique opportunity to revisit the idea and practice of defining Panama and creating new vocabularies for the multiple spaces Afro-Caribbean Panamanians had, could, and would call home. New York City offered many parallels to Panama. Both had rich Black migrant populations, an inclusionist discourse alongside entrenched segregation, and unequal educational opportunities that undermined students of color. The two settings provide a unique opportunity to further explore Afro-Caribbean diasporic world making at both a micro- and a hemispheric level.

Afro-Caribbean Panamanians in New York

Sarah Anesta Pond Samuel, better known as Anesta Samuel to her contem-poraries, made her first trip to New York in 1940. She enrolled in the La Robert's Beauty School and resided with relatives in Brooklyn. After her graduation in 1941, she returned to Panama. Samuel was then twenty-three years old, a married woman, and the mother of a three-year old son.[3] These circumstances, and her status as a mother, made Samuel a rather atypical foreign student in New York. Yet, given the social expectations and economic constraints of her time, being married and having a husband with steady employment in the Canal Zone made acquiring a visa and financing her beauty school courses possible.[4] Another factor made Samuel's New York stay significant—she culminated her studies in New York a week following the passage of a new constitution in Panama that denationalized all those with foreign-born parents belonging to "prohibited races."

As I discussed in earlier chapters, the 1941 Constitution made acquiring citizenship nearly impossible for Black people with parents from the non-Spanish-speaking Caribbean. Samuel was born in Panama City, but both her parents had been born in Montserrat. Her husband, also born in Panama City, had parents from Barbados and Antigua. As a result of the 1941 Con-stitution, both Samuel and her husband became ineligible for Panamanian citizenship (and by extension, passports). By 1946, a new constitution had removed explicit racial exclusions to citizenship but still required all indi-viduals with foreign-born parents to petition for their citizenship. Samuel, and those who like her had traveled before 1941, temporarily avoided the brunt of these changes. Those traveling after 1941, including Samuel and the future members of Las Servidoras, did so entangled by the citizenship and exclusion debates of the time. By choosing to travel overseas, Samuel and her peers, especially those with Canal Zone connections, risked being dubbed selfish and unpatriotic.

Afro-Caribbean Panamanian travel to New York and other parts of the United States nevertheless continued into the 1940s and early 1950s. According to US immigration statistics, from mid-1946 to mid-1949, more than ten thousand non-US citizens departed from Panama (including the Canal Zone) for the United States.[5] One such traveler was Ann Rose Mulcare, an eventual Las Servidoras member. In July 1946 Mulcare boarded the SS *Acadia* in Balboa, Canal Zone, with New York City as her destination. In her passenger manifest, Mulcare indicated her place of birth as Gorgona, La Boca City, Panama; her citizenship as Panamanian; and her last place of residence as Panama City. She also listed her race as "Negro," denoted English and Spanish as her spoken languages, and dressmaker as her profession.[6]

At the time of her move to New York, Mulcare was fifty-four years old. Securing employment at that age was likely difficult, though as a seamstress she had more flexible employment options. Mulcare was also the widow of a reverend in La Boca (John Talbert Mulcare) and may have secured financial assistance from US-based members of her church community.[7] Mulcare had her daughters in mind when she chose to migrate. Ann Rose (her namesake) and Louisa made the journey to New York with her and celebrated their twentieth and eighteenth birthdays in 1946. Both had been trained as typists. Finding employment in New York as bilingual typists—both Ann Rose and Louisa also declared English and Spanish as their languages—likely offered more stable options than the seamstress business.[8]

The Mulcares' travel to New York fit a pattern that would become more pronounced among Afro-Caribbean Panamanians by the 1950s. Many chose to make Brooklyn their new residence. Before this, in the immediate post–canal construction period, migration from Panama to Harlem was the norm. In Harlem migrants like Maida Springer, Kenneth B. Clark, and Guyanese-born and Panama-raised Eric Walrond made their international careers in labor organizing, psychology and social service, literature, and civic organizing.[9] By the early 1940s some Panamanians already lived in Brooklyn, among them Anesta Samuel's relatives and successful entrepreneurs such as Ethelbert Anderson, a neighborhood association developer.[10] The bulk of the women who formed and joined Las Servidoras in the 1950s were all Brooklyn residents.

Why then did Brooklyn become a communal space for Las Servidoras and other Afro-Caribbean Panamanians? One answer lay in the growth of Brooklyn as a Black urban center by the 1940s. Black southerners, Black migrants from outside the United States, and Black people born in New York formed part of this urban community. The completion of subway lines connecting central Brooklyn to Manhattan in the late 1930s facilitated this demographic trend. Prior to these subway lines, most people of African descent in New York chose to live in Manhattan, mostly in Harlem. With eased commuter options, Brooklyn became a borough of interest. By 1940 Brooklyn also offered cheaper rents and more home ownership opportunities than Harlem or Manhattan as a whole.[11] For the founders and the future members of Las Servidoras, home ownership was especially important. By law, no one in the Canal Zone could own property since all land came under the purview of the US government. In Panamá and Colón, rampant overcrowding made the possibility of owning a home very difficult. Those seeking home ownership also had to find a way to finance and build their residences.[12]

The presence of other Black migrants from throughout the Caribbean increased the appeal of Brooklyn for Afro-Caribbean Panamanians. Many of these new residents came from the Anglophone Caribbean, especially Barbados and Jamaica, in addition to Puerto Rico and Haiti.[13] Although most Panamanian migrants of the 1940s had never lived in the Anglophone Caribbean, some had attended school there and, even for those who had not, the culture of the region informed their identity. Puerto Ricans, like Afro-Caribbean Panamanians, had familiarity with US imperial governance. Although the majority of Puerto Ricans who moved to New York starting in the early twentieth century settled in Manhattan, a portion, by the 1940s and 1950s, made their way to Brooklyn and joined the US-born and migrant Black populations of the borough.[14]

By the mid-1940s, some Black New Yorkers had secured elected office in Brooklyn, and a plethora of race-specific associations (both local and national) addressed the civic, communal, and legal needs of the borough's residents. Afro-Caribbean migrants also operated their own associations at this time.[15] In terms of leadership potential and entrepreneurship, 1940s Brooklyn held key similarities with Colón. Here too a handful of Black people held municipal offices, and civic associations served Black migrants and their descendants. Rampant racial segregation posed a challenge to Black migrants in Brooklyn. By the 1940s, banks, landlords, and insurance companies had mapped Brooklyn into desirable (South Brooklyn) and undesirable (North Brooklyn) areas. A high number of residents of color effectively sealed a neighborhood's fate with these designations. This racial mapping of Brooklyn coincided with loan practices. As a result, white residents secured home loans in South Brooklyn and surrounding suburbs, whereas African Americans, Puerto Ricans, and Afro-Caribbean migrants were limited to home ownership and rentals in North Brooklyn and parts of Central Brooklyn. Such segregationist practices mirrored those in the Canal Zone, though there, segregation was established by a canal commission and upheld via appointed zone governors from the 1910s into the 1960s. In Brooklyn, de facto segregation existed alongside a political and legislative discourse of liberalism and integration.[16]

Despite labels of "undesirability," people of color made their way to North and Central Brooklyn neighborhoods like Bedford-Stuyvesant and Crown Heights. Others also pushed against these boundaries.[17] Among these people of color were Afro-Caribbean Panamanians. For those who had lived through Canal Zone apartheid, Brooklyn segregation probably came as no surprise. Notably, New York segregation also operated at the corporate and jurisdictional levels. Segregation made profits for some, while it punished others. People of color scrambled for the same homes in older areas. White residents, in turn, like their Canal Zone counterparts, secured access to newer neighborhoods with amply funded schools and other community services.[18] This pattern of racial districting also had strong parallels in Panama, as seen in New Cristóbal and El Chorrillo. Afro-Caribbean Panamanians navigating through Brooklyn were familiar with segregation practices orchestrated by both governmental and private agents.

For Afro-Caribbean Panamanians making homes in areas deemed "undesirable" and "unprofitable" by corporate and municipal authorities, a good neighborhood did not require white residents. Such areas needed only to offer a better quality of life and more abundant opportunities than previous residencies. The Afro-Caribbean Panamanians choosing to reside in Brooklyn in the 1940s and 1950s were especially prepared to take advantage of these opportunities. Like other Afro-Caribbean migrants, many had some level of education, had worked for years in their places of birth, and had some savings. They often sought out a small network of relatives or friends who had migrated before them.[19] Relocation to Brooklyn was not just about the racial politics of the time but also about the ways in which Afro-Caribbean Panamanians could make this space their own. As migrants, they brought histories of previous homes and connected them to the racial and ethnic politics of New York. They were, therefore, familiar with diaspora (as Afro-Caribbeans), migrants who understood national politics (as Panamanians), and self-defined Black women and men ready to engage in hemispheric conversations about race.

The 1952 birthday/welcome home party for an Afro-Caribbean Panamanian couple, featured in the *Amsterdam News*, offered one example of these intertwined histories and identities in Brooklyn. According to the coverage of the party, approximately sixty friends of Mr. and Mrs. George Campbell congregated at the couple's Brooklyn brownstone to "stage a typical Panamanian fiesta" in honor of their joint birthdays and their return from vacation. The fiesta included tamborito dances and the wearing of folkloric costumes like the pollera and the montuno.[20] By the mid-1950s, poets, writers, and scholars of folklore on the isthmus promoted these practices as emblems of an authentic mestizo and raceless Panamanian nation—practices that differentiated true Panamanians from the interior from more questionable elements in Panamá and Colón.[21] At this Brooklyn party, however, rather than emblems of a static Panamanian identity, the dances and customs became the domain of Afro-Caribbean Panamanians. Their bodies, their mobility, and their ability to gather a wide array of other Black men and women challenged the fixity of notions like ser panameño. Afro-Caribbean Panamanians could, as they danced the tamborito, speak in English and Spanish, share stories about their friends and family back on the isthmus, and discuss New York City politics. The party guests, with English, Spanish, and bilingual first names and a plethora of English last names, along with a sprinkling of Spanish and French last names, represented a culturally diverse Black community brought together by Afro-Caribbean Panamanians and the tides of transnational migration.

The party also pointed to the unique position of Afro-Caribbean Panamanians within a culturally diverse Brooklyn. To be Panamanian in Brooklyn blurred the distinctions among Latinx, African American, Latin American, and Caribbean identities. The multidiasporic Blackness that Afro-Caribbean Panamanians encompassed remained outside any defined racial or ethnic category in early 1950s New York. Certainly, some New Yorkers already understood that Caribbean migrants brought with them additional perspectives on Blackness and culture.[22] But fully understanding Afro-Caribbean Panamanians required addressing the layered history they embodied. These layers included hemispheric citizenship debates, multiple migrations, and a direct experience of US neocolonialism.

Creating Las Servidoras

Joyce Daphne Gumbs, a founding member of Las Servidoras (later the second president of the organization), was among the guests at the "Panamanian fiesta" featured in the *Amsterdam News*. Gumbs and her husband had made the move to Brooklyn in the late 1940s.[23] Like Samuel, Gumbs had studied in the United States before 1941. She trained as a seamstress in Roxbury, Massachusetts.[24] Both women used what was available to them in the Panamanian Republic and the Canal Zone and opted to expand their professional development in the United States. In Panama, Samuel also attained success as an entrepreneur. She owned and operated a successful beauty parlor in the Río Abajo neighborhood of Panama City, the very neighborhood that decades later would include Parque Sidney Young.[25] Of the nine women—Anesta Samuel, Nella Gunning, Joyce Gumbs, Catherine Grace, Rosa Binnom, Edith Kirton, Ruby Lindo, Marie Neilson, and Noemi Straker—who founded Las Servidoras, four were self-employed, and three had studied abroad. To an observer, the livelihoods these nine women had created bespoke success, at least for that time. A desire for greater opportunities and more freedom underwrote the motivation of Samuel and her peers.

Migrating and making a home in New York in the late 1940s and early 1950s occurred in the shadow of two important shifts in Panama and the Canal Zone. Arnulfo Arias won the presidency again in late 1949 and sought to reinstate the constitution that denied Afro-Caribbean Panamanians birth-based citizenship. For those concerned about resurgent legalized xenophobia, and with the means and networks to leave Panama, this marked a seminal moment for migration. By 1952 the Canal Zone government had also begun its depopulation policy, which shut down robust Afro-Caribbean towns like La Boca. This policy denied Afro-Caribbeans the cultural centers that had made the zone unmistakably their own, with population numbers and a communal presence that rivaled those of white US citizens. The goal was to chip away at these numbers so that the Afro-Caribbean Panamanians living in the Canal Zone would never again match the numbers of white US citizens. In this environment, Afro-Caribbeans who already had some financial security grappled with how these changes on the isthmus might affect the future they envisioned for themselves and their families.

Samuel was the first in her family to establish a steady economic base, doing so without a high school diploma. Her niece Grace Ingleton remembered that Samuel had foregone this degree not by choice but because of lack of opportunity. Schooling in the zone where she lived had only extended to the eighth grade in the 1930s. Her parents had secured private tutors when possible (usually Afro-Caribbean teachers in Panamá or the Canal Zone), but time and money were constant limiting factors.[26] Samuel likely knew how much more success she could have achieved with more education. With her husband and son, she made her second trip to New York in 1950, the first year of Arias's second presidency. Once settled into Brooklyn, and before starting Las Servidoras, Samuel earned her high school degree with the aim of going to college, all while working in a neighborhood beauty salon.[27]

Rosa Binnom followed a similar path on arriving in New York. Binnom had lived in the Canal Zone and attended school there up to the eighth grade. She initially worked with Samuel at her beauty salon but eventually clerked at a zone commissary. Few women held this position in the zone, something Binnom recognized. Even so, like Samuel, Binnom sought to extend her educational opportunities. After moving to Brooklyn in 1951, she enrolled in high school night classes and later attended the Central School for Practical Nursing. With this training, Binnom started her nursing career once she had settled in New York.[28]

Even among the founding members of Las Servidoras with high school or vocational degrees premigration, New York held the promise of expanded occupational and educational options. Ruby Lindo, born in the Canal Zone and a resident of La Boca for much of her young adult life, sought such an opportunity. As a teenager she attended the Phillips Private School, one of the dozens created by Afro-Caribbean educators in Panama. Lindo went on to the Taller de Modestería in Panama City, where she trained as a seamstress. Her education encapsulated the options embraced by various Afro-Caribbeans who came of age during the 1930s—public primary schooling in the Canal Zone, English-language private schools in Panama City or Colón, and Spanish-language vocational/training schools usually in Panama City. Once in New York, Lindo continued her trade as a seamstress in the garment district.[29]

Marie Neilson, the only founding member to attend high school in the Caribbean (Queens College in Barbados), held degrees in liberal arts and secretarial skills on her arrival in New York. In Panama City, she worked as a secretary for the British Legation and hosted a half-hour radio program called *The Women's Hour*. As a Brooklyn resident in the 1950s, Neilson enrolled in medical secretary classes and continued with this career until her retirement. Through her work with Las Servidoras, both as a founding member and as the group's historian, Neilson nourished her creative and organizational talents.[30]

Piecing together the lives of the four other founding members of Las Servidoras poses a greater challenge, although the organization's records do offer some answers. Three of them—Nella Gunning, Catherine Grace, and Edith Kirton—were married. Gunning, as I note in chapter 2, also had prior experience with civic associations. Back in Panama, she had contributed financially to the Afro-Caribbean Panamanian–led Liga Cívica Nacional and served as a translator to the organization. She and her husband migrated to New York in 1948.[31] In all, seven of the nine founding members were married and had made the journey to New York with their husbands. The founders and most eventual members of the group were in their thirties when they settled in New York. Seven made Brooklyn home, and two lived in Manhattan. Most did not have children and had at least ten years of work experience before migrating.[32] By the mid-1950s, Samuel was also a homeowner of a three-story brownstone in Brooklyn.[33]

The 276 Lafayette Avenue brownstone owned by Anesta and Henry Samuel hosted the first meeting of the group in 1953. Based on the group's records, Samuel proposed this first meeting. The group, as she envisioned it, would offer scholarships to Panamanian students in the United States who required financial assistance to attend or to complete college.[34] During this first meeting, the founding members and invited guests elected a board of officers to a two-year term that included a president, vice president, secretary (recording secretary), assistant secretary (corresponding secretary), and a treasurer. Nella Gunning and Joyce D. Gumbs, the two members of the group with the longest period of residency in New York, were elected president and vice president.[35] Marie Neilson and Anesta Samuel were selected for the posts of assistant secretary and treasurer. Esmé Parchment, the only elected official not part of the founding membership, held the position of secretary.

Parchment, like the groups' founding members, had a career prior to migrating to New York and personally experienced the denationalization attempts that targeted her community. She, as noted in chapter 2, wrote to President Arias to petition for recognition of her birth-based citizenship but had to wait five years until a new constitution secured it. In the interim Parchment worked in the Canal Zone colored schools as a Spanish teacher. In 1948, with her Panamanian passport in hand, she and an older sister left Panama for Los Angeles, California. Parchment eventually settled in New York.[36] Given her long interest in education, as part of Las Servidoras, Parchment took on the role of chairperson of the Scholarship Committee. The committee reviewed and nominated prospective scholarship recipients.

The decisions reached by this committee, in turn, determined the organization's fund-raising goals for any given year.[37]

From its establishment, Las Servidoras made the decision to recruit only women, mostly Afro-Caribbean Panamanians, as members, although the group invited men to participate in the Scholarship Committee.[38] Two spouses—Len Gunning, who was a schoolteacher, and Henry Samuel, another teacher in training—were invited as outside members. So too were former Canal Zone teacher Robert Beecher and James Haughton, an Afro-Caribbean Panamanian physician who had made New York home since the late 1930s.[39] Outside this committee men could participate only as financial contributors and guests.

The idea of a female-led and female-only group was rooted in a history of women's entrepreneurship. Samuel had run a beauty shop in Panama. She interacted with women customers and employees and likely became familiar with major events in their lives, learned of community affairs, and also used the salon to promote events or other businesses. As scholars of beauty culture have argued, beauty salons have served as sites where women candidly brainstorm about present and future possibilities. The beauty business also afforded women the potential for economic independence.[40] While no longer running a beauty shop in New York, Samuel still had the experience of working with and for women. Some of the founding and future members of the group may have been patrons at Samuel's salon or knew of her business.

Gumbs, Lindo, and Straker as seamstresses also understood what it meant to work for a female clientele. Women came to them seeking an important item—clothing for themselves and their families. Each seamstress depended on these women for her livelihood, both in remuneration and word-of-mouth advertising. Neilson, in turn, had experience organizing female-only platforms through her radio program *The Women's Hour*. Transcripts or recordings of Neilson's program are unfortunately not available, but the show's title suggests that it provided a space to articulate women's ideas. This notion of women coordinating and collectively acting on their own ideas also resonated with the group's name choice. Las Servidoras, "those who serve," neatly indexed women who came together in service of a greater good.

The name also spoke to a desire within the membership to recapture part of Panama in New York. In 1953 Club Alpha was the working name of the group, but in 1957, having obtained a New York charter as an educational and civic organization, the group chose the official name: Las Servidoras.[41] While *Club Alpha* denoted leadership and a Christian subtext—most of the women in the group identified as Christian—the name did not reference their unique histories. Within New York, they were likely viewed as a group of Black women with roots in the United States or the Anglophone Caribbean, as many spoke English with a creole or patois accent. As *Las Servidoras*, the founders and members referred to a place, a history, and an experience that had shaped the first decades of their lives. By choosing a Spanish title, while conducting meetings in English, they also laid claim to a bilingual and multidiasporic understanding of Panama and New York.[42] In this way they defied nationalist expectations of the time that focused on a single language, nation, and identity.

Choosing the name Las Servidoras did pose the problem of inadvertently perpetuating the image of women happily serving those around them. Here it becomes important to recognize the religious grounding of the organization. Protestant Christianity informed the day-to-day lives of many of the women who came together as Las Servidoras. All had attended Episcopalian, Anglican, or Baptist churches in Panama, the Canal Zone, and later New York. Serving voluntarily through all-women auxiliary associations and other similar outlets formed the basis of proper Christian womanhood. In Panama City, Samuel had volunteered as a Sunday school teacher and later became the leader of the Girl's Friendly Society. In Brooklyn she volunteered as leader of the Pre-Teen Girls Club at her home church.[43] Dorothy Haywood, who joined Las Servidoras in 1959 and served for many years on the Scholarship Committee, emphasized this idea of Christian selflessness and duty to others: "I'm a Christian. I never expected recognition or a reward for my work.... I guess my mother's church work back in Panama served as my inspiration."[44]

While rooted in a Protestant tradition of service, the membership chose to meet in a private home and not in a church. Women were the leaders of the group, not the auxiliaries to a male-led organization. By proceeding in this manner, Las Servidoras deployed the religious language of service while also guaranteeing the group's autonomy as a private space under the full jurisdiction of women. Because Las Servidoras preceded the creation of any similar organizations by their male counterparts, they set the stage for organizational building among Panamanians in New York that placed women at the center of this project.

To Be Young Black Migrants

During the first years of operation, Las Servidoras raised funds through crochet sales, food sales (including food delivery), cocktail parties, and dances. These activities gained them local coverage, primary from the Black press though not the Spanish-language press. At this time, a preoccupation with "delinquent" African American and Puerto Rican youth dominated the local and national reporting on New York.[45] Samuel had a personal incentive to keep the organization going; she and her husband had teenagers at home. In addition to serving as the headquarters for Las Servidoras, their brownstone was also home to three of the Samuels' teenage relatives: Grace Brown Ingleton, Velma Brown Armstrong, and Ruthwin Samuel, who joined the couple in Brooklyn in 1953, 1955, and 1959, respectively. All three would pursue higher education in New York City (albeit R. Samuel's studies would be interrupted by his conscription into the US Army), making them some of the first young post-1950 Afro-Caribbean Panamanian migrants to study in and make New York their home. The Samuels' two nieces and their nephew, in ways paralleling the growth of the organization and debates that preoccupied their ancestors on the isthmus, juggled questions of self-identity, public versus private education, and the possibilities and future of racial solidarity.

Grace Ingleton, the Samuels' eldest niece, moved to Brooklyn at the age of seventeen. Her parents arranged the move in the hope of furnishing Grace, and later her sister, Velma, with better educational and job opportunities. During our interview, I asked Ingleton about her first impressions of and experiences in 1950s and 1960s Brooklyn. As she recollected: "The neighborhood [surrounding the Lafayette house] was primarily a white community. At my high school there were also very very few Black students." At school, she explained, she was very attracted to other Caribbean students. Most students in the school, including the few African Americans present, she confided, labeled her "not really Black" because she spoke Spanish.[46] Ingleton's gravitation toward other Caribbean students made sense since she had spent her young life in Panama, a quintessential Caribbean diasporic space. Accusations of questionable Blackness because of language usage proved ironic given that in 1950s Panama, critics dubbed Afro-Caribbean people speaking English as questionable citizens. Language, whether in Panama or in the United States, had the potential for categorizing inclusion or exclusion.

Regarding her experiences in high school and beyond, Ingleton recalled trying to make both Caribbean and African American friends and how this effort differentiated her from some of her older relatives in Brooklyn. "One of my aunts, not Aunt Anesta," she recalled, "would see me outside on the stoop at night talking to my African American friends and she would say that I was emulating negative African American behavior. She created such tension."[47] This recollection by Ingleton holds parallels to some of novelist

Paule Marshall's own memories of growing up Bajan in Brooklyn. As she wrote in a 1987 essay, "My mother and her friends perceived themselves as being more ambitious than Black Americans ... 'If only we had had our own language,' my mother used to lament—meaning by that something which would have clearly established that they were different, foreign and, therefore, perhaps more acceptable."[48] Ingleton had a language that set her apart, yet a shared racial heritage offered her a desired sense of communion.

Once she graduated high school, Ingleton attended the Lincoln School of Nursing in the Bronx, an in-residence Black nursing school. She deliberately chose to attend an all-Black institution following a very negative experience at a nursing school in Prospect Heights, one of the whitest areas in central Brooklyn. "I went to take an admissions test and was given a psychological test where I was asked to draw a man. I can't draw two sticks! From this drawing it was concluded that I had difficulties with my father and would probably not be able to interact very well with male residents and patients. This made me decide I would go to Lincoln."[49] Ingleton described her time at Lincoln as one of the most rewarding experiences of her life. Here she joined the Black sorority Links and established friendships that lasted several decades. By graduating with her nursing degree, she also fulfilled the expectations of her Brooklyn and Panama-based families.[50]

For Ingleton's sister, Velma Armstrong, finding a way to honor both her Spanish-speaking heritage and her Afro-Caribbean ancestry became a priority once she moved to Brooklyn. "I never lost my Spanish because I sort of gravitated to folks who spoke Spanish ... two girlfriends [from Panama] who had traveled at the time, we spoke over the phone a lot, and friends at home, in Panama, we would call each other." Armstrong also recalled the growing enrollment of Puerto Ricans and Dominicans at both her high school and neighboring schools. "After school, walking home or to the bus stop, we sort of formed a clique." While happy to congregate with fellow Spanish speakers, Armstrong nonetheless grew unsettled by classmates who refused to recognize her as a Black person. "They always considered you different. We're Black. We are all Black together. We went to an integrated school, a lot of white kids at the time at Prospect Heights, but they did not consider us Black, and I became very offended. They said, 'You are Spanish, you are different.' ... I'm Black.... That got me into a lot of tiffs.... I'm Panamanian but I'm Black.'"[51] Her self-identity as a Black woman encouraged Armstrong to partake in the struggle to create Black studies programs at Hunter and Brooklyn Colleges in the early 1960s. "The movement was especially strong at Brooklyn College because there were so many Black students," she informed me. Many of these students, like her, had migrated from or had ancestry in the Caribbean.[52] The struggle to establish Black studies at Brooklyn College proved challenging because of an administration willing to use police violence and surveillance to intimidate student organizers. Yet they and their Black professors and allies, such as Carlos E. Russell, an Afro-Caribbean Panamanian migrant and Pan-Africanist, prevailed by the early 1970s.[53]

Ruthwin Samuel, like his cousins, fully identified as a Black person, but unlike them, he felt that he had to become an African American. "When I came, I had to assimilate to being a Black American. When people saw me, they saw a Black man. They did not know I was from Panama. So, some of the same issues that Black Americans had to go through, in terms of discrimination, I had to go through."[54] Samuel also recalled navigating Brooklyn's racial lines, especially after he and a group of friends were cornered by a white gang. "We were meeting Velma and her friends at a skating rink and got off the bus early. Some white guys grabbed the three of us, threw us up against a fence, and asked us 'what the hell are you doing in this neighborhood?' That was in 1960."[55] Samuel and his friends emerged from the incident unharmed but never forgot it. Racial segregation was rampant in 1960s New York, but as noted by Brian Purnell, "one of the main challenges activists faced in the Jim Crow North was convincing elected officials, newspaper editorialists, and the masses of citizens that racial discrimination existed."[56] Instead, teenagers like Ruthwin learned firsthand how to handle the dangers of this unspoken but very real segregation while making home and community in neighborhoods that received very little government support.

When not in Brooklyn, Samuel spent his time in Harlem, working several part-time jobs. There, he listened to speeches by Adam Clayton Powell Jr. and Malcolm X, men he grew to admire. Powell, as noted in chapter 3, visited Panama in the late 1940s and, with research provided by George Westerman, advocated before Congress for Panamanian workers in the Canal Zone. Malcom X was not as yet well known in Panama, and much of his advocacy focused on opportunities for African Americans. Some young people on the isthmus were nonetheless drawn to the message of the Black Power movement, and through dress, music, and organizations like the Asociación Afro-Panameña (Afro-Panamanian Association), they called for Black pride and the end to racial discrimination.[57] Malcolm X shared with Samuel, his cousins, and Las Servidoras an ancestry in the Anglophone Caribbean. His mother, Louise Norton Langdon Little, was born in Grenada. She, alongside Malcolm's father, Earl Little, played an active role in UNIA branches in

Nebraska and Michigan during the 1920s.[58] Such branches were also active in Colón and Panamá in this period.

Ruthwin Samuel's first years in New York were interrupted, however, after he was drafted to the US Army to serve in the Vietnam War. At the time he was a student at Brooklyn College.[59] Neither Ingleton nor Armstrong made similar trips to Harlem, but Ingleton recalled the heated debates in the Lafayette brownstone regarding Martin Luther King Jr's nonviolence message and Malcom X's call for a more militant Black liberation. Robert Beecher, she recalled, often interceded as a mediator. Beecher by then was a schoolteacher in Manhattan and was completing his PhD in education psychology at New York University School of Education. For his dissertation project he examined interactions between African American and Puerto Rican students in New York City public schools. Such a study, he believed, could shed light on future relations among communities of color, particularly between Caribbean migrants and African Americans, in the city.[60]

As Ingleton, Armstrong, and Samuel completed their educations and secured jobs in New York, their aunt and uncle made similar advances. Anesta Samuel began training as a nurse but stopped her studies shortly after giving birth to a daughter. Soon afterward she worked as a teacher in a day care center. In the interim, her husband completed his BA and by 1960 was a public school teacher in Crown Heights.[61] In his classroom he witnessed some of the racial shifts and tensions his nieces and nephew experienced. By this time, the couple and their nieces had also become US citizens.[62] Similarly, by the early 1960s, more than half of the initial members of Las Servidoras became US citizens.[63]

Las Servidoras members becoming US citizens directly connected to the citizenship struggles many heard about or were affected by in Panama. As noted in chapter 1, after October 1928, Afro-Caribbeans born on the isthmus had to formally petition for their citizenship. No examinations or reviews formed part of this process, but it created a precedence for questioning birth-based citizenship. For those who came of age between 1941 and 1946, or who had not petitioned for their citizenship prior to this time, birth-based citizenship was not guaranteed. In fact, having an Afro-Caribbean parent automatically foreclosed the possibility of Panamanian citizenship. Compared to this hostile process, becoming a US citizen was rather transparent. Naturalization required a set number of years of residency, paying a fee, and taking an exam. According to the US Constitution and relevant laws passed over time, citizenship could not be retroactively denied on the grounds of parental heritage.[64] Ironically, by the time many of the Las Servidoras members became US citizens, the Panamanian National Assembly had finally eliminated the nationality law. This change came too late, however, for those who had suffered more than thirty years of discrimination based on racism and xenophobia.

While US citizenship offered certain protections and opportunities, especially in a Cold War world obsessed with citizens versus foreigners, being new US citizens of color in the 1960s also meant contending with narratives about growing "urban ghettos" and underperforming students of color. Brooklyn was stigmatized as an area rife with young "Black hoodlums" and crime.[65] Studies proposing to investigate the "Black and Puerto Rican problem" also emerged at this time. What to do about youth of color, the fastest growing population in the city, received particular attention.[66] Few of these studies addressed the educational ambitions of this group and the role of institutionalized discrimination in thwarting their ambitions. None, for example, investigated the preponderance of students of color graduating high school with general or vocational diplomas as opposed to academic ones. Parents of color and African American and Puerto Rican activists were among the loudest voices calling for an end to these practices.[67]

Ingleton recalled how a high school chemistry teacher, commenting on her difficulties in class, suggested that she obtain a general diploma as opposed to an academic one. "My aunt was not having that. 'I did not bring you to this country for you not to be able to get into college,' she told me."[68] Ingleton graduated with an academic diploma, but many in her position, particularly first-generation migrants, did not. Not surprisingly, through their scholarship-granting work, Las Servidoras focused on first-generation college students who, like Samuel's nieces and nephew, faced the challenges of navigating the educational system of a new country while dealing with systemic racism.

Celebrating Success and Hope in 1960s New York

Starting in the early 1960s, Las Servidoras enhanced their fund-raising ventures by coordinating dinner dances and luncheons that paid tribute to prominent members of the Afro-Caribbean Panamanian diaspora in New York. Each guest of honor or honoree, with their presence, showcased a vision of progress by people of color quite contrary to the depictions of poverty, disillusionment, and despair gaining attention in the city. Las Servidoras held one of their first formal dinner dances in April 1963, at the St. George's Hotel in Brooklyn. The event marked the organization's tenth anniversary. In conjunction with a debutante ball coordinated a year later and a luncheon held in 1966, these events gave the group an opportunity to publicly express their stance on civil rights, education, and Black progress. The group's decision to celebrate their anniversary event in Brooklyn also belied critics who continued to view the borough in a racist light.

For their tenth anniversary dinner-dance, Las Servidoras brought together their membership's histories in Panama with the politics of 1960s civil rights New York. They accomplished this goal in two ways. First, the organization invited Leonor Jump Watson, a prominent educator in Panama and New York, to serve as their guest speaker.[69] She had taught in the Canal Zone for several years, including as an instructor and a principal in the Normal School. She migrated from Panama to New York in the late 1940s.[70] Once in New York, she married but maintained her maiden name (Jump), a bold move for the time. She also continued to pursue her passion for bilingual education. By 1963 she was the project assistant for the Higher Horizons Program, an experimental leadership program that focused on students of color on Manhattan's Lower East Side.[71]

In her speech, Jump Watson commented on the vital role played by organizations like Las Servidoras in assisting foreign-born students of color in financing their college education. As she noted, Las Servidoras was the "second largest Latin group" providing scholarships to students in the city. Jump Watson also congratulated Las Servidoras for taking on the responsibility of educating future citizens, "not simply by awarding scholarships, but by helping to create in youth a self-image of capable, responsible citizens who walk in dignity among their fellowmen, regardless of race, color, creed or national origin." In describing citizenship as something not connected to a particular national identity or race, she emphasized the kind of educated global citizen who had informed much of her thinking since the early 1930s. This citizen had the skills to go forth into the world and make a path for the educating of others.[72]

In addition to inviting Jump Watson as their guest speaker, Las Servidoras used the occasion of their anniversary to announce their decision to become lifelong members of the NAACP. Following their honoree's speech, they presented Rev. Henry B. Hucles III, a Brooklyn-based NAACP official and an Episcopalian minister, with a $100 check for that purpose.[73] Around two hundred guests attended the dinner-dance. A picture of three members of Las Servidoras, Lurlene Johnson (scholarship committee chairperson), Anesta Samuel (founder and vice president; figure 5.1), and Mavis Tait (president; figure 5.2), presenting Reverend Hucles with the group's check made

FIGURE 5.1 Anesta Samuel, founder of Las Servidoras. From Las Servidoras, "Tenth Anniversary Scholarship Dinner-Dance of the Club Las Servidoras, Inc.," April 20, 1963. George W. Westerman Papers, 16/30, Schomburg Center for Research in Black Culture, New York Public Library.

FIGURE 5.2 Select Officers of Las Servidoras in 1963. From Las Servidoras, "Tenth Anniversary Scholarship Dinner-Dance of the Club Las Servidoras Inc.," April 20, 1963. George W. Westerman Papers, 16/30, Schomburg Center for Research in Black Culture, New York Public Library.

it into the pages of the *Panama Tribune*. The *Tribune* article also included the text of Jump Watson's speech and noted that Panamanian ambassador to the UN César Quintero had attended the event. Notably no mention was made of Quintero's vocal opposition, only two years earlier, to eliminating the nationality law. This made sense given the nature of the event featured. His presence nevertheless affirmed that Panamanian officials could not ignore Afro-Caribbean Panamanian New York, especially as highlighted by the triumphs of Las Servidoras.[74]

The appearance of this article in the *Tribune* was not coincidental. Earlier in the year, Ann Rose Mulcare, during a visit to Panama, contacted George Westerman regarding the newsweekly's coverage of Las Servidoras. She hoped the newspaper could feature a piece, or a series of articles, on the organization's tenth anniversary celebration.[75] The group also approached newspapers in New York. Of these, the *New York Amsterdam News* offered a brief blurb on the April celebration. Their coverage, a photo of Jump Watson and Mavis Tait and a one-paragraph write-up, focused on Jump Watson's participation as the guest speaker. The paragraph also noted that the proceeds of the event would be "used by this Panama-born women group to continue a scholarship assistance program in the community."[76]

The one-line description offered by the *New York Amsterdam News* roughly summarized the organization's history, at least as it was outlined in Las Servidoras's own journal commemorating the anniversary dinner. Along with celebrating the organization, Las Servidoras used the 1963 dance as an opportunity to promote a self-history and introduce another fund-raising method. In a feature that would become standard for all the subsequent journals published by the group, the 1963 edition offered a one-page history of Las Servidoras. In this first public self-history, the group described its beginnings: "Ten years ago Mrs. Anesta Samuel called together a group of women to meet the challenge of fulfilling one of the many needs of Panamanian youth.... The challenge of maintaining the scholarship fund has not been easy; nevertheless, a growing membership, a commendable public support, and the determination to carry out plans soon brought about the realization of this objective."[77] This statement made clear that Panama and Panamanians formed part of the identity of Las Servidoras. By doing so, it established who could and should support the group. That is, anyone interested in Panamanian youth, back in Panama or in the United States, had an opportunity to contribute to the Las Servidoras cause.

The journal format further facilitated a broad vision of community by allowing those in Panama, New York, and other parts of the United States to contribute messages, ads, and general greetings. Businesses could purchase advertisements in the journal. These messages and ads came at a fee per page, which, combined with the proceeds from the dance, ensured that two students, a young man and woman, received scholarships for the 1963 calendar year.[78] The use of the commemorative journal also showcased Las Servidoras's entrepreneurial spirit. As Jump Watson noted in her speech, the "alertness" of Las Servidoras, came at a time when "education [wa]s becoming a practical necessity for survival."[79] She had made a similar statement in 1930, during her early years as a teacher in the Canal Zone. Thirty years later, she returned to these sentiments and pointed to the centrality of Las Servidoras in procuring this survival. The women of Las Servidoras understood this struggle. A spirit of survival had shaped their lives back in Panama and during their first years in New York. They personified a burning desire to help a generation of dreamers and thinkers not only to survive but to thrive. The recipients of their scholarships represented this diasporically inspired generation.

The introduction of cotillions, or debutante balls, by Las Servidoras also touched on this idea of shaping new generations.[80] Gumbs brought the concept of these balls to the group. Her home church had sponsored a cotillion, and she decided that Las Servidoras could have great success doing the same.[81] Haywood and other active members at the time agreed that the growing body of Panamanian young women and men in Brooklyn and other parts of the city might enjoy such an affair.[82] The first cotillion took place in 1964 at the Savoy Manor in the Bronx. All cotillion participants, but especially debutantes, raised a certain amount of funds that formed part of the general scholarship fund. The debutantes who raised the greatest amount of money received individual prizes. The 1964 cotillion proved so successful that the group held the event for two subsequent years and eventually made the ball a biannual event. Indeed, as evidenced by figures 5.3 and 5.4, the attendance grew exponentially between the first and second ball.[83]

In addition to being popular, the balls suggested that a "respectable success," including propriety and marriage, formed part of the vision Las Servidoras held for Afro-Caribbean Panamanians in New York. The young women who participated in the balls received careful instruction on proper etiquette, makeup application, and attire—all skills meant to make them "proper ladies." Each young woman was also paired with a male escort. Significantly, only students in good academic standing could participate in the cotillions, a requirement that emphasized the group's mantra of placing education first. All debutantes declared their intended career choice

FIGURE 5.3 Debutante ball, Las Servidoras Club, Savoy Manor, September 5, 1964. Private collection, Gift of Marva Christie Kester.

FIGURE 5.4 Club Las Servidoras, second debutante ball, Waldorf Astoria Hotel, September 4, 1965. Private collection, Gift of Marva Christie Kester.

as part of the cotillion process. Las Servidoras then published this information, along with pictures of the debutantes, in the journals commemorating the balls.[84] While the notion of female propriety as a prerequisite for personal and communal advancement informed the cotillion, so too did academic performance and upward mobility. Given the growing talk of broken homes and welfare dependency among communities of color in New York, emphasizing a stylized form of upward mobility formed a strategic goal for these balls. The cotillions showcased young Black women as queens of the ballroom and as aspiring professionals who, together with their gallant male escorts, their parents, and the young children in attendance, projected a future full of possibilities. The emphasis on young women as queens harkened back to the popular carnival queens of Panama, also communal celebrations though more populist and bacchanalian than these respectable cotillions. By centering young Black women in the New York balls, the participants upended the traditional exclusion of Black women as Panamanian carnival queens.[85]

For Bernice Alder, a former Canal Zone teacher who migrated to Brooklyn in 1960, the bourgeois ideals promoted by Las Servidoras hindered their inclusivity. "Not many people," she noted "could afford to attend a cotillion at the Waldorf Astoria."[86] Alder never joined Las Servidoras, though she too shared their ethos of education and progress. Unlike most members, she had made the move to New York on her own and chosen not to marry. Alder was a generation younger than the founders of the group. Contrary to the other former zone teachers in the organization, she eventually returned to teaching once in New York. For her, teaching offered the best mode of service for the growing body of Black migrant youth in the city.[87]

For Haywood, who taught in the Canal Zone for fourteen years, the cotillion was about much more than the debutantes, pomp, and circumstance. Along with raising scholarship funds, the cotillions offered Panamanians an opportunity to connect and socialize: "I was actually president when we had our first cotillion. . . . I have a letter that Leonor Jump Watson wrote to me after the cotillion. This was from a long time ago and I still keep it. At that time we also had a little social entertainment before the cotillion. We had some Panamanians in their native costumes dancing. We also sang our national anthem from Panama at the beginning of the program. She [Jump Watson] mentioned that this was such a thrilling experience for her."[88] Haywood's recollections highlight the cultural and socializing components of the debutante balls. The dance performed at the first and subsequent cotillions was the tamborito, with a professional couple leading the membership. The debutantes, in turn, performed the quadrille (a dance with roots in eighteenth-century France) and, along with the general membership, sang the national anthem of the United States.[89] The singing of one or multiple national anthems and the Black national anthem ("Lift Every Voice and Sing") would typify the Las Servidoras events during this period.[90] The first ball also served as an opportunity to honor a member of the Afro-Caribbean Panamanian community in New York. Albert Robertson, a dentist based in Harlem, received the ball's first tribute, which inspired the group to initiate a series of luncheons to honor outstanding members of the community.[91]

With their first luncheon in 1966, Las Servidoras distributed honors but also explicitly spoke about the contemporary civil rights movement. The invitations for the luncheon displayed the motto "Las Servidoras recognizes Education and Civil Rights as one and the same." In taking this stance the members affirmed that quality education was a right and not a privilege, and in this way, they joined with parents and organizers from across New York City demanding the end to the systematic neglect of students of color in public schools. The invitations also reiterated the Panamanian roots of the organization, noted its lifetime membership to the NAACP, and described their scholarship recipients as "deserving youths." This left open the possibility that future scholarship recipients need not be Panamanian migrants.[92] Starting in 1966, most of the organization's scholarship winners would be young men and women born in the United States.

Still, a shared racial heritage remained central to Las Servidoras membership and scholarship decisions throughout the decade. Self-identity as members of an African diaspora typified the membership and all those invited to speak or be honored at its events. By 1969 all scholarship recipients were Black: Afro-Caribbean descendants (born in Panama or the United States) and African Americans.[93] The 1966 luncheon guest speaker, William Booth, was an African American born in Queens, New York, who headed New York City's Human Rights Commission. Prior to this appointment, Booth had also served as president of the local NAACP and a judge in the New York State Supreme Court.[94] The honoree at the luncheon, Dr. James Haughton, was Afro-Caribbean Panamanian and New York City's first deputy commissioner in the Department of Hospitals. Haughton had long served as an outside member of the group's Scholarship Committee.[95]

Collectively, the anniversary dinner-dance, the luncheons, the cotillions, and the awarded honors and scholarships offered Las Servidoras two unique opportunities—to speak against stereotypes that marginalized communities of color and to place the unique perspectives of Afro-Caribbean Panamanians at the center of ongoing New York civil rights campaigns. These events also highlighted a gendered imbalance in terms of recognition. They mostly focused on men as the source of pride for the expanding Afro-diasporic community promoted by Las Servidoras. This proved ironic given the crucial role played by women in building an organizational structure in New York. Of the eight scholarships awarded by Las Servidoras from 1958 to 1965, five went to young men. This percentage was better than those honored by the organization but suggested room for greater equity from a women-led group to assist women's higher education. Making up for this shortcoming, in 1966 the organization awarded five of its scholarships to women. One of these recipients, Barbara Gardner, a high school student from Brooklyn, received a four-year scholarship, the first of its kind awarded by the group.[96] Following this milestone, Las Servidoras would assess the role of gender and national belonging more carefully in their future events and awards.

Gendering Honors, Activism, and Leadership

The group's third and fourth spring luncheons in 1968 and 1970 addressed unfolding questions of multiple national histories and communal progress. The 1968 luncheon combined three of the major histories that informed the group's trajectory, the Afro-Caribbean experience in Panama, the growing presence of the US-born generation, and the continued search for adequate representation of the goals and achievements of Black women, especially Afro-Caribbean Panamanian women. The 1970 luncheon, by showcasing the achievements of a particular Afro-Caribbean Panamanian woman, explicitly engaged this third history. Las Servidoras, through their choice of honorees and guests, also used these luncheons to depict how the histories of Panama and New York, and of Afro-diasporic political thought, intertwined.

The June 1968 luncheon paid tribute to George W. Westerman and Alvin K. Wilks. Westerman's activism was familiar to New York Afro-Caribbean Panamanians. Principal editor for the *Panama Tribune* since 1959, he had often commented on this community. Between 1956 and 1960 he also spent time in New York as Panama's UN ambassador. The second luncheon honoree, Wilks, a native of Missouri, was the first non-Panamanian to receive an honor from the group. He came to the attention of the organization through his assistance in the choreography and general arrangements for the cotillions. Wilks was also the director of recreation and cultural affairs for the New York City Youth Board.[97]

The two honorees came from different backgrounds. Westerman through the *Tribune* had kept the public in Panama informed about the affairs of the group. In 1963 and 1967, he had purchased full-page ads, on behalf of the *Tribune*, in the group's commemorative journals.[98] Wilks, as the male choreographer for the 1965 and 1967 cotillions, had worked alongside the members of the Las Servidoras cotillion committee.[99] Honoring them highlighted the achievements of two prominent Black men, one with roots in Panama and the other with roots in Missouri and New York. Their presence also gave Las Servidoras an opportunity to acknowledge two public supporters. Given Westerman's international and community fame, Las Servidoras could count on a good turnout from the general Panamanian community in New York. Wilks's presence could also encourage the attendance of other city officials and African Americans interested in organizations working with New York City youth. A big turnout for the event would increase monies for the scholarship fund.

This honoring of a prominent Panamanian and a US citizen came at a time of tense relations between both countries. Four years earlier the Panamanian government had ended diplomatic relations with the United States following the deaths of twenty-two Panamanian protestors, including Afro-Caribbean Panamanian youths, at the hands of the Canal Zone police and US military. Protestors had been demanding that the Panamanian flag be flown in the Canal Zone, alongside the US flag, at fifteen specific sites as agreed to in the 1963 Kennedy-Chiari accord. US students at Balboa High School in the zone, not one of the designated sites, flew their flag without the Panamanian flag beside it, which led to a confrontation between US and Panamanian students, the latter from the nearby Instituto Nacional. This flag conflict between rival groups of students centered on who held sovereignty in the zone and sparked the January 1964 popular uprising as it spread to the neighborhoods of El Chorrillo and Colón. Diplomatic relations resumed between both nations six months later, but they remained strained, and the issue of sovereignty over the Canal Zone would lead to two new sets of canal treaty discussions, one starting in 1964 and the other in 1971.[100] Honoring Westerman, as someone who had worked as a journalist and a diplomat on canal matters since the 1940s, offered hope for a new diplomatic future between the two nations. Wilks in turn represented the kind of solidarity that US citizens could offer their fellow Black allies in the United States and throughout the diaspora. His work with young people highlighted the necessity to think of future generations and the promises of young Black potential.

About five hundred people attended the luncheon; clearly, Las Servidoras had remained "alert" entrepreneurs fifteen years into the group's establishment.[101] The decision to honor two men nonetheless raised the question of the place of women honorees in the organization's events. Both Westerman and Wilks had done great work throughout the years, and honoring them made strategic sense, but where were the women? The first cotillion and luncheon had honored men of the community. The second luncheon now honored two men. Were there no women, in either Panama or the United States, that the group wished to recognize? A review of the commemorative journal created for the 1968 luncheon offers some answers. The journal revealed the tensions between women organizing as leaders and the continued use of race-pride agendas centered on manhood. This focus on men as the vectors of race pride had a long and deep-rooted history, in the context of Afro-Caribbean Panamanian experiences, as far back as the creation of the *Panama Tribune* and its presentation of male editors as the only legitimate representatives of the community.

The luncheon journal, along with providing information on the male honorees, featured a brief presidential address and details on a guest speaker that reflected awareness within the group of the peculiar nature of honoring two men and no women. Lurlene Johnson, the group's president at the time, devoted most of her address to thanking all those involved in making the luncheon and the organization a success. She extended her congratulations to the event's two honorees. Johnson ended her comments, though, by quoting Mary McLeod Bethune's last will and testament. Bethune, prior to her death in 1955, had founded the Bethune-Cookman School in Florida, and by 1935 had created the National Council of Negro Women in New York.[102] A former teacher in Panama, Johnson sought out the words of another Black woman, born in an earlier century and in another part of the Americas, to express her final thoughts on the power of education and enlightened leadership:

> I leave you the thirst for education.
> I leave you a respect for the use of power.
> I leave you faith.
> I leave you racial dignity.
> I leave you desire to live harmoniously with your fellow men.
> I leave you finally, a responsibility to our young people.[103]

These verses coincided with the mission of Las Servidoras. Education, faith, dignity, and serving young people were foremost on the organization's agenda. The organization represented women "living harmoniously with one another," but the presence of foundational "race men" remained unquestioned.[104] Progress remained centered on brotherhood and fraternity, making it difficult to celebrate women without first invoking men.

The presence of Shirley Chisholm as guest speaker at the 1968 luncheon indicated an attempt by Las Servidoras to go beyond a male-centered race-pride agenda. Chisholm, a passionate educator and later New York Assemblywoman, had received the kind of academic training most of the women in the group had been unable to access. She had a BA from Brooklyn College and a MA in early childhood education from Columbia University.[105]

Chisholm was also a generation younger than the leaders of Las Servidoras but, like them, had connections to the Caribbean. Though born in New York, Chisholm received her elementary education in Barbados. Given the number of people in Panama with Bajan ancestors, tapping Chisholm as guest speaker was especially meaningful. Barbados gained its independence as a Black nation in 1966. Its postcolonial future was of great interest to Bajans and other Caribbean descendants throughout the diaspora.[106] Politics also factored into Chisholm's participation. Many attendees lived in the Brooklyn district she represented. Their votes could seal her congressional victory.

By asking Chisholm to speak at the luncheon, Las Servidoras showcased their political acumen. In her speech Chisholm focused on education debates, especially around community control of schools, and invoked the importance of engagement and activism to solve the political problems of the city.[107] With Chisholm's presence, Las Servidoras gestured to the bright futures that awaited scholarship recipients.

Six Black women awardees benefited from the proceeds of the luncheon.[108] Writing to the group in 1970, Barbara Gardner expressed her deep thanks to Las Servidoras. "My four years at American University have meant a great deal to me. I will never forget how instrumental members of Club Las Servidoras have been in making it possible. On behalf of myself and my family, I would again like to express my thanks." Throughout her scholarship, Gardner sent the group updates on her work in the Black Students Union, her volunteer service with children in southeast Washington, DC, her chartering of a women's sorority devoted to international service, and her work in the Decent Housing Federal Community Program. She also made note of plans to enroll in a master's program in international service and continue work with federal agencies on international development.[109] Gardner not only succeeded but thrived as a Las Servidoras scholarship recipient.

Marcia Bayne Smith, a 1967–70 scholarship recipient, credited Las Servidoras for her formation as an activist and a scholar. She was working in Panama City and attending classes in a newly built Canal Zone Junior College constructed in La Boca when she learned of Las Servidoras. La Boca had been converted to a US-rate community, a blow to the once thriving Afro-Caribbean community there, but the college remained open to tuition-paying US and Panamanian citizens. This concession allowed zone officials to comply with school desegregation mandates while generating a profit when the Canal Zone no longer received US federal assistance. On attending the college and connecting with Las Servidoras, Bayne Smith recalls:

I had no money to go to school full time and I was working in the day-time. It [had taken] me two and a half years to accumulate one year of credits.... The [Las Servidoras] founder and her family were all friends of my family [back in Panama] so I knew of their work and applied for a scholarship. I completed my SATs in Panama and once I got into school and got scholarships I then moved to New York. I met regularly with the scholarship committee and they were constantly in touch with the school and paid the school directly. It was not just about money.... They [Las Servidoras] gave me a lot of emotional support and spiritual guidance.[110]

After completing college and graduate school, Bayne Smith worked as a social worker. Many of the adults and families she assisted were migrants of the post-1965 period. As a migrant Black woman and bilingual speaker, she had a particular connection to the people she served. Eventually, her frustration at "implementing policies that were created by people who did not have a clue about the communities they were servicing" pushed Bayne Smith to start her own organization targeted at the needs of Caribbean women in New York (Caribbean Women's Health Association) and begin a doctoral program in social work.[111]

In Las Servidoras's efforts to inspire a new generation of scholarship awardees, they also paid tribute to Leonor Jump Watson and Waldaba Stewart. By offering a two-page biography on Jump Watson, the group gave their honoree the kind of recognition that she had not received in either Panama or the United States.[112] Her life in many ways paralleled the values and aspirations of the women who seventeen years prior had founded Las Servidoras. Like them, she also viewed the start of the 1970s as an opportunity to engage with the next generation of leaders. In her acceptance speech, Jump Watson raised this very issue:

> As a community organization, Las Servidoras has done a remarkable job in stimulating and helping young people attain their goals of higher education by providing substantial scholarships; and it has helped them to improve their personal and social images by sponsoring elegant debutante activities. But a greater challenge, perhaps, imposes itself at this crucial time—HOW TO WORK WITH YOUNG PEOPLE IN IMPROVING THE QUALITY OF LIFE NOT ONLY FOR THEMSELVES, BUT FOR OTHERS LESS FORTUNATE IN THEIR COMMUNITIES?[113]

By also honoring New York state senator Waldaba H. Stewart at the 1970 luncheon, Las Servidoras offered one possible suggestion to this younger generation. Stewart, who was Jump Watson's junior by two decades, also had roots in Panama, the Canal Zone, and New York. Born in Panama City, he received the bulk of his education in the Canal Zone. His father, a reverend, still lived in Panama City. Before becoming a state senator in 1968, Stewart had taught in the New York City public school system and later joined Bedford-Stuyvesant Youth in Action, a federally funded antipoverty program. He served as an associate director for the program between 1966 and 1968.[114] Stewart's presence at the luncheon, with that of two other politicians of color (state assemblyman Thomas Fortune and state senator Basil A. Patterson), was tied to a new political wave sweeping through New York in the late 1960s.[115] All three men had roots in the Caribbean, although Stewart was the only one born outside the United States. Along with women like Chisholm, they represented a civil rights generation of Black migrants (and their descendants) who were reshaping the cultural and political landscape of New York.

The honors bestowed on Jump Watson and Stewart by Las Servidoras pointed to another phase of Afro-Caribbean Panamanian diasporic formation. This phase comprised an engagement with education-centered civil rights struggles and electoral debates in New York, as well as the centrality of women in making the Black diasporic histories of Panama and New York visible to thousands. The existence of Las Servidoras showed how independent cohorts of Afro-Caribbean Panamanians could start other organizations that simultaneously laid claim to Panama, the United States, and wider diasporic possibilities. Already in Jamaica, at least one such organization brought together recent migrants to share in dance, comedy, and politics. Through businesses like the Panama-based Agencias Giscome/Giscome Travel, Afro-Caribbean Panamanians also forged cultural and economic links between Panama, Jamaica, and New York. While not matching the scale and tenure of Las Servidoras, these organizations and businesses successfully tapped into the spirit of innovation and invention that long guided Afro-Caribbean diasporic world making.[116]

Panama in New York, New York in Panama

By 1971 a branch of Las Servidoras began operating in Panama and, along with its parent branch in Brooklyn, adopted a new name—The Dedicators, Inc. The change, as explained by past members of the organization, coincided with seeking a name that would make the group more accessible within the New York City area. Just as this name change went into effect, the group had an opportunity to expands its reach to Panama. A group of women and men there, including former New York residents who were inspired by the work of Las Servidoras/The Dedicators, requested permission to establish a new branch of the organization. Black students would remain the focus, centering on the needs of students in Panama. Unlike the Brooklyn-based group, men would also serve in elected positions. By 1974 the Panama branch counted eleven members and offered two scholarships that year to Panama City–based students, bringing the total distributed by the Dedicators to fourteen.[117]

Las Servidoras/The Dedicators thrived as an organization after its humble Brooklyn beginnings. Its history allows for a richer understanding of diaspora making by Afro-Caribbean Panamanians. A Brooklyn brownstone became the base for Las Servidoras, and the city as a whole became transformed by the luncheons, dinner-dances, cotillions, and scholarship awards coordinated by the organization. Their events brought together a multilingual and multidiasporic Black New York but also revealed generational differences. These differences, like those back on the isthmus, posed questions about self and community, identity, progress, and belonging. The work of Las Servidoras contended with gender inequities as they pertained to recognition, opportunities, and leadership platforms in Panama and the United States. Women were active agents on the isthmus and used venues like newspapers, school rooms, beauty shops, churches, radio stations, and small independent businesses to share their opinions about the present and their visions for the future. This backdrop of action allowed for the emergence of Las Servidoras rooted in the belief that women had the capacity to organize and to serve a wider community. The honoring of mostly men for some time typified the actions of the group, but with each event, a realization that Black women in Panama, New York, and the Caribbean shared points of commonality emerged. That few Afro-Caribbean women had ever been recognized for their work, and that young women continued to seek avenues for educational advancement, also registered into these events and scholarship decisions. Issues of class and propriety never disappeared from the equation, but in highlighting the work and intelligence of women, Las Servidoras/The Dedicators challenged longstanding masculinist frameworks of community activism and diasporic world making.

Conclusion

Afro-Caribbean Panamanians and the Future of Diasporic World Making

I began *Panama in Black* discussing the opening of Parque Sidney Young in 1960s Panama City and how this event offered a glimpse at the long, complex history of diasporic world making among Afro-Caribbean Panamanians. I end by exploring other openings, such as the first major conference of Panamanians in the United States in 1974 and the creation of congresses and cultural and academic centers in Panama that privileged Afro-Caribbean and Afro-diasporic experiences throughout the Americas beginning in the 1980s. This conclusion points to the indelible connections that united various facets of Afro-Caribbean Panamanian diasporic world making, returning to some of the people, places, ideas, and organizations that guided much of this study. It also emphasizes how a diasporic experience invested in educating against anti-Blackness and advocating solidarities among Black people in the Americas formed the crucial core of claiming, remapping, and reinventing the Panamanian isthmus.

The lives and dreams nourished on the isthmus during struggles against exclusions and racism sustained Afro-Caribbean world making into the late twentieth century. As in the early 1900s, Afro-Caribbean community leaders mapped strategies that grappled with entrenched class and gender hierarchies, looked to and beyond the isthmus, and reckoned with imperial and nationalist debates. In all, the work of diasporic world making continued in this post-1960s period. New movements and generations took up the mantra of the *Tribune* to "bring light" in service to a now global community.

They did so on their own terms, with agendas that purposefully connected multiple histories and geographies.

Revisiting Racial Histories and Assessing Nationalist and Diasporic Potentials

On May 17, 1974, more than two hundred Panamanians living in the United States gathered in Poconos, Pennsylvania, as part of the First US Conference of Panamanians. The decision to meet in the Poconos demarcated the class standing of many participants (middle class) and represented a meeting ground for most in the community who called the Northeast home. The three-day conference counted on the sponsorship of fourteen US-based Panamanian organizations, although the Brooklyn-based Panamanian Cultural Action Committee (PCAC), or Comité de Acción Cultural Panameño, led the way in envisioning and planning the program. The PCAC had existed for one year at this time, but it included as core members experienced organizers such as Anesta Samuels of Las Servidoras/The Dedicators; Carlos Russell, a respected scholar activist who also held a deanship at Brooklyn College; as well a handful of other professionals with networks that extended throughout the United States. Eight women and four men in total, most of Afro-Caribbean background, formed the core of the original conference coordinating committee. This breakdown reflected the central role of women in the development of a US-based Afro-Caribbean Panamanian community.

The conference, the product of diaspora, formed in the shadow of a self-proclaimed revolutionary government in Panama that came to power in 1968 through a military coup and in 1971 began agitating for a new canal treaty with the United States.[1] Not surprisingly, governmental agendas and sovereignty claims over the Panama Canal and Canal Zone emerged as topics of discussion at the conference. Organizers placed these concerns second to discussing a wide range of economic, political, cultural, educational, and health challenges affecting Panamanians within and outside the isthmus. In this way the 1974 conference highlighted another phase of Afro-Caribbean diasporic world making, one that connected Panamanians in the United States to one another and included Panamanian officials seeking to court them.

From the planning stages of the conference, the PCAC leadership focused on recruiting well-known figures within Panama and the United States to serve as expert panelists and speakers. These guests would participate in workshops tasked with formulating recommendations for the conference leadership and any relevant government officials. Some of the invitees from Panama included George W. Westerman, teacher and sociologist Armando Fortune, and philosopher and historian Ricaurte Soler. Uniting these men was a shared reputation as public intellectuals and scholars whose writings were familiar to the organizers. Westerman had both a national and an international reputation by the late 1960s. Fortune dedicated his career to writing about African-descendant contributions to colonial and early modern Panama and had the distinction of being the only Afro-Caribbean member of the Academia Panameña de Historia (the Panamanian Historical Academy).[2] Ricaurte Soler, a white Panamanian, through his writings and the creation of the academic journal *Tareas*, had gained a reputation as one of the foremost theorists on Panamanian nationalism. No Black women scholars formed part of this invitee list. Marion Clarke de Martin, a microbiologist, and Melva Lowe Ocran, a literary scholar, were both young professors at the Universidad de Panamá at the time but did not catch the attention of the committee. The focus on established experts left unaddressed the reality that many Black women in Panama had only begun their research trajectories. Las Servidoras/The Dedicators would compensate for this slight later in 1974, by inviting Lowe Ocran to serve as guest speaker during the organization's first ever tribute program held in Panama City.[3]

In addition to inviting scholars from Panama, the PCAC reached out to Panamanian government officials. They invited as guest speakers General Omar Torrijos, leader of the new military-dominated government, and Juan Antonio Tack, minister of foreign affairs. The invitation of these government representatives was not without controversy. Press censorship and police repression dominated the first years of the Torrijos government, leading activists such as Clarence Beecher, Robert Beecher's younger brother, to leave Panama after being jailed by the regime. Westerman and other older-generation Afro-Caribbeans also initially criticized the government. A military coup went against their beliefs in moderation and democracy. Torrijos expanded his base of support by promoting literacy and scholarship campaigns targeting poor and working-class Panamanians, promising agricultural land reforms, and implementing a new labor code backed by unions. He also recruited Black men and women to leadership positions in government and called for sovereignty over the Panama Canal and Canal Zone. The conference coordinators focused on these latter parts of Torrijos's record as they envisioned their own progressive reforms for the isthmus.[4]

Of those invited, Tack attended along with other Panamanian officials: Nicolas González Revilla, ambassador to Washington; Aquilino Boyd, permanent delegate to the United Nations; Nander Pitti, representative of the Organization of American States; Rómulo Escobar Bethancourt, the rector of the Universidad de Panamá, the first Black man to hold this position; and Marcela Hutchinson, legal counsel for the National Guard. The balance of guests from the isthmus privileged government officials over scholars and public intellectuals. Because the conference aimed to workshop ideas from experts in their fields, the imbalance of officials over scholars threatened to overshadow the conference goals. Government authorities, particularly the keynote speakers, focused their speeches on how Panamanians in the United States could promote Panamanian nationalism and the goals of the revolutionary government. As noted by George Priestley, one of the coordinators, such assistance and leadership would be crucial in the upcoming treaty talks. The Poconos Conference marked an early effort to secure Afro-Caribbean Panamanian support for the new canal treaty, one that would finally transfer the canal to the republic.[5]

Even with the overrepresentation of government officials, the conference maintained its workshop structure through an impressive recruitment of US-based Panamanian scholars and activists as panelists. Many had years of experience and advanced degrees in education, community organizing, healthcare, fund-raising, and advocacy ventures. Clarence Beecher, now a resident of Chicago, was among those sharing their knowledge as education experts. His participation indicated that for some, supporting the conference did not equal supporting the military government.[6] Another commonality shared by these panelists and guest speakers was their background as Afro-Caribbean Panamanians. The significant presence of that US-based community at the conference ensured that the thoughts and opinions of this group received attention. Members of this group represented the trailblazers who had made places like New York, New Jersey, Chicago, Philadelphia, Washington, DC, and Los Angeles key sites of activism for Afro-Caribbean Panamanians. Almost all shared the experience of upbringing in Panama at a time when debates about "true Panamanians" prevailed and when being of Afro-Caribbean descent and speaking English were still considered offenses. This practice, of deriding English spoken with a Caribbean intonation, continues to this day. Also bringing these US-based Afro-Caribbean Panamanians together was an understanding that whether in Panama, the United States, or any other part of the world, their identities as Black men and women connected them to a broader African diaspora. Participants like Carlos Russell forged connections with journalists and activists in Central and West Africa, and through the founding of Black Solidarity Day and the organizing of forums like the Black Liberation Rally, they championed antiracist and antiimperialists causes within and outside the United States.[7]

At the conference this awareness of a global Black diaspora was made most evident in the speech delivered by Joel E. Mitchell. He, like many at the conference, had migrated from Panama to the United States in pursuit of higher education and remained there. He earned a BA in social welfare at San Francisco State University and was among those who raised funds for the Angela Davis Defense Committee. By the time of the conference, he worked for the California Youth Authority Board as an advocate for parolees.[8] Mitchell in his speech emphasized the "necessity for the complexity of multiple identification," particularly among Black people.[9] As he stated:

> It is legitimate that we identify with the just causes of Panama at the same time that it is tellingly moral that we understand the plight of Black people throughout the world. None of us will be free until all of us are free! Therefore, at the same time that we diligently call for sovereignty over the Canal Zone, we must agitate for demonstrated equality of treatment in the Republic. We must intimately understand that the problems in Guinea Bissau, Mozambique, and Angola are simply reflections of a basic character configuration in the United States, other parts of the world, and Panama.[10]

Mitchell's message was significant given that most other speakers at the conference focused on the progress of the new Torrijos government. Mitchell sought support for Panamanian sovereignty over the zone but linked this struggle to Black liberation against the Portuguese Empire in Africa. Effective anti-imperialist struggles, he suggested, had to oppose the systematic discrimination of Black people in every corner of the globe.

The guest speakers from the isthmus also discussed discrimination but as a legacy from the past that no longer shaped Panamanian society. All allusions to Black lives and experiences were relegated to the pre-Torrijos era. Minister Tack, in his speech, for example, spoke of sectarianism as something that in previous decades "weakened the human potential of the country" by privileging individual interests over those of the collective.[11] This, he claimed, was no longer the case with the administration he represented. Torrijos, in conjunction with the executive cabinet, ensured that the people, the collective, were at the heart of all policies. This explained the creation of the Constituent National Assembly as well as new programs to eradicate illiteracy and expand health care. Tack, in his rhetoric, mimicked Torrijos's own speeches, which lionized Indigenous military men and runaway slaves who fought against Spanish colonial authorities as the spiritual forefathers of the revolutionary government.[12] The focus on these two groups ran counter to the exaltation of the nation's Iberian and whitened mestizo ancestry during much of the republic's history. Tack moved away from the anti-Black bigotry of the 1941 Constitution and the raceless understanding of ser panameño presented by Ernesto de la Guardia in the 1950s. This stance by Tack and Torrijos, while it denounced decades of prejudice, still relegated Black and Indigenous people to the historical past and ignored the grave economic, educational, and health conditions they suffered in twentieth-century Panama.

Rómulo Escobar Bethancourt vigorously condemned the history of discrimination on the isthmus but pointed to these acts as aberrations embraced by only a select few. He acknowledged that discriminatory policies had disproportionally targeted Afro-Caribbean descendants. He blamed this intolerance on a purposeful alignment between US officials and members of the Panamanian oligarchy who benefited equally by excluding and marginalizing this community.[13] Such an assessment held some validity but failed to address the discrimination in all facets of social and political life for generations that still existed in 1974 Panama. Not every member of the national assemblies who voted to deny citizenship rights to Afro-Caribbeans formed part of the oligarchy. Those who joined the PPP (Panamá Para los Panameños/Panama for the Panamanians), threatened forceful expulsion, and wrote letters denouncing the "cultural incompatibility," "working class status," and "inferior language skills" of this group did not all form part of the oligarchy. What made their protests so effective was the extent to which they represented a cross-class and cross-racial alliance of similarly minded citizens to excoriate the "other" as a pariah. The focus on US officials as the second half of the problem perpetuated the myth that no discrimination existed in Panama prior to the arrival of US North Americans. US officials practiced their own form of discrimination against Afro-Caribbean Panamanians, and the decision to exploit this group united legislators and citizens in both the Canal Zone and the republic. To acknowledge the role of everyday citizens in discrimination, however, contradicted the message of a "people" united against oligarchs and US empire. Most in the republic never acknowledged that the canal had been built almost entirely by Afro-Caribbean workers who suffered high death rates to achieve this monumental task, fundamental to the making of modern Panama. White Zonians also underplayed their role, extoling their own ancestors' work as engineers and foremen. And US officials focused on extracting labor from Afro-Caribbeans while benefiting from an anti-Black xenophobic rhetoric that deflected attention from US occupation. Recognizing these intertwined histories of discrimination and exclusion challenged the simplistic narrative of a heroic small nation versus an imperialist goliath.

A similar focus on differentiating between "the people" on the one side and "the oligarchy" and privileged foreigners on the other shaped Bethancourt's remarks on updates to dual citizenship. According to the republic's laws, foreigners could become Panamanian citizens without losing their previous nationality. This was not the case for Panamanians who left the isthmus and became citizens elsewhere. They lost their citizenship and could only recover it by going before the National Assembly. The new constitution of 1972 specified that Panamanians who became citizens of another country would not lose their citizenship.[14] Speaking before a room of many Panamanians who had become US citizens, this point likely aroused interest and curiosity. The new policy stood in stark contrast to the citizenship mandates that had wounded Afro-Caribbean Panamanians since the late 1920s. Living now hundreds of miles from their original homes, with established lives in the United States, US-citizen Panamanians encountered isthmian officials who reassured them of their birth-based rights. This only confirmed something that several Afro-Caribbean Panamanians had always held true—the idea of Panama as the center of their diasporic world and their ability, whether within or outside the isthmus, to lay claim to this space.

The Role of Citizenship and Place in Diasporic Solidarity Efforts

The findings that emerged in the conference workshops revealed the difficulties in bridging national and diasporic agendas articulated in both Panama and the United States. Those in the culture workshop expressed concern that the continued migration of Panamanians to the United States represented a brain drain for Panama. Conference attendees professed how discrimination and xenophobia thwarted the republic's opportunity to flourish as a modern nation. The workshop participants suggested that the Panamanian government create an agency to publicize job opportunities in the republic for Panamanians living abroad. An interest emerged among Panamanians living in the United States to give back and possibly return to Panama.[15]

Even as the members of the culture workshop emphasized possible contributions by those residing in the United States, they also pointed to job discrimination patterns in Panama that might impede these efforts. One recommendation was that in addition to ending racial discrimination in hiring, the government offer preferential considerations to those of Afro-Caribbean background applying for jobs. Such a policy would mitigate years of discrimination faced by this group and would mirror similar US government efforts for underrepresented groups. Whether additional considerations could also be applied to Afro-Caribbean Panamanians living abroad was not fully explained.[16]

Twenty years after the US Conference of Panamanians, campaigns calling for the end to photo requirements and the criteria of *buena presencia*, or "good appearance," in job applications made progress throughout the isthmus. Among those leading the efforts were Afro-Panamanians of Afro-Caribbean descent.[17] No similar campaigns to offer additional job considerations to this community ever emerged. In advocating for such a practice in the 1970s, the culture workshop participants likely drew from the affirmative action debates in the United States. Three US-based scholars and activists, including Joel Mitchell, served as panelists for the workshop. Marcela Hutchinson, as lawyer for the National Guard, which by the 1960s continued to heavily recruit Black Panamanians, saw the appeal of such proposals. Executing them, though, in a context where governmental agencies did not collect statistics on race posed a problem.

The 1940 census was the last to include such statistics. Thereafter mestizaje and discourses of a raceless Panama permeated in official and bureaucratic spaces. Black organizations of the 1960s and throughout the twentieth century contested these discourses. Communal memories and histories, documented in media like the *Panama Tribune*, also challenged attempts to deracialize Panamanian identity. In 2010, following extensive campaigning among Black and Indigenous groups in Panama, census officials finally included racial and ethnic classifications. The 2010 census results confirmed economic and educational disparities, in addition to high incarceration rates among African descendants and Indigenous populations. As of this writing, no opportunity-based program like those in the United States, Brazil, or Colombia has been proposed in Panama.[18]

Another recommendation made by the culture workshop called for the end to hyphenated identities. Panelists claimed the media needed to reflect the reality that Panama was not a melting pot but a mosaic of cultures and races. Through such an approach, the history of Afro-Caribbean Panamanians could be included in film, literature, history books, and school curriculums. This would replace the need to identify as West Indian, Afro-Caribbean, or Afro-Panamanian given that a multicultural and diverse nation automatically made room for these identities. In contrast to this recommendation, groups that explicitly conveyed a hyphenated or racial identification through names or membership grew in strength throughout the isthmus from the late 1960s into the late 1970s. These groups included the Asociación Afro-Panameña (Afro-Panamanian Association), the Unión de Afro-Panameños (Union of Afro-Panamanians), and Alternativa (Alternative). Young professionals, educators, and community organizers formed the core of these three groups. Two years after the 1974 conference, another organization, Acción Reinvidicadora del Negro Panameño (ARENEP), or Action for the Revindication of the Black Panamanian, enjoyed popular appeal and recognition from the Torrijos regime.[19]

The gap in this focus on ending hyphenated identities while emphasizing multiculturalism and multiracial traditions reflected the lack of participants, especially in this workshop, from the Black activist networks on the isthmus. Had these men and women attended, they could have demanded a recognition of Panama not just as a racial mosaic but as a country where people of African descent should occupy positions of leadership, and where the population as a whole stood to benefit from education against anti-Black racism.

Other workshops in the conference addressed the importance of ongoing communication between Panama and the United States. Participants in the education workshop stressed binational exchanges in education and curriculum building. One recommendation included a summer exchange program where educators from Panama and the United States could trade ideas on pedagogical practices. They called for the creation of a student exchange program whereby students could study and live in the United States and Panama. They also proposed the formation of a committee for recruiting Panamanians in the United States to fill positions in the republic's school system. As a final recommendation, participants called for a task force of "individuals of Panamanian origin" with specialties in history, education, and public relations to develop "a sound fusion of the historical and contemporary contributions of Black Panamanians in all official publications that describe Panama."[20] The wording suggested that those recruited would be US residents, which missed an opportunity to connect Black Panamanians in Panama and the United States, even as it emphasized the unique expertise those living on the isthmus could offer.

This focus on the contributions of Panamanians residing abroad also shaped key proposals by the political workshop. US-based Panamanians who held dual citizenship, they proposed, should participate in the election of candidates in Panama through absentee ballots. This interest in electoral power reflected the participation of two politicians, former New York state senator Waldaba Stewart (chair) and New York Assemblyman Edward Griffith (panelist), in the workshop. Thirty years after the conference and with continued advocacy from New York–based Afro-Caribbean Panamanians, this practice became a reality.[21] The workshop also sought input in the appointment of Panamanian representatives to the United States, although they left unclear the logistics behind this proposal. As part of Afro-Caribbean world making, the group asked that a Panamanian consular office be opened in Kings County, Brooklyn. Most Panamanians living in New York called this area home. The participants also flipped the idea of what they could offer Panama and instead asked for what the Panamanian government could provide its citizens living abroad. They requested a guarantee that "in the event of a United States (peaceful) demonstration by Panamanian citizens supporting a Panamanian issue with the United States, [where] a demonstrator is arrested, and/or persecuted by the United States government, the Panamanian government representative, with the support of the Central government, will come to the total aid of the individual."[22] Given that Foreign Minister Tack called on US Panamanians to take up the fight for a just canal treaty, this made sense.[23] Protesting US policy could involve fines and prosecutions, and Panama's consulates could offer assistance.

The confidence with which conference participants made these recommendations to the Panamanian government reflected their security as members of a stable middle class in the United States. Attending the conference cost one hundred dollars, not including travel expenses to Pennsylvania. Still, more than two hundred people felt secure enough in public speaking and finances to attend. The class imbalance of the conference did pose some challenges, as those with advanced degrees and steady middle-class incomes made up a majority of the participants. Working-class Panamanians were far less represented.[24] While people of all class backgrounds could write to the editor of the *Tribune*, join labor unions, march in rallies, and attend community meetings in the Canal Zone, Colón, and Panamá, only a select few had the means to attend the Poconos Conference. The danger, thus, rested in closing off access to diasporic world making on the basis of class, something critics had earlier cautioned against.

Gendered imbalance regarding leadership positions also threatened inclusivity. Women formed the majority of the original organizing committee but made up a distinct minority of chairs or panelists. Grace Ingleton, who by 1974 was a member of Las Servidoras/the Dedicators and a registered nurse, chaired the health workshop, and Marian Holness-Gault served as one of its panelists. Grace Tait cochaired the economics workshop and in this capacity criticized the lack of a Panama-based economist who could offer an isthmian perspective on what proposals could be beneficial. This ability to be self-critical denoted the transformative potentials of the conference. Because of the presence of established patriarchs at the helm of workshops, the conference missed the opportunity to fully advocate inclusivity along the racial, gender, geographic, and class lines to which it aspired.

Afro-Caribbean Diasporic World Making after 1974

The 1974 US Conference of Panamanians was the first and only one of its kind. The vision of creating a national organization for US Panamanians, a goal promoted in the conference, never became a reality. Individual organizations created by Afro-Caribbean Panamanians in New York and other parts of the United States nonetheless continued. Anesta Samuel would by 1982 also receive the Vasco Núñez de Balboa honor from Panama in recognition for the work of Las Servidoras/The Dedicators.[25] Within Panama, Black professionals, artists, and scholars continued making contact with other people of African descent in the hemisphere, as well as in other parts of the world. One example included the Segundo Congreso de Cultural Negra de las Américas (Second Congress of Black Culture in the Americas) held in Panama in 1980. Universidad de Panamá professors, mostly Black men, who had attended the first congress in Colombia organized this one. Between two hundred and four hundred delegates, including literary scholars, social scientists, researchers, and students mostly from Latin America, but with some participants from Africa and Europe, attended. The congress was also the first to include delegates from the English-, Spanish-, and French-speaking Caribbean. Panama's continued salience as a multilingual Caribbean space, a reality that hypernationalists failed to understand, facilitated this process.[26]

The Segundo Congreso explored four major themes: the position of African descendants in the class structure, the importance of Black culture in formal and informal education, cultural pluralism within national unity, and perspectives on the future of Black people in Panama.[27] As articulated by one its coordinators, this approach could address the factors that led to marginalization while also affirming racial consciousness. This awareness could in turn "deepen [Black] contributions to society and the production of culture."[28] In calling for racial consciousness, the congress harkened back to the messaging in the *Panama Tribune* of the 1920s and 1930s. Those article writers had identified as UNIA members, men and women who embraced race pride, and members of diaspora community uncertain if the Western Hemisphere could ever prove welcoming to Black people. Segundo Congreso participants parted ways in this last regard. They understood Panama and the Americas as their rightful home. Like their ancestors who created civic organizations, language clubs, libraries, and worked as teachers and community organizers, they acknowledged the centrality of staking a claim to the isthmus. Yet, the call to race pride connecting these sixty years of history reaffirmed the continued appeal of this diasporic approach.

The creation of Sociedad de Amigos del Museo Afro-Antillano de Panama (SAMAAP), or Society of Friends of the West Indian Museum of Panama, a year after the Segundo Congreso, provided another example of diasporic world making emanating from the isthmus in the post-1970s period. The group sought economic and social assistance to maintain the Museo Afro-antillano. The activism of groups like ARENEP and university professors such as Reina Torres de Araúz, Aminta Núñez, and Coralia Hassán de Yorente resulted in the creation of the Museo in December 1980.[29] The founding members of SAMAAP, fifteen in total, with Melva Lowe de Goodin (Lowe Ocran) serving as president, feared that national funds alone could not maintain the facility. The museum received partial aid from the government's national institute of culture, INAC. As a result, the founders proposed the creation of a sister affiliate, which would use its membership fees to ensure the museum obtained necessities such as books, computers, and an adequate archival system. Membership to SAMAAP remained open to all, regardless of citizenship, residency, race, or class, since the organization sought as much support as possible to honor men and women who led diasporic lives.[30] Through cultural events and strong local support, SAMAAP and the Museo still operate today. Both institutions celebrate Afro-Caribbean economic and cultural contributions to Panama, from the building of the railroad and the canal to the growth of bilingualism in Panama. The largest of these events includes the Gran Feria Antillana (Grand Antillean Fair) organized every year during carnival weekend. As part of festivities of El Día de la Etnia Negra (the Day of Black Ethnicity), which began May 30, 2001, SAMAAP coordinates month-long educational and cultural events.[31]

Afro-Caribbean diasporic world making also inspired the creation of the Centro George Westerman in Panama City in 2001. The center marked the first research institution named after an Afro-Caribbean Panamanian. Among the organizations at the center included the Centro de Investigación y Desarrollo de la Diáspora del Sur (Center for Investigation and Development of the Global South Diaspora), Instituto Internacional de Intercambio Tecnológico y Capacitación (Institute for the International Exchange of Technology and Training), and Taller de Mujeres de las Américas (Women of the Americas Workshop). The Taller held particular significance, given the work of Afro-Caribbean Panamanian intellectuals like Agatha Williams, who through her work since the 1970s called for a recognition and celebration of the vital role of Black women in Panama's history. It responded to the rise of similar scholarship, generated and promoted by Black women, throughout the Americas.[32] The center housed the Museo Diggers (Diggers Museum), which maintained archives connected to the history of Afro-Caribbean participation in the building of the Panama Canal, as well as Respuesta Afropanameña (Afro-Panamanian Response), a nonprofit committed to sustainable development projects in predominantly Black neighborhoods.[33]

These late twentieth-century and early twenty-first-century organizations pointed to the continued balancing of national and diasporic realities that shaped the evolution of Afro-Caribbean diasporic world making from the start of the twentieth century. Newspapers like the *Tribune* and *Workman* had helped to promote the idea of Panama as a diasporic site by the 1920s. This proved crucial as talk of forced and voluntary returns caused Afro-Caribbean Panamanians to alter, expand, and at times retract their identification as diasporic world makers and citizens of the isthmus. From the 1930s into the 1950s, educators, labor activists, and lawyers advocated for citizenship and worker rights that demanded full participation, equality, and social mobility. Here the work of the Liga Cívica Nacional, the Canal Zone Colored Teacher's Association, and the legal activism of Pedro N. Rhodes was vital.

Canal treaty debates of the 1950s included input from Afro-Caribbean Panamanian labor leaders along nationalist and internationalist lines that shaped their community's diasporic world making. Anticommunist rhetoric, complaints about "privileged workers," and unequal access to citizenship threatened to upend cross-class solidarities. But the coexistence of conflicting ideological and economic views formed the parameters of their larger diasporic visions. For some, this meant challenging the white washing of activist histories, and for others, seeking alternative spaces for Black liberation connected to the isthmus and the Americas. From the mid-1950s through the mid-1970s, organizations like Las Servidoras/The Dedicators highlighted the extent to which migration and community formation remained key components to this process. Through it all, the isthmus, as a geographic space and an idea, continued to nourish diasporic possibilities.

Demands for justice, equity, and citizenship rights connected these eighty years of history spanning from the isthmus to the United States. Seeking to participate while residing abroad and rallying all members of their international community distinguished the latter part of this history. Overall, the work of the Segundo Congreso, combined with that of SAMAAP and the Centro George Westerman, highlighted that looking from Panama to the world constituted a key component of ongoing diasporic formations.

Debates regarding the forging of richer alliances between diasporic communities, and what this means for world making continue to be relevant in the present moment. *Panama in Black* is a product of these debates. While this book emerges from a specific time, place, and history, it poses questions that connect Black people across space and time in numerous ways: What does it mean to be a citizen? What does it mean to create diaspora? What do we do about the ever-present reality of anti-Blackness? For those whose activism formed the core of this book, the answers to these questions were purposefully complex. Citizenship at times meant movement. At others it meant embracing a multitude of identities including West Indian, Panamanian, Jamaican, Bajan, British West Indian, Black, Isthmian, American, Afro-panameño, Afrodescendiente, and Caribbean, while rooted in one space or navigating between spaces. Through this evolution of self and communal identity, resisting anti-Blackness remained a reality. From state-sanctioned discrimination and exclusion to the policing of speech, education, and livelihoods, anti-Blackness at times felt all consuming.

Panama in Black rejects the logic of anti-Blackness and its rendering of Black people as foreign and suspect during periods of hypernationalism. It also offers one additional path for writing about and reflecting on Black life in Panama, the United States, and the wider Americas. Specifically, it questions the veracity of histories of the region that neither engage with questions of Blackness and anti-Blackness nor feature Black people at the center of unpacking these questions. It also challenges discussions of race, nation, and belonging that center around linguistic and cultural commonality. Both Spanish and English are languages of colonization. They are also languages that through formal and vernacular practices have been used to challenge discrimination and exclusion. Speaking one and not the other, speaking both or none at all does not make a person less a member of a nation, a culture, or a diaspora.

Recognizing the kinds of histories that can be written and how the archive remains a powerful tool of censure and possibility is likewise important. Writing this book required reading against sources that trumped nationalism above all else and sitting with the anger and sadness brought forth by terms like *ciudadania no comporada, alien, silver worker, chombo*, and *undesirable*. Government archives can be traumatic, particularly when those being dehumanized resemble your kin and family. Finding life histories that countered this dehumanization was essential. This is where hearing from those who came before me proved vital. Writing about these life stories was an important first step, but equally important was reckoning with the lasting impacts of discrimination, nativism, xenophobia, and bigotry. *Panama in Black* is neither a patriotic history nor an anti-imperialist manifesto. It is a book about Black men and women who practiced local internationalism and nourished diasporic communities. It is about how they laid claim to Panama, within and beyond the isthmus, and the imperative of understanding their diasporic world making. *Panama in Black* affirms Afro-Caribbean history as Panamanian history, Afro-Caribbean Panamanian history as Latin American and US history, and world making as African diaspora history.

Notes

Introduction

1   S. Hall, "Cultural Identity and Diaspora," 225.

2   Some of the scholarship critical of mestizaje narratives that I build on and push further include Euraque, "Threat of Blackness"; Appelbaum, *Race and Nation*; Múnera, *Fronteras imaginadas*; Hooker, "Beloved Enemies"; and Euraque, Gould, and Hale, *Memorias del mestizaje*.

3   S. Hall, "Cultural Identity and Diaspora," 235.

4   Morris, "Becoming Creole, 171.

5   Patterson and Kelley, "Unfinished Migrations," 20.

6   Kelley, *Freedom Dreams*, 2.

7   Putnam, "Citizenship from the Margins." Lok C. D. Siu, in her study of the Chinese diaspora in Panama, and Tao Leigh Goffe, in her examination of Afro-Asian intimacies, both point to similar practices of vernacular citizenship. Siu, *Memories of a Future*; Goffe, "Albums of Inclusion."

8   For more on the denationalization of Haitian descendants in the Dominican Republic and the work of activist communities, see Evangelista, "Reshaping National Imaginations"; Shoaff, "Right to a Haitian Name"; and Estrella, "Muertos Civiles."

9   Stephens, *Black Empire*, 5.

10 By the early nineteenth century, descendants of enslaved Africans, many born in Jamaica and other parts of the eastern Caribbean, alongside Afro-Caribbean migrants from the islands of San Andrés and Providence, had created small fishing and trading communities in Bocas del Toro, Panama. Here they joined Ngäbe and Buglé Indigenous communities that had long called this area home. Westerman, *Los inmigrantes antillanos*, 21; Crawford, "A Transnational World," 31–32; Araúz Monfante, *Bocas del Toro*, chap 5.

11 Senior, "Colon People"; Newton, *Silver Men*, chap. 8. For more on the building of the Panama railroad, including its connections to US expansionism, see García B., *La doctrina Monroe*. On the cross-national and cross-racial interactions that formed part of the railroad construction, see McGuiness, *Path of*

Empire. On the presence of the United Fruit Company in Panama (specifically in Bocas del Toro), see Bourgois, *Ethnicity at Work*. For more on the monopoly held by United Fruit in Central America, see Chomsky, *West Indian Workers*; Harpelle, "Bananas and Business"; and Colby, *Business of Empire*.

12 On the vital role played by Caribbean migrants in the building of the Panama Canal, see Newton, *Silver Men*, chaps. 4, 5, and 9; Conniff, *Black Labor*, chap. 3; Maloney, *El Canal de Panamá*; Greene, *Canal Builders*, chap. 3; and Senior, *Dying to Better Themselves*.

13 Westerman, *Los inmigrantes antillanos*, 109–23; Westerman, "Historical Notes on West Indians," 344; "News of the Churches," *Panama American*, May 26, 1928; "West Indians Originators of Panama's Now Immense Motor-Bus Service," *Panama Tribune*, December 30, 1928; Brown Valdés and Castillero Cortés, "El afroantillano en la sociedad," 97; Salabarría Patiño, *El Colón de ayer*, 178; O'Reggio, *Between Alienation and Citizenship*, 78–79. For a rich examination of the creation of lodges among Afro-Caribbean migrants in Panama, see Zenger, "West Indians in Panama," chap. 2.

14 Albert E. Bell, "Jingles," *Panama American*, May 26, 1928; Burnett, "Are We Slaves or Free Men?," 6, 67–69; Ewing, "Caribbean Labour Politics," 23–45, 33. For more on local branches of the UNIA in other parts of Central America and the Caribbean, see Garvey and Hill, *Marcus Garvey*; Harpelle, "Cross Currents in the Western Caribbean"; MacPherson, "Colonial Matriarchs"; McLeod, "Sin Dejar de Ser Cubanos"; Guridy, *Forging Diaspora*, chap. 2; Leeds, "Toward the 'Higher Type of Womanhood'"; and Sullivan, "'Forging Ahead' in Banes."

15 Labor strikes beginning during the railroad construction period were not uncommon, but none compared in terms of numbers and duration to the 1920 strike. For these earlier strike movements, joined in part by Afro-Caribbeans, see Martinez H., "Luchas populares en Colón," 86–96; and Salabarría Patiño, *La ciudad de Colón*, 139–41.

16 Conniff, *Black Labor*, 53–61; O'Reggio, *Between Alienation and Citizenship*, 56–60; Burnett, "Unity Is Strength," 39–64.

17 For more on the history of African descendants in Panama prior to and during the arrival of Afro-Caribbean migrants, see Fortune, *Obras selectas*; Castillero Calvo, *Los negros y mulatos*; and Lowe de Goodin, *Afrodescendientes en el Istmo*.

18 Navarro, *Dominio y sociedad*, 342–44; Lizcano, "La población negra," 32; Porras, *Papel histórico*, 381; Sanders, *Contentious Republicans*, chaps. 6 and 7; McGraw, *Work of Recognition*, chap. 6.

19 Pizzurno Gelós, *Memorias e imaginarios*, 15. On the fear of "another Haiti" in various parts of the Americas, see Geggus, "Sounds and Echoes of Freedom," 19–36.

20 Quoted terms from Pizzurno Gelós, *Memorias e imaginarios*, 13, 16; de la Rosa Sánchez, "El negro en Panamá," 264; Szok, *La Última Gaviota*, 7–8, 19–20; Lasso, *Erased*, 32, 49–50. Fernando Aparicio notes that for some members of the elite, such as Justo Arosemena, fears of US expansionism, particularly given what occurred with the building of the Panama railroad in the 1850s, tempered

their full support of a canal project. Control of commerce through the canal nonetheless was viewed as an important means of gaining independence from Colombia. Aparicio, *Liberalismo, federalismo y nación*, 20–22.

21 Newton, *Silver Men*, 151–52.

22 For a brief snapshot of some letters sent by Caribbean migrants to British consular officials detailing these abuses, see May McNeil, "Traducción de la correspondencia," 5–61.

23 Araúz Monfante, *El imperialismo y la oligarquía criolla*; McGuiness, *Path of Empire*, 191. In 1920, Tomás Gabriel Duque temporarily held the presidency. Pizzurno Gelós, *Memoria e imaginarios*, 152.

24 Szok, *La Última Gaviota*, 86–104.

25 Szok, *Wolf Tracks*, chap. 2; Maloney, "Los afropanameños y la cultura nacional," 410; Chirú Barrios, "Liturgia al héroe nacional," 71–99. For more on discourses of mestizaje and blanqueamiento in Latin America, particularly in Central America and the circum-Caribbean, see Múnera, *Fronteras imaginadas*; Hooker, "Beloved Enemies"; and Gudmundson and Wolfe, *Blacks and Blackness*.

26 Gudmundson and Wolfe, introduction, 16.

27 For more on the connections between Iberian culture, mestizaje, and the discourse of panameñidad, see Watson, *Politics of Race*, chaps. 1–2; and Sigler, Amen, and Dwyer, "Heterogenous Isthmus," 232–33. On eugenicist practices in Panama, see Pizzurno Gelós, *El discurso eugenésico*, 85–112. For more on the degree to which scientific racism shaped the construction of the Canal Zone, see Lasso, *Erased*. On the idea of "foreign coastal cities," especially in opposition to an idolized interior, see Pizzurno Gelós, *Memorias e imaginaros*, chap. 5.

28 Greene, *Canal Builders*, 22–25. For a rich analysis of how the very term *sovereignty* as it appeared in the 1903 treaty (the English and subsequent Spanish version) was interpreted by US and Panamanian officials, see King, *El problema de la soberanía*, chap. 3; and Zien, *Sovereign Acts*, 6–12. For a detailed examination of how US officials incrementally excluded Panamanian governance and commerce from the zone area between 1903 and 1915, see Lasso, *Erased*, chaps. 3–4.

29 The gold/silver system originated with the Panama railroad construction of the mid-nineteenth century and the actual use of gold and silver coins as wages for US citizens and non-US citizens. The system was also employed during the French canal construction efforts of the late 1890s, but skill not citizenship determined payment. During the start of canal construction by the United States in 1904, US officials kept the system's name (gold/silver) but paid in dollars and soon added citizenship and racial criteria to their wage policies. On the evolution of the gold/silver system and how it operated in the US canal-building efforts, see Westerman, "Gold vs. Silver Workers," 93–94; Donoghue, *Borderland on the Isthmus*, chap. 2; Zien, *Sovereign Acts*, chap. 2.

30 Corinealdi, "Envisioning Multiple Citizenships," 88–89.

31 Both Michael Donoghue and Katherine Zien offer a rich engagement with the Americanization of Zonians in the zone schools and other communal

spaces. Donoghue, *Borderland on the Isthmus*, chap. 2; Zien, *Sovereign Acts*, chap. 2.

32 As US citizens, African American workers would be paid in the "gold scale." For more on African Americans in the Panama Canal Zone, see P. C. Brown, "Panama Canal"; and Greene, *Canal Builders*, 99–107.

33 Donoghue, *Borderland on the Isthmus*, 27.

34 Conte-Porras, *Arnulfo Arias Madrid*, 67–78; Pearcy, "Panama's Generation of '31," 694–96, 699–702; Lasso, "Nationalism and Immigrant Labor," 556–57; García B., "Chiarismo vs. Acción Comunal."

35 "Ley 13 de 1926 (de 23 de Octubre)," *Gaceta Oficial* 4977 (October 28, 1926).

36 Alfaro, *El peligro*. Alfaro had no direct ties to national politics, but as a white Panamanian-Ecuadorian whose father was twice president of Ecuador, he had the opportunity to study, travel, and live around the world. By the mid-1920s he was back in Panama, contributing to national and international newspapers. Pérez Pimentel, "Olmedo Alfaro Paredes," 8–17. For a study exploring how Alfaro's text connected to hemisphere-wide white supremacist debates, see Milazzo, "White Supremacy, White Knowledge."

37 Alfaro, *El peligro*, 3, 7.

38 Alfaro, *El peligro*, 15–16.

39 Conniff, *Black Labor*, 5–6; R. A. Davis, "West Indian Workers," chap. 1.

40 R. A. Davis, "West Indian Workers," 144; Zumoff, "1925 Tenant's Strike," 537.

41 Alfaro, *El peligro*, 7, 16.

42 Prior to 1923, the term *Turks*, or *turcos*, was used to identify anyone migrating from the Ottoman Empire.

43 Durling Arango, *La inmigración prohibida*, 33–44. On the creation of hierarchies of immigrant undesirability in Panama and neighboring Colombia by the first decades of the twentieth century, see Lasso, "Race and Ethnicity in the Formation"; and Rhenals Doria and Flórez Bolívar, "Escogiendo entre los extranjeros 'indeseables.'"

44 I. Reid, *Negro Immigrant*, 63–66; Duncan, "El negro en Panamá," 71; Putnam, "Eventually Alien." For a careful study of the policies implemented against Caribbean migrants in Costa Rica, see Harpelle, *West Indians of Costa Rica*. On anti–West Indian policies in Guatemala, see Opie, *Black Labor Migration*. On the treatment of Caribbean migrants in Honduras, see Chambers, *Race, Nation, and West Indian Immigration*. On anti-Asian policies in the Americas, see E. Lee, "Yellow Peril"; Lee-Loy, "Antiphonal Announcement"; and A. P. Lee, *Mandarin Brazil*.

45 Putnam, "Eventually Alien," 295.

46 Putnam, "Eventually Alien," 291–92; Ngai, *Impossible Subjects*, 9–10, 19, chap. 1.

47 Bourgois, *Ethnicity at Work*. On United Fruit in other parts of Central America and their involvement in national politics, see Purcell, *Banana Fallout*; Chomsky, *West Indian Workers*; and Harpelle, *West Indians of Costa Rica*, chaps. 1–4.

48 Franks, "Property Rights and the Commercialization"; Harpelle, "Bananas and Business"; Casey, *Empire's Guestworkers*.

49 "Ley 15 de 1927 (de 27 de Enero)," *Gaceta Oficial* 5058 (February 28, 1927).

50 "Ley 16 de 1927 (de 31 de Enero)," *Gaceta Oficial* 5058 (February 28, 1927).

51 Ngai, *Impossible Subjects*, 7–8, 25–27, chap. 1.

52 My study joins and expands the work of historians such as Ronald Harpelle, Lara Putnam, Jorge Giovannetti-Torres, and Richard Turits. Harpelle, *West Indians of Costa Rica*; Putnam, *Radical Moves*; Giovannetti-Torres, "Elusive Organization of 'Identity'"; Giovannetti-Torres, *Black British Migrants in Cuba*; Turits, "World Destroyed." The work of historians Aviva Chomsky, Barry Carr, Edward Paulino, Keith Tinker, Andrea Queeley, and Asia Leeds also informs this study. Chomsky, *West Indian Workers*; Chomsky, "Barbados or Canada"; Carr, "Identity, Class, and Nation"; Paulino, "Erasing the Kreyol"; Tinker, *Migration of Peoples*; Queeley, *Rescuing Our Roots*; Leeds, "Toward the 'Higher Type of Womanhood.'"

53 Trouillot, *Silencing the Past*, 29.

54 Vinson, "African (Black) Diaspora History," 13.

55 Hull, Scott, and Smith, *All the Women Are White*; Williams, "La mujer negra"; Gonzalez, "Racismo e seximo na cultura brasileira"; Boyce Davies, *Black Women, Writing, and Identity*; Carby, *Race Men*; Collins, *Black Feminist Thought*; Barriteau, "Relevance of Black Feminist Scholarship"; Ransby, *Eslanda*; Alvarez and Caldwell, "Promoting Feminist Amefricanidade"; K. J. Brown, *Repeating Body*; K. M. Q. Hall, *Naming a Transnational Black Feminist*.

56 S. Hall, "Culture Identity and Diaspora"; Gilroy, *Black Atlantic*; Patterson and Kelley, "Unfinished Migrations"; U. Y. Taylor, *Veiled Garvey*; Edwards, *Practice of Diaspora*; Jason Parker, "Capital of the Caribbean"; Boyce Davies, *Left of Karl Marx*; Guridy, *Forging Diaspora*; Makalani, *In the Cause of Freedom*; Crawford, "Transnational World Fractured"; Nwankwo, "Bilingualism, Blackness, and Belonging"; Blain, Leeds, and Taylor, "Women, Gender Politics, and Pan-Africanism."

57 Bryce-Laporte, "Voluntary Immigration," 28–41; Andrews, *Afro-Latin America*; Nwankwo, *Black Cosmopolitanism*; Marable and Agard-Jones, *Transnational Blackness*; Moreno Vega, Alba, and Modestin, *Women Warriors*; Queeley, "El Puente"; Dixon and Burdick, *Comparative Perspectives*; Alvarez and Caldwell, "Promoting Feminist Amefricanidade"; García-Peña, *Borders of Dominicanidad*; Ariail, "Between the Boundaries"; Corinealdi, "Creating Transformative Education"; Fuente and Andrews, *Afro-Latin American Studies*; K. M. Q. Hall, *Naming a Transnational Black Feminist*.

58 For some seminal examples of this work, see Priestley and Maloney, "El grupo antillano"; Westerman, *Los inmigrantes antillanos*; Maloney, *El Canal de Panamá*; Williams, "La mujer negra"; Priestley, "Etnia, clase y cuestión nacional"; Russell, *Old Woman Remembers*; Lowe de Goodin, *De Barbados a Panamá*; Lowe de Goodin, "La fuerza laboral afroantillana"; Barrow and Priestley, *Piel*

oscura Panamá; Maloney, "Significado de la presencia y contribución"; and Lowe de Goodin, *Afrodescendientes en el Istmo*.

59 Scholars such as Michael Conniff and more recently Julie Greene, Michael Donoghue, Katherine Zien, and Marixa Lasso have offered rich studies on US policies and ideologies surrounding the Panama Canal Zone, with some attention given to the lives of Afro-Caribbean migrants and their descendants in this space. Rather than devote specific chapters or sections to Afro-Caribbean Panamanian experiences, this study affirms that any examinations of Panamanian nationalism or US empire making in Panama must seriously engage with how the lives, ideas, and work of members of this group fundamentally shaped the realities of the isthmus. Conniff, *Black Labor*; Greene, *Canal Builders*; Donoghue, *Borderland on the Isthmus*; Zien, *Sovereign Acts*; Lasso, *Erased*.

60 For more on the activism of Afro-Caribbeans and their descendants in early to mid-twentieth-century New York City, see James, *Holding Aloft the Banner*; Hoffnung-Garskof, "Migrations of Arturo Schomburg"; Hoffnung-Garskof, *Racial Migrations*; Stephens, *Black Empire*; Opie, "Eating, Dancing, and Courting"; Jiménez Román and Flores, *Afro-Latin@ Reader*; and Mirabal, *Suspect Freedoms*.

61 McKittrick, *Demonic Grounds*, xix.

62 Lara Putnam has also examined the work of the *Tribune*, albeit without the level of detail present in this book. See Putnam, *Radical Moves*, chap. 4; and Putnam, "Circum-Atlantic Print Circuits."

Chapter One: Panama as Diaspora

1 Sidney A. Young, "Making Our Bow," *Panama Tribune*, November 11, 1928.

2 S. Young, *Isthmian Echoes*, vii.

3 S. Young, *Isthmian Echoes*, 216.

4 This high literacy trend was initially a legacy of labor recruitment policies in the British Caribbean during the US-financed canal construction project, whereby those seeking to migrate increasingly had to prove financial soundness. Those able to migrate were quite often both financially sound and among the most educated in their places of birth. *Censo Demográfico*, 11, 115; McLean Petras, *Jamaican Labor Migration*, 143–46; Newton, *Silver Men*, 6–66; Frederick, *"Colón Man a Come,"* 29. After the canal construction, the Panamanian government, when not barring Anglophone Afro-Caribbean labor, also followed a finances-based migration requirement, and this too coincided with a growth in migration by the literate and most educated in the British Caribbean. Durling Arango, *La inmigración prohibida*, 44–46.

5 Sidney A. Young, "Panamanian Students in Jamaica," *Panama Tribune*, January 26, 1930.

6 Putnam, "Sidney Young," 3.

7 Sidney A. Young, "Sid Says Adios," *Panama American*, May 28, 1928.

8   "Acto Legislativo de 1928 (de 19 de Octubre)," *Gaceta Oficial* 5388 (October 20, 1928): 18432; *Constitución de la República de Panamá*, 1929, 6–7.

9   S. Young, *Isthmian Echoes*, i.

10 Philip Lewis, "Who Is to Be Blamed," in S. Young, *Isthmian Echoes*, 68–70.

11 Corinealdi, "Being Fully Human."

12 Linda Smart Chubb, "Will Trinidad Spurn the Call?," in S. Young, *Isthmian Echoes*, 137–41.

13 Smart Chubb, "Will Trinidad Spurn the Call?," 139.

14 Cespedes Burke, "'If It Is Worth While, What Does This Mean to You,'" *Panama Tribune*, November 11, 1928.

15 L. C. Williams, "There Is Need for the Panama Tribune," *Panama Tribune*, November 11, 1928.

16 St. Hill, *Panama Tribune*, November 11, 1928, sec. Views. This was likely Louis St. Hill. St. Hill by this time had contributed to the *Workman*, led the Women's Life Problem Association (a Canal Zone–based organization created by Afro-Caribbean women), and was a concert vocalist as well as a beauty shop owner. Jeffrey W. Parker, "Sex at the Crossroads," 210.

17 Corinealdi, "Section for Women."

18 *Censo Demográfico*, 21.

19 Sidney A. Young, "Our Steady Growth," *Panama Tribune*, March 10, 1929. The *Workman*, at its peak in the early 1920s, had a circulation of six thousand copies. Thus a circulation of three thousand after just six months was impressive. Burnett, "Are We Slaves or Free Men?," 53.

20 Karl Schillos, "Greetings to the Tribune from the Land of the Incas," *Panama Tribune*, January 9, 1929.

21 *Panama Canal Zone Population*, 2, 6. The *Workman* provided half a page of news on events in the Canal Zone, mainly in La Boca and Silver City. See "Canal Zone News," *Workman*, 1924–1927.

22 "Happenings in the Canal Zone Towns," *Panama Tribune*, August 25, 1929; November 3, 1929; November 5, 1929; January 26, 1930; February 2, 1930; June 1, 1930; May 7, 1933; November 5, 1933; December 24, 1933. For more on some of the other cultural events that took place in zone segregated communities, and how these compared to events hosted in whites-only/gold towns, see Zien, *Sovereign Acts*, chap. 2.

23 Women's sections began appearing in Panama's Spanish-language press in the early 1910s, first in anarchist magazines and eventually in large dailies like the *Diario de Panamá*. For more on these early sections see, Marco Serra, "Los debates." On women's sections in the international Black press see, Edmondson, *Caribbean Middlebrow*, chap. 2; U. Y. Taylor, *Veiled Garvey*, chap. 4. In this text Taylor also carefully examines how Jacques Garvey sought to push against a similar content limit as the creator and editor of the *Negro World*'s women's section. For more on the *Tribune*'s women's section, see Corinealdi, "Section for Women."

24 "France Succumbs to Color Prejudice," *Panama Tribune*, July 7, 1929; "No Color Bar for New York Teachers," *Panama Tribune*, July 7, 1929; "Thirty London Hotels Refuse Accommodations to Colored Editor," *Panama Tribune*, September 29, 1929; "Ku Klux Klan Organized in Cuba Opens Attack against Colored Natives," *Panama Tribune*, November 5, 1933. For more on Afro-Caribbean migration from Panama to early twentieth-century New York, see Watkins-Owens, *Blood Relations*, chap. 2.

25 Edwards, *Practice of Diaspora*, 9.

26 B. Anderson, *Imagined Communities*, 36.

27 "UNIA Seeks Second Emancipation," *Panama Tribune*, August 11, 1929; "20,000 Garveyites in Procession," *Panama Tribune*, August 4, 1929; Sidney A. Young, "Ajax and the Lightning," *Panama Tribune*, February 23, 1930; Sidney A. Young, "Garvey's Decision," *Panama Tribune*, February 22, 1931; Louise Arthurs, "Lack of Race Unity as Sin against Heaven," *Panama Tribune*, May 14, 1933.

28 Hector Connor, *Panama Tribune*, August 11, 1929; "Garvey Issues Call for Worldwide Conference in Jamaica from August 1–31," *Panama Tribune*, June 3, 1934; "Garvey's Day Today by Div. 187," *Panama Tribune*, May 7, 1933; L. M. Williams, "Colon Div. U.N.I.A. to Teach Racial Uplift," *Panama Tribune*, April 4, 1937.

29 George A. Todd, "Students Graduate with Honors," *Panama Tribune*, February 9, 1936; "Honor Graduates of Silver City School," *Panama Tribune*, June 27, 1937.

30 Sidney A. Young, "Our Contribution," *Panama Tribune*, January 9, 1929.

31 Sidney A. Young, "What of 1930?," *Panama Tribune*, March 1, 1930.

32 A New Providence Reader, "To the Editor," *Panama Tribune*, February 23, 1930.

33 A New Providence Reader, "To the Editor."

34 For more on these educational options with particular focus on the Canal Zone, see Corinealdi, "Envisioning Multiple Citizenships."

35 Engelhardt, *Report of the Survey*, 7.

36 Sidney A. Young, "Commencement," *Panama Tribune*, July 7, 1929.

37 S. A. Young, "Commencement."

38 Las Servidoras, "Third Spring Luncheon Honoring Senator Waldaba Stewart and Mrs. Leonor Jump Watson," June 14, 1970, George Westerman Papers (GWP) 16/30, Schomburg Center for Research in Black Culture (SCRBC), New York Public Library.

39 Leonor Jump, "Higher Education," *Panama Tribune*, April 13, 1930.

40 Jump, "Higher Education."

41 Amy Denniston, "Finding Time," *Panama Tribune*, January 20, 1929.

42 Amy Denniston, "Au Revoir to Our Readers," *Panama Tribune*, March 2, 1930.

43 S. A. Young, "Panamanian Students in Jamaica." Jamaica had the largest number of secondary schools throughout the region. Schooling options for girls and women, however, came much later than those for their male peers and in

some areas remained confined to domestic arts training. Altink, *Destined for a Life of Service*, chap. 3; King, *Education in the British West Indies*, 7–8.

44 Amy Denniston, "Commercial Teaching in Jamaica," *Panama Tribune*, June 1, 1930.

45 "Commission Visited Woman's Industrial School," *Workman*, August 12, 1922; Cantón, *Desenvolvimiento de las ideas*, 150; Marco Serra, "El movimiento sufragista en Panamá," 58–59, 90.

46 "A Survey of Zone Schools," *Panama Tribune*, October 27, 1929.

47 Engelhardt, *Report of the Survey*, 170–71.

48 Amy Denniston, "Quarks in Our Private Schools," *Panama Tribune*, July 13, 1930.

49 Denniston, "Quarks in Our Private Schools."

50 A. S. G., "A Reply on the Question of Private Schools," *Panama Tribune*, July 27, 1930.

51 Amy Denniston, "Comparing Conditions Here and There," *Panama Tribune*, May 18, 1930.

52 "Ley 26 de 1932 (de 1 de Diciembre)," *Gaceta Oficial* 6464 (December 5, 1932); "Drastic Immigration Bill Becomes Law with Signature of Pres.," *Panama Tribune*, December 4, 1932.

53 J. J. Vallarino, "Decreto No. 50 de 1931 (de 23 de Junio)," in *Memoria que el Secretario* (1932), 6; J. D. Arosemena, *Memoria que el Secretario* (1934), v.

54 Between 1929 and 1933, canal officials eliminated 3,400 "silver roll" jobs. Conniff, *Black Labor*, 75.

55 Araúz, *Cien años de colonalismo*, 4.

56 "Hundreds Sign Petition," *Panama Tribune*, July 19, 1931.

57 On hemispheric-wide exclusionist policies, see Putnam, "Eventually Alien"; E. Lee, "Yellow Peril." For more on various anti-Asian immigration acts in the United States from the early to the mid-twentieth century, see Ngai, *Impossible Subjects*.

58 Sidney A. Young, "To Your Tents," *Panama Tribune*, July 19, 1931.

59 Sidney A. Young, "An Intolerable Situation," *Panama Tribune*, June 18, 1933.

60 "'PPP' Society Will Halt Jobless Moving from Zone at Border," *Panama Tribune*, June 18, 1933.

61 "'PPP' Society Will Halt Jobless."

62 For nationalist and fascist-leaning groups in Europe and their connections to the Americas, see Finchelstein, *Transatlantic Fascism*; and Reggiani, "Depopulation, Fascism, and Eugenics." For more on antiforeigner nationalist policies in Cuba and the Dominican Republic that specifically targeted African descendants, see McLeod, "Undesirable Aliens"; Turits, "World Destroyed"; Whitney and Chailloux Laffita, *Subjects or Citizens*, chap. 4; and Giovannetti-Torres, *Black British Migrants*, chaps. 8 and 9. For more on the degree to which Haitians and Dominicans of Haitian descent were victims of the 1937 massacre in the Dominican Republic, see García-Peña, *Borders of Dominicanidad*, chap. 3.

63 "'PPP' Society Will Halt Jobless."

64 "Asks for Protection against Foreigners," *Panama Tribune*, July 16, 1933.

65 "Ultimate Deportation Hinted for Alien Unemployed," *Panama Tribune*, July 30, 1933.

66 "Gov. Schley Advises 'Self Help' for Community," *Panama Tribune*, July 23, 1933.

67 "To West Indian British Subjects," *Panama Tribune*, June 18, 1933.

68 Castillero Pimentel, *Panamá y los Estados Unidos*, 277–94.

69 Conniff, *Black Labor*, 78.

70 E. A. Lewis, "Better Return Home than Swallow Insults," *Panama Tribune*, July 9, 1933.

71 E. A. Lewis, "Better Return Home."

72 William Thompson, "Inquiries about Holdings of Persons Repatriated," *Panama Tribune*, July 1, 1934.

73 Frederick, *"Colón Man a Come"*; Senior, *Dying to Better Themselves*. Beginning in August 1954, the Panama Canal Company provided chartered planes to ship household effects and baggage to Jamaica. The first such set of chartered flights carried a total of 41,405 pounds worth of items. "Charters Plane to Carry 31 Repatriates to Jamaica," *Panama Tribune*, August 8, 1954.

74 C. A. Dixon, "Time to Change Our Way of Thinking," *Panama Tribune*, July 9, 1933.

75 Denniston, "Comparing Conditions Here and There"; E. A. Lewis, "Better Return Home."

76 Hector Connor, Facing Issues column *Panama Tribune*, August 11, 1929.

77 C. Greenidge, "The Delusion that Is Keeping Us Apart," *Panama Tribune*, November 26, 1933.

78 "Repatriation of Jobless Begins," *Panama Tribune*, June 25, 1933; "Pres Arias Insists Unemployed West Indians Must Be Repatriated by Zone," *Panama Tribune*, July 1, 1934; *Annual Report of the Governor* (1934), 84. A small portion of retirees who worked for the railroad company secured some cash relief, starting in 1928. Conniff, *Black Labor*, 79.

79 "P.C.W.I.E.A. Takes Up Alleged Irregularities in Repatriation of W. Indians.," *Panama Tribune*, September 23, 1934.

80 "First Group of Repatriates Reaches Barbados; Tell Sad Tale," *Panama Tribune*, August 26, 1934.

81 *Annual Report of the Governor* (1934), 84; *Annual Report of the Governor* (1936), 86.

82 Arosemena, *Memoria que el Secretario* (1934), 372–74.

83 Narciso Garay, *Memoria que el Secretario* (1936), 300–303.

84 Sidney A. Young, "A Printing Plant of Our Own," *Panama Tribune*, June 21, 1931; Sidney A. Young, "An Exceptional Offer," *Panama Tribune*, January 26, 1936.

85 Sidney A. Young, "Adios to the Benedetti Shop," *Panama Tribune*, July 26, 1936.

86 Jack Jamieson, "Tributes to Tribune," *Panama Tribune*, August 2, 1936.

87 Sidney A. Young, "Battling the Cause of West Indians and Their Offspring," *Panama Tribune*, April 4, 1937.

Chapter Two: Activist Formations

1 Esmé Parchment, "Carta a su Excelencia Señor Presidente de La República," September 9, 1941, Presidencia de Arnulfo Arias Madrid, 1940–1941 (PAAM), box 59/folder 194, Archivo Nacional de Panamá (ANP). All subsequent citations from this archive are cited as PAAM box/folder.

2 Arias, *Discurso del Excelentísimo*, 6, 11–14.

3 Arias, "El mejoramiento de la raza," 3–5; Robinson, "Arias Madrid Brothers," 79; Turits, "World Destroyed"; Paulino, "Erasing the Kreyol"; Hintzen, "Veil of Legality."

4 The reform project included provisions from proposals authored by Galileo Solís and Fabián Velarde at the behest of the Juan Demóstenes Arosemena administration (1936–39). The Solís proposal had called for denationalization. Velarde, who also formed part of the Arias commission, recommended extending the length of time between when the children born in the republic of foreign-born parents could petition for their citizenship from one year to two years after reaching legal age. Those calling for full-scale denationalization on the basis of race won the debate. "Sesión especial de los miembros de la nueva Asamblea Nacional de 1940–1944," August 30, 1940, PAAM 140/211; "Carta de Píndaro Brandao a Arnulfo Arias," September 8, 1940, PAAM 64/211; "Sesión de los miembros de la comisión encargada del estudio de reforma de la constitución," September 9, 1940, PAAM 140/211.

5 "El Pdte. Arias presenta personalmente mañana a la Asamblea Nal. el proyecto de reformas panameñistas a la constitución," *La Tribuna*, October 16, 1940; "Se avecina la discusión de las reformas constitucionales," *El Panamá América*, October 16, 1940, sec. Editorial; "Texto de las reformas constitucionales," *El Panamá América*, November 22, 1940; "La constitución panameñista," *La Tribuna*, October 17, 1940; "Los designados para ejercer el poder ejecutivo del 1940–1942," *La Estrella de Panamá*, October 1, 1940; "Proyecto de reformas a la constitución nacional," October 17, 1940, PAAM 140/211; McLean Araúz, *Xenofobia*, 146–47.

6 Sidney A. Young, "Men without a Country," *Panama Tribune*, October 20, 1940. The *Tribune* also reported on rumors of citizenship changes prior to the official unveiling of the reform project. "Vital Change in Citizenship Rights Planned in New Arias Constitution," *Panama Tribune*, October 13, 1940.

7 S. A. Young, "Men without a Country."

8 Robinson, "Panama for the Panamanians," 189.

9 "Honorables Diputados de la Asamblea Nacional," October 25, 1940, GWP 17/11, SCRBC. *El Panamá América* and the *Panama Tribune* also published a copy of the petition. "Respetuosa solicitud elevan los antillanos a la cámara," *El*

Panamá América, October 26, 1940; "Ask Assembly to Amend Clause in New Constitution Revoking Citizenship," *Panama Tribune*, October 27, 1940.

10 "Honorables Diputados de la Asamblea"; "Respetuosa solicitud"; "Ask Assembly to Amend."

11 "Sugiere modificaciones al proyecto de reformas comisión de la cámara," *El Panamá América*, October 29, 1940. This wording of Articles 12 and 13 remained intact by the final approval of the 1941 constitution. *Constitución de la República de Panamá* (1941), 5.

12 Fabián Velarde abstained from voting on the nationality law. "Assembly Passes Clause in New Constitution Revoking Citizenship," *Panama Tribune*, November 3, 1940. Tam, "Huellas Chinas en Panamá," 31.

13 "Habrá plebiscito," *El Panamá América*, November 20, 1940, sec. Última Hora; "Llamarse al pueblo panameño a plebiscito," *La Tribuna*, November 23, 1940; "Se prepara el decreto ejecutivo convocando al llamado plebiscito," *El Panamá América*, November 25, 1940; "Ley 9 de 1940 (de 26 de Noviembre)," *Gaceta Oficial* 8409 (December 10, 1940); "Sesión especial de los miembros."

14 "Carta de Cristóbal Rodríguez a Ricardo Adolfo de La Guardia," November 29, 1940, PAAM 140/211; "Desinterés notable se advierte con respecto al plebiscito del domingo," *El Panamá América*, December 11, 1940; "Como se esperaba, anúnciase como un gran éxito el plebiscito de ayer," *El Panamá América*, December 16, 1940.

15 J. D. Vásquez G., "Las reformas constitucionales y el problema antillano," *La Tribuna*, November 8, 1940; "Carta de Secretaría General del Partido Nacional Revolucionario a Arnulfo Arias," December 3, 1940, PAAM 64/211; Esteban Huertas Ponce, "Panameño del pueblo asista al mitin del sabado," *La Tribuna*, December 4, 1940; "El Pdte. Dr. Arias quiere con estas reformas hacer de Panamá país verdaderamente libre," December 8, 1940; "El Presidente Dr. Arnulfo Arias lanzó anoche manifiesto al país," *El Panamá América*, December 15, 1940.

16 "Ley 8 de 1941 (de 11 de Febrero)," *Gaceta Oficial* 8453 (November 2, 1941).

17 "All Pending Solicitations for 'Citizenship' to Be Decided in Next 30 Days," *Panama Tribune*, July 16, 1944.

18 Ernesto B. Fábrega, "Memorandum para el Excelentísimo Señor Presidente de La República," August 20, 1941, PAAM 59/194.

19 Osborne, "Biographical Sketches," 12.

20 Parchment, "Carta a su Excelencia."

21 Arnulfo Arias, "Carta a La Señorita Esmé Parchment," September 16, 1941, PAAM 59/194; "Esme Parchment," *Passenger Manifests of Airplanes Arriving in Miami, Florida*, July 7, 1946, Record Group (RG) 85, Records of the Immigration and Naturalization Services, 1787–2004, National Archives and Records Administration (NARA), Washington, DC; "Esme Madelina Parchment," *Index to Naturalization Petitions of the United States District Court of the Eastern*

District of New York, 1865–1957, November 11, 1954, RG 85, NARA Northeast Region; Osborne, "Biographical Sketches," 16.

22 *Censo Demográfico*, 24, 146; Salabarría Patiño, *La ciudad de Colón*, 171; R. Reid, "Don Pedro N. Rhodes."

23 "Demetrio Porras Names Rhodes for 2nd Vice-Pres as Gesture against Color Bar," *Panama Tribune*, December 16, 1934.

24 "Supreme Court Asked to Rule on 'Citizens,'" *Panama Tribune*, March 15, 1942.

25 "Three Professions Discussed Sunday at Symposium," *Panama American*, October 14, 1940; "Sesión de los miembros de la comisión encargada"; "El Pdte. Arias presenta personalmente." Marixa Lasso notes that in the early 1930s, Escobar was among those nationalist writers who promoted the myth of peaceful race relations in Panama prior to the arrival of Americans and West Indians. Curiously, this mentality perhaps informed his decision to fight a legislative act that threatened to further upend race relations in the country. For Afro-Caribbeans who viewed him as an ally, these racial myths alone did not apparently cancel his ability to support their cause. Lasso, "Nationalism and Immigrant Labor," 559–60.

26 "'Nationality Is a Natural Right' Says Escobar in Opinion to Court," *Panama Tribune*, April 5, 1942; "Nationality Is a Natural Right Escobar Tells Supreme Court Upholding Memorial by Rhodes," *Panama Tribune*, April 12, 1942; "Nationality Is a Natural Right Which Cannot Be Taken Away," *Panama Tribune*, April 19, 1942.

27 "Supreme Court Upholds Law on 'Disnationalization,'" *Panama Tribune*, July 5, 1942.

28 *Memoria que el Ministro*, 135–63, 1183–99.

29 "Form Group to Seek Reform in Constitution," *Panama Tribune*, January 23, 1944.

30 Oscar Cragwell, "Week after Week," *Panama Tribune*, January 30, 1944.

31 Del Vasto Rodríguez, *Historia del Partido del Pueblo*, 24–27. For more on the Popular Front movement in other parts of Latin America, see K. A. Young, *Making the Revolution*, particularly the essays by Barry Carr, Marc Becker, Margaret Power, and Kevin A. Young.

32 Britton, *Legado patriótico*.

33 "Assembly Passes Clause"; "New Gov't of Panamá to Maintain Democracy," *Panama Tribune*, October 12, 1941; LaFeber, *Panama Canal*, 76–77; Conte-Porras, *Arnulfo Arias Madrid*, 99–110. Arias's supposed lukewarm relationship with the United States has also been cited by historians as another reason for his successful deposal. De la Guardia would go on to sign the Fábrega-Wilson Treaty, which granted the United States 135 additional military bases in Panamanian territory. Araúz Monfante and Pizzurno, "Panamá bajo el imperio," 14.

34 "Constitutional Reform to Restore 'Nationality' Proposed by Committee," *Panama Tribune*, June 11, 1944; Turner Yau, *La constitución de 1946*, 38.

35 Sidney A. Young, "Removing the Restrictions," *Panama Tribune*, June 18, 1944.

36 "Estatutos de la Liga Cívica Nacional," 1944, 1, 5, GWP 17/11, SCRBC; Nella Gunning, "Recibo de pago," July 18, 1944, GWP 17/11, SCRBC; "Untitled List of Donations Received," August 24, 1944, GWP 17/11, SCRBC.

37 "Estatutos de la Liga," 1.

38 George Westerman, "Reporte del Presidente del Comité Memorialista," July 20, 1944, GWP 17/11, SCRBC.

39 "Why the Liga Cívica Nacional Honors George Washington Westerman," 1948, GWP 1/2, SCRBC; Murphy, "Antillean Pioneers," 12–13.

40 "1,000 Signatures to Petition to Lift 'Citizenship' Ban," *Panama Tribune*, July 23, 1944.

41 "1,000 Signatures."

42 "Panama Suspends 1941 Laws," *Panama Tribune*, December 31, 1944; Turner Yau, *La constitución de 1946*, 38, 53.

43 "Renovador Party Names Candidates for Assembly," *Panama Tribune*, April 8, 1945.

44 Turner Yau, *La constitución de 1946*, 40; Oscar Cragwell, "We Can Do No Less," *Panama Tribune*, March 18, 1945.

45 Oscar Cragwell, "The Challenge to Our Women," *Panama Tribune*, February 4, 1945. The 1941 Constitution had the curious effect of restricting citizenship to men aged twenty-one and older, while also suggesting that elected officials could allow women to vote. Prior to 1941, citizenship had not been gendered, and female exclusion from voting, while accepted, had not been codified. With the 1941 Constitution, women's ability to vote was connected to a distinctly male right that only men could diffuse to the remainder of the population. Law 98 of 1941, promulgated after the constitution, allowed women with a secondary or university education to vote in provincial-level elections. Women could not run for any political offices. Marco Serra, "El movimiento sufragista," 120–21; Turner Yau, *La constitución de 1946*, 30.

46 "Assimilation of 'Criollos' Urged as a Solution to Problem by Local Paper," *Panama Tribune*, February 6, 1944.

47 "New Constitution Promulgated: Affords Nationality Status for All Persons Born in R.P.," *Panama Tribune*, March 3, 1946; *Constitución de la República* de Panamá (1946), 4; Turner Yau, *La constitución de 1946*, 93–97.

48 Corinealdi, "Envisioning Multiple Citizenships," 89.

49 In contrast to the Canal Zone, by 1930 two out of every three teachers in the republic were women. *Censo Demográfico*, 26.

50 "Governor Schley Approves Normal School to Train Young Teachers on Zone," *Panama Tribune*, December 30, 1934; Corinealdi, "Redefining Home," 199; La Boca Normal Training School, *Thinker*, 8, 22.

51 La Boca Normal Training School, *Thinker*, 8, 44.

52 La Boca Normal Training School, *Thinker*, 31; Westerman, *Pioneers in Canal Zone Education*, 8.

53 "Teacher's Assn. to Hold Presentation Program Today," *Panama Tribune*, December 14, 1941.

54 R. A. Davis, "West Indian Workers," 209–11; Westerman, *Los inmigrantes antillanos*, 80, 153; O'Reggio, *Between Alienation and Citizenship*, 109–15.

55 Gaskin, *Blacks Played Significant Role*, 23; Harper, *Tracing the Course*, 165–66; Club El Pacífico, "The Roasting of Ed Gaskin," October 12, 1975, 3, GWP 47/19, SCRBC.

56 "Teacher's Assn. to Hold Presentation"; "Petition for a High School," *Panama Tribune*, August 1, 1943; Westerman, *Plea for Higher Education*; Westerman, *Pioneers in Canal Zone Education*, 16.

57 Canal Zone Colored Teacher's Association, GWP 28/6, SCRBC.

58 "La Boca Athenaeum to Hold Quarterly Debate," *Workman*, April 7, 1923; William Jump, "To Our Literary Societies," *Panama Tribune*, January 5, 1936; William Jump, "The Political Conduct of the Partido Liberal Renovador," *Panama Tribune*, February 4, 1945; Osborne, "Biographical Sketches," 16–17; Club El Pacífico, "Roasting of Ed Gaskin"; Conniff, *Black Labor*, 92–95.

59 Westerman, *Plea for Higher Education*, 5–6; Aston M. Parchment et al., "Memorandum for Executive Secretary, Balboa Heights," October 3, 1942, GWP 28/6, SCRBC.

60 Edward A. Gaskin, Aston M. Parchment, Leonor Jump, and Robert Beecher to the Honorable John W. Studebaker, Commissioner of Education, Washington D.C., October 1, 1943, GWP 28/6, SCRBC.

61 "C.Z. Joins in Disfranchising 5000 Persons Born on Isthmus," *Panama Tribune*, February 8, 1942.

62 Gaskin et al. to Studebaker.

63 Gaskin et al. to Studebaker.

64 Gaskin et al. to Studebaker.

65 Gaskin et al. to Studebaker.

66 Gaskin et al. to Studebaker.

67 In February 1945, the Isthmian Negro Youth League (an organization spearheaded by Aston Parchment, George Westerman, Sidney Young, and Alfred Osborne, comprising young people in the Canal Zone town of La Boca in 1942) launched the first ever Negro Week program. The program included art, music, essay contests, and readings. The success of this program partly inspired an adaptation of a similar model in the CZCS, albeit without addressing the issue of a full curricular integration of Black history. Starting in 1945, George Westerman would also edit A Negro in History section in the *Panama Tribune*. Gaskin, *Blacks Played Significant Role*, 16; George W. Westerman, "The Passing Review," *Panama Tribune*, February 18, 1945, sec. The Negro in History; "Schools to Observe Negro History Week," *Panama Tribune*, February 10, 1946; "The Panama Canal, Canal Zone Division of Schools, School Bulletin," March 1946, 1, GWP 28/9, SCRBC. On some of the cultural events, particularly concerts, organized by the Youth League, see Zien, *Sovereign Acts*, 95–100.

68 "School Bulletin," March 1946, 1.

69 George W. Westerman, "Stresses Need for Teaching Spanish in Canal Zone Schools," *Panama Tribune*, May 19, 1946.

70 Panama Canal Zone, Division of Schools, "Circular of Information for Applicants," February 15, 1946, GWP 28/9, SCRBC.

71 T. M. Nolan, "Matters Relating to the P.C.W.I.A.E.A.," *Panama Tribune*, January 27, 1946; Conniff, *Black Labor*, 50, 77.

72 A Young Blood, "Will Get Support of 20,000 Members," *Panama Tribune*, January 20, 1946; Nolan, "Matters Relating"; Conniff, *Black Labor*, 112. The CIO had briefly operated in the zone in 1939, after a white US zone worker secured a charter that created a union local open to all zone employees. The local was promptly disbanded, however (and the ban on "silver" unionizing reinforced), on the grounds that such a grouping could adversely affect the US war effort. R. A. Davis, "West Indian Workers," 160–61.

73 "Enroll Over 500,000 Negroes in C.I.O.," *Panama Tribune*, November 21, 1943; George F. McCray, "C.I.O. Names 2nd Negro on Board," *Panama Tribune*, December 5, 1943.

74 R. A. Davis, "West Indian Workers," 165; Biondi, *To Stand and Fight*, 149; C. Gerald Fraser, "Ewart Guinier, 79, Who Headed Afro-American Studies at Harvard," *New York Times*, February 7, 1990.

75 George W. Westerman, "Working Conditions on the Panama Canal Zone as of August 1949," 1949, 29, GWP 45/4, SCRBC; Conniff, *Black Labor*, 112.

76 "Native Canal Workers Protest: Say Merchants Seek Oppressive Measures," *Panama Tribune*, February 24, 1929; R. A. Davis, "West Indian Workers," 144–45.

77 Gaskin, *Blacks Played Significant Role*, 17, 20.

78 Robeson, *Undiscovered Paul Robeson*, 125–26; Zien, "Race and Politics in Concert," 111–19; Donoghue, "Race, Labor, and Security," 72.

79 Abram Flaxer, "Officer's Report [on Behalf of the International Officers] to the 2nd Biennial Convention, United Public Workers of America—CIO" (Atlantic City, NJ, May 17, 1948), 41, 43, Abram Flaxer Papers (AFP) 2/15, Tamiment Library and Robert F. Wagner Labor Archives (TLRWLA), New York University; Zien, "Race and Politics in Concert," 113–19.

80 Donoghue, "Race, Labor and Security," 72; Zien, "Race and Politics in Concert," 113.

81 United Public Workers of America, *Jim Crow Discrimination against U.S. Employees in the Canal Zone*, 1948, Ewart Guinier Papers, 9/9, SCRBC.

82 Joseph A. Loftus, "CIO Committee to Attempt Purge of Communist Ties," *New York Times*, December 16, 1946; Conniff, *Black Labor*, 113–14. This charge of communist affiliation was not the first made regarding UPWA representatives in the Canal Zone. In September 1946 Len Goldsmith (the first US organizer sent to the zone after the union's official charting) was accused by former associates and by members of Congress of supporting communist groups in the United States. Goldsmith left the zone shortly thereafter. Brodsky and Sachs

were then recruited to work in the zone in late 1946. American Business Consultants, Counterattack: Research, "Report on Leonard Goldsmith," June 10, 1948, 2, TAM 148, 27/14–113, TLRWLA.

83 "Local 713 Refuses to Take Stand against Communism," *Panama Tribune*, March 28, 1948.

84 Westerman, *Blocking Them*, vii–viii; "Zero Hour has Struck to Rid Local 713-CIO of Pro-Red Leaders," *Panama Tribune*, February 22, 1948. George Priestley also documents some of the feud between Westerman and Sachs. Priestley, "Raza y nacionalismo," 109–12. On the details of what unfolded between Sachs and the Canal Zone district attorney, from the former's point of view, see Joseph Sachs, "History of the First Three Years of Local 713," n.d., AFP 2/9, 19–21.

85 Westerman, *Blocking Them*, vii–viii, 13–4; Sachs, "History of the First Three Years," 7, 13, 21; Priestley, "Raza y nacionalismo," 109–12; Du Bois, *Correspondence*, 212–13.

86 For more on the uses of anticommunism by US white southerner segregationists starting in the early Cold War period, see Noer, "Segregationists and the World," 141–62; Katagiri, *Black Freedom*.

87 George W. Westerman, "Sachs Case Must Be Lesson for Community Now Besieged by 'Character Assailants,'" *Panama Tribune*, August 1, 1948. Sachs would eventually serve jail time (nine months of hard labor at the Gamboa penitentiary in the Canal Zone) for charges of criminal libel. Flaxer, "Officer's Report," 66.

88 George W. Westerman, "UPWA Leadership Proving Itself Willful, Malicious and of Questionable Motives," *Panama Tribune*, September 5, 1948.

89 George W. Westerman, "Honest Program of Trade Unionism Needed to Stir Enthusiasm and Loyalty of Tropical Workers," *Panama Tribune*, March 28, 1948.

90 George W. Westerman, "The Proof," *Panama Tribune*, July 17, 1949, in Westerman, *Blocking Them*, 45–46.

91 "Adam Powell to Study J. C. In Canal Zone," *New York Amsterdam News*, October 29, 1949, 2; Report of Adam C. Powell, Jr., Chairman, Special Investigating Sub-Committee on the Committee on Education and Labor in the House of Representatives, October 20, 1950, GWP 49/27, SCRBC.

92 Biondi, *To Stand and Fight*, 163–64.

93 Westerman, "Gold vs. Silver Workers." The Common Council for American Unity, a membership- and contributions-based organization comprising academic and literary intellectuals and journalists, published *Common Ground*. Langston Hughes served as a member of the advisory editorial board for several years. The council listed as its goals the promotion of democracy, freedom of difference, culture inclusiveness, and the assistance of migrants "adjusting" to America.

94 George W. Westerman, "Working Conditions on the Panama Canal Zone as of August 1949," 1949 GWP 45/4, SCRBC.

95 Westerman, "Working Conditions," 37.

96 "Adam Off on Biz Trip to Panama," *New York Amsterdam News*, December 3, 1949, 3.

97 Robinson, "Panama for the Panamanians," 193

98 "Congressman in Panama: Urges People of Panama Work with U.S. for Rights," *New York Amsterdam News*, January 7, 1950; "Adam Powell Reports on Canal Zone—Tells What He Observed during December Visit Here," *Panama Star and Herald*, October 24, 1950.

99 "CIO Expels Union of Public Workers," *New York Times*, January 17, 1950.

100 Special to the Panama American, press release, "Local 900 GCEOC-CIO," July 24, 1950, GWP 46/13, SCRBC; Club El Pacífico, "Roasting of Ed Gaskin," 3.

101 Conniff, *Black Labor*, 115.

102 Former Local 713 president Pascual Ampudia also proposed that Local 713 be transferred "as a fully organized and established union." This would have meant maintaining the old local leadership. Ampudia was outvoted. Hector Connor, "Facing Issues, Radio Broadcast over Station HOG," March 16, 1950, GWP 46/3, SCRBC; Pascual Ampudia to Abram Flaxer, March 20, 1950, AFP 2/9, TLRWLA; Westerman, *Blocking Them*, ix.

103 "CIO Is Uniting Welfare Workers to Supplant Own Left-Wing Union," *New York Times*, September 31, 1949; Philip Murray, "C.I.O to Organize Panama Canal Zone Workers: Murray Pledges C.I.O. Aid to Panama Canal Workers," *CIO News*, 1950, 1, 3; "Ed Welsh, Labor Organizer," 1979, Edward K. Welsh Papers (EWP) 7/1, TLRWLA; Black Trade Unionists Leadership Committee of the New York City Central Labor Council, AFL-CIO, "The Ed K. Welsh Award," 1980, EWP 7/1, TLRWLA.

104 Club El Pacífico, "Roasting of Ed Gaskin," 3.

105 The Liga Cívica eventually published a bilingual edition of Westerman's paper; Westerman, *Minority Group*, 10, 29.

106 Westerman, *Minority Group*, 10, 29.

107 A rich scholarship exists that traces the ways in which anticommunism discourse both stimmed more radical activism by African Americans in the United States while also foreclosing some of the Black leftist international-ism that had categorized the 1915–1945 period. Among these studies are Von Eschen, *Race against Empire*, chaps. 6 and 8; C. Anderson, "Bleached Souls and Red Negroes"; Berg, "Black Civil Rights and Liberal Anticommunism"; and Arnesen, "Civil Rights and the Cold War at Home." For more on Black Left internationalism in the postwar period and the crucial role played by Black women during the height of anticommunism, see Boyce Davies, *Left of Karl Marx*; McDuffie, *Sojourning for Freedom*.

108 George W. Westerman, "Address Delivered at the Trinity Methodist Church," October 1, 1950, 14, GWP 65/11, SCRBC.

Chapter Three: Todo por la Patria

1   "Agradecen al Pdte. Remón honor hecho a Westerman," *La Nación*, August 16, 1953.

2   "Westerman Raps C.Z. Policy in Chicago Speech," *Panama Tribune*, October 26, 1952; Westerman, "Canal Zone Paradise for North Americans while Natives Classed Inferior," *Panama Tribune*, November 2, 1952; William G. Arey, "Address at International House Chicago by Panamanian Newspaperman George W. Westerman: 'Sore Spots in United States–Panama Relations,'" U.S. Embassy in Panama, Panama City, November 18, 1952, RG 59, Records of the Department of State, Central Decimal Files, 611.19/11-1852, NARA, College Park, Maryland.

3   "Westerman Raps"; Westerman, "Canal Zone Paradise"; Arey, "Address at International House."

4   Arey, "Address at International House."

5   Corinealdi, "Section for Women"; Smart Chubb, "Will Trinidad Spurn the Call?"

6   Joseph and Grandin, *Century of Revolution*; Iber, *Neither Peace nor Freedom*.

7   "Sobre nuestros problemas con la Zona versó charla de G. Westerman en Chicago," *El Panamá América*, October 24, 1952; "El Norteamericano promedio es alérgico a la política del buen vecino—G. Westerman," *La Hora*, October 24, 1952; "Westerman Raps"; "Las relaciones entre Panamá y los Estados Unidos de América—Un interesante discurso de George Westerman," *La Nación*, October 28, 1952.

8   "30 de Octubre de 1952," Asamblea Nacional de Panamá, GWP 88/25, SCRBC; "Discurso de G. W. Westerman en los anales de la Cámara," *La Estrella de Panamá (LEP)*, October 31, 1952; "El discurso de Westerman en Chicago fue incluido en el acta de ayer de la Asamblea," *La Hora*, November 1, 1952; "Panamá en defensa de sus derechos," *El Mundo Gráfico*, November 23, 1952.

9   St. Clair Drake and Cayton, *Black Metropolis*. For more on St. Clair Drake's Caribbean roots, see Bryce-Laporte, "Black Immigrants," 45. As noted by Hazel V. Carby, as part of his dissertation work, St. Clair Drake focused on the Afro-Caribbean population of England. St. Clair Drake, thus, had both personal and research interests as these pertained to Afro-Caribbean migrants in the Americas and across the Atlantic. Carby, *Imperial Intimacies*, 90.

10 Conniff, *Black Labor*, 102. When the issue of discrimination was raised, it focused on the gold/silver system and US vs. Panamanian workers, not the concerns raised by the majority Afro-Caribbean workforce. For more on the hypocrisy of antiracism rhetoric as used by Panamanian officials, see Herman, "Global Politics of Anti-Racism."

11 George W. Westerman to John Gibbs St. Clair Drake, November 2, 1952, GWP 84/2, SCRBC.

12 José A. Remón Cantera, "Discriminación racial, discurso de campaña," May 29, 1952, Presidencia José Remón Cantera (PJRC), 177/504, ANP.

13 "La democracia será una farsa si no cesa en la Zona del Canal la discriminación racial—Declaró el Excmo. Pdte. Remón a los periodistas," *La Nación*, November 20, 1952.

14 The death of Domingo Díaz Arosemena was but one factor in the drama surrounding Arias's return to the presidency. Arias had apparently won the popular vote in 1948, but the National Electoral Board shifted the votes in favor of Díaz Arosemena. Following Díaz Arosemena's death and two unsuccessful temporary presidents, Arias and José Remón Cantera, then head of the national police, reached an agreement whereby the National Electoral Board agreed to a recount and confirmed that Arias had been the 1948 popular vote winner. Robinson, "Panama for the Panamanians," 193–94.

15 Conniff, *Black Labor*, 130

16 Priestley, "Raza y nacionalismo," 119.

17 José A. Remón Cantera, "Carta a Beresford A. Hansell F., John Stewart Harding, Alma Best, Horacio Sinclair y amigos," July 18, 1953, PJRC 177/502, ANP; Peña, *José Antonio Remón Cantera*; Pippin, *Remón Era*, 5–25; Lawson, *Panamá y sus hijos*, 8–11. As noted by Thomas Pearcy, the eventual militarization of the national police was due to changes as early as the 1930s, including the creation of paramilitary groups to spy on political opponents. Remón joined the force in 1932, just as these changes were unfolding. Pearcy, "Panama's Generation of '31," 703–4, 707–8.

18 Pippin, *Remón Era*, 35–89; "Courier Special Correspondent Praises Col. Remon's Semblance of Democracy," *Nation*, October 23, 1952; Central Intelligence Agency, "Panama: Communists Involved in Student Strike," CREST report, 1951, 15–17; del Vasto Rodríguez, *Historia del Partido Comunista*, 26.

19 "Courier Special Correspondent."

20 Conniff, *Black Labor*, 115–16.

21 "El mejoramiento de las relaciones entre Panamá y la Zona del Canal es objetivo principal, dijo Seybold a los periodistas," *LEP*, June 10, 1952.

22 John S. Seybold to Edward A. Gaskin and Local 900-GCEOC-CIO, February 12, 1953, 2, GWP 46/11, SCRBC.

23 For more on the history of the ISB, see Donoghue, "Imperial Sunset," 552.

24 "Robert C. Walker, Edward A. Gaskin—Local 900 Activities," Balboa Heights, Canal Zone Internal Security Branch, Panama Canal–Canal Zone Government, February 27, 1953, RG 84-3080A, Panama City embassy: confidential file 1953–1958, b15, NARA.

25 Edward Gaskin, "Discurso de radio," March 1, 1953, 1, Robert H. Beecher Papers (RBP) box 2, SCRBC.

26 Gaskin, "Discurso de radio," 5

27 Gaskin, "Discurso de radio," 1–3, 10.

28 Gaskin, "Discurso de radio," 10.

29 "El gobierno y pueblo panameño insistirá en la revisión del Tratado de 1903, Remón—Y que se nos haga la justicia a la que tenemos derecho, subrayó el Pdte. en la convención de CPN," *LEP*, March 16, 1953.

30 King H., *El problema de la soberanía*; LaFeber, *Panama Canal*, 69–70, 79–80; Conniff, *Black Labor*, 86–87; Acosta, *Influencia decisiva*.

31 "De todos los sectores del país respaldan las declaraciones del Sr. Presidente de la República—Numerosos mensajes recibe el Jefe del Estado," *LEP*, March 17, 1953; "De todos los sectores del país respaldan las declaraciones del Sr. Presidente de la República," *LEP*, April 9, 1953; "De todos los sectores del país respaldan las declaraciones del Sr. Presidente de la República, *LEP*, May 24, 1953. *La Estrella* continued to publish letters of this kind, albeit with less frequency, into late May.

32 "El Sindicato de Industriales ofrece su entusiasta concurso a las gestiones del presidente," *LEP*, March 21, 1953; "Respaldo nacional tendrá Remón para la revisión del Tratado del Canal de 1936," *La Hora*, March 18, 1953.

33 ISB, "Local 900-GCEOC-CIO," Balboa Heights, Canal Zone Internal Security Branch, Panama Canal–Canal Zone Government, March 20, 1953, RG 84-3080A, b15, NARA.

34 An example of such media reports included "El Canal mantendrá los jornales de salario local por lo menos en paridad con los que se pagan en Panamá por oficios comparables," *LEP*, March 1, 1953.

35 ISB, "GCEOC-Local 900-CIO Protest Rally," March 25, 1953, RG 84-3080A, b15, NARA; Robert B. Memminger, "Local-Rate Labor Rally in Colon; Increased Panamanian Interest in Local-Rate Objectives," U.S. embassy in Panama, counselor of embassy, April 2, 1953, RG 84-3080A, b15, NARA. For more on the history of the Guna Yala people in the international and national affairs of Panama, particularly during the first half of the twentieth century, see Howe, *People Who Would Not Kneel*. For a study focused on issues of sovereignty during the Spanish colonial period to the present moment, see Martínez Mauri, *La autonomía indígena en Panamá*.

36 ISB, "GCEOC-Local 900-CIO Protest Rally," 2–3.

37 ISB, "GCEOC-Local 900-CIO Protest Rally," 2; Memminger, "Local-Rate Labor Rally in Colon," 1–2.

38 Rabe, *Eisenhower and Latin America*; McPherson, *Yankee No!*; Joseph and Grandin, *Century of Revolution*; Grandin, *Last Colonial Massacre*.

39 Robert Memminger, "Public Reaction to Treaty Revision Campaign," Panama City, RP, US embassy, April 1, 1953, RG 59, 611.1913/4-153, NARA.

40 Memminger, "Public Reaction"; "Por un tratado comercial con Estados Unidos aboga el ex-Presidente de la Guardia," *LEP*, March 24, 1953.

41 "La posición de nuestro gobierno," *LEP*, March 24, 1953.

42 Memminger, "Public Reaction"; José Manuel Faúndes, "No debe festinarse ni especular con las negociaciones próximas a discutirse en los Estados Unidos," *LEP*, March 20, 1953; "Especulaciones contraproducentes," *LEP*, March 27, 1953.

43 J. R. Guizado, Ministro de Relaciones Exteriores de Panamá, "Aide Memoire to John Foster Dulles, U.S. Secretary of State," April 7, 1953, RG 59, 611.19/4-753, NARA.

44 John Foster Dulles, "Nota Verbal to Panamanian Foreign Minister," April 21, 1953, RG 185-147 Canal Zone Government/Panama Canal Co., Office of the

Executive Secretary, Records Relating to Negotiations for the 1955 Treaty, b1/f1, NARA, College Park, MD.

45 "Carta del Secretario de Estado Foster Dulles," LEP, April 30, 1953. Remón did eventually visit the White House in September 1953, but under the auspices of a "friendly visit" with Eisenhower to discuss general relations between both countries. Samudio, *El Canal de Panamá*, 189–91. Remón and his cabinet viewed the visit as an opportunity to get the negotiations back on track. Panamanian negotiators expressed frustration at the refusal by US delegates to address requests presented as treaty revisions on the grounds that revisions did not form part of the negotiations. Victor N. Juliao, "Acta de La Sesión Celebrada Por El Consejo de Gabinete," September 25, 1953, PJRC 179/511, ANP.

46 Robert Walker, "Edward A. Gaskin, Panama-US Relations," Balboa Heights, CZ, Internal Security Branch, Panama Canal-Canal Zone Government, April 28, 1953, RG 84-3080A, b15, NARA.

47 Robert B. Memminger, "Local-Rate Union Meets with Governor; Panamanian Government Interest in Canal Zone Labor Conditions May Weaken Union." U.S. embassy in Panama, May 5, 1953, RG 84-3080A, b15, NARA.

48 "Ministro Guizado consultará con sindicato de trabajadores panameños del Canal," *La Nación*, June 13, 1953.

49 Welsh left the Canal Zone later that year. Officially he was reassigned by the CIO to New Jersey to work with the United Rubber Workers of America. It also seems that Welsh requested a placement close to New York City, where his wife resided. John V. Riffe (CIO Executive Vice President) to Ed K. Welsh, September 29, 1953, EWP 1/4, TLRWLA. Regarding tensions between Gaskin and Welsh, in a December 1954 letter to a Local 900 official, Welsh expressed dismay at what he viewed as the basic problem of the union, Gaskin's "personality problem." This "problem," he declared, would inevitably lead to the fall of the union. Ed Welsh to Leonard Williams, December 21, 1954, EWP 1/7, TLRWLA.

50 "Westerman's 'Sore Spots' Recorded by U.S. Congress," *Nation*, February 7, 1953.

51 "Westerman's Study on Canal Treaty Placed in Circulation," *Panama Star and Herald*, August 12, 1953.

52 Westerman, "Press Statement Issued in the Embassy of Panama," Washington, DC, September 25, 1953, 4, GWP 82/5, SCRBC.

53 "Existing Iniquities against Panama Outlined by Panamanian Newspaperman," *Americas Daily*, September 28, 1953; George W. Westerman, "La política de discriminación en la Zona del Canal debe ser abandonada rápidamente," *El Mundo Gráfico*, October 3, 1953.

54 "Westerman Defends Panama's Interest in NY Radio Address," *Atlántico/Atlantic*, August 22, 1953.

55 "Westerman Defends."

56 Myers Asch, *Chocolate City*, 286.

57 "Agradecen al Pdte. Remón"; Jack Jamieson, "Group Shows Gratitude in 'Thank You' Letter to President Remón," *Panama Tribune*, August 23, 1953.

58 "'Toda mi vida he repudiado la discriminación racial,' declaró el Presidente Remón," *El Panamá América*, October 20, 1953.

59 Gaskin, "Summarized Statement on Socio-Economic Problems Affecting Panamanian Nationals Employed by the United States Government on the Panama Canal Zone," Panamá, RP, President, Local 900, Government and Civic Employees Organizing Committee-Congress of Industrial Organizations, August 1953, RBP, box 2, SCRBC.

60 Gaskin, "Summarized Statement," 10.

61 Joaquín C. Beleño, "Y los criollos brillaron por su ausencia," *La Hora*, August 29, 1953.

62 In 1951 Beleño published *Luna Verde*, the first of three novels published between 1951 and 1961 (now popularly known as La Trilogía Canalera / The Canal Trilogy), which critiqued the US presence in Panama, particularly US control of the Canal Zone. *Luna Verde*, which received the Ricardo Miró prize for fiction in 1949, allowing for its eventual publication, centered on the dynamics of the dollar economy (the green moon) in Panama and the Canal Zone. It placed patriotic mestizo Panamanians in opposition to Afro-Caribbean workers willing to tolerate unjust zone policies. The main character, who is, interestingly, born of a Panamanian mother and a French father (perhaps a reference to the infamous Bunau-Varilla), becomes a nationalist vis-à-vis the Universidad de Panamá and dies in a heroic attempt to expel US military forces from Panama. For examinations of Beleño's novels, particularly their depictions of Afro-Caribbeans and their descendants, see Wilson, "Aspectos de la prosa panameña"; Watkins, "Los aspectos socio-políticos"; and Watson, *Politics of Race*, chap. 2.

63 Beleño, "Y los criollos."

64 Beleño, "Y los criollos."

65 Alfonso E. McFarlane, "Los criollos sí fueron a la manifestación del 27 pero no se encontraban uniformados," *La Hora*, September 2, 1953.

66 "A Sieve of Inaccuracies," *Nation*, September 2, 1953.

67 Joaquín Beleño, "A Sieve of Inaccuracies," *La Hora*, September 3, 1953.

68 Beleño, "Sieve."

69 Alfaro, *El peligro antillano*, 9–12.

70 Escobar, *Arnulfo Arias*, 53–54; Biesanz, "Cultural and Economic Factors," 775. Mendeita and Husband, "Contribución del afro-antillano," 207. For a careful examination of the resonance of these labels in contemporary Panama, see Craft, "Una Raza, Dos Etnias."

71 Beleño, "Sieve."

72 Jamieson capitalizes the term *criollo* to differentiate his use of the term and that of xenophobes. His continued use of the term nonetheless pointed to his own status as a member of an older generation of Afro-Caribbean Panamanians for whom the term criollo could be a powerful self-identifier.

73 Jack Jamieson, "'Criollos Will Fight Bigots' Fire with Fire for Country and Fatherland," *Panama Tribune*, September 5, 1953; "Our Jack Comments on

Beleño-Criollo Dispute," *Nation*, September 5, 1953. I mainly quote from Jamieson's article in the *Nation*.

74 Beleño, "Replicando," *La Hora*, September 14, 1953.

75 Manuel de J. Berrocal, "Amigo Beleño," *La Hora*, September 14, 1953.

76 Juan B Olivera G., "Estimado Señor," *La Hora*, September 14, 1953.

77 Joaquín Beleño, "Una clara prueba del sectarismo criollo," *La Hora*, September 28, 1953.

78 Eduardo Archibold P., "Letter to the Editor," *Nation*, September 22, 1953.

79 Beleño, "Una clara prueba."

80 "Remon Asks Justice for R.P. Labor in Canal Zone," *Panama Star and Herald*, January 25, 1954; "Más de 10.000 personas asistieron al grandioso mitin," *La Nación*, January 26, 1954; "Over 10,000 Hear Remón, Arias Declare RP Support of Local 900," *Panama Tribune*, January 31, 1954.

81 "Remón Asks Justice"; Robert Memminger, "Canal Zone Local-Rate Labor Rally Addressed by President of Panama," US embassy in Panama, January 29, 1954, RG 84-3077A, Panama City embassy: general records 1953–1958, b3, 1–2, NARA.

82 "Remon Asks Justice"; "Más de 10.000"; "Over 10,000"; Memminger, "Canal Zone Local-Rate Labor Rally," 1–3.

83 For more on the relationship between the government of Jacobo Arbenz and the United States, see Gleijeses, *Shattered Hope*; Cullather, *Secret History*; and García Ferreira, *La CIA y el caso Arbenz*.

84 "La concentración del CIO," *LEP*, January 25, 1954 (Reprinted in *La Nación*, January 26, 1954); "El gobierno y los trabajadores," *El País*, January 27, 1954.

85 "Discordant Note in CIO Rally," *Nation*, January 26, 1954.

86 "Discordant Note in CIO Rally."

87 "Over 10,000 Hear Remón."

Chapter Four: To Be Panamanian

1 De la Guardia, *Segunda conversación*.

2 The term *depopulation* was first used by George Goethals, the first governor of the Canal Zone. He used the term to describe the act of purposefully denying housing in the zone to non-US-citizen workers and their families. He pursued an extensive depopulation policy between 1914 and 1925. Conniff, *Black Labor*, 47. For more on the first depopulation policies in the Canal Zone, see Marixa Lasso's *Erased*.

3 The tropical differential added a 25 percent bonus to all US citizen salaries. For more on the Canal Zone as a socialist space, see Knapp and Knapp, *Red, White, and Blue Paradise*; and Donoghue, *Borderland on the Isthmus*.

4 Conniff, *Black Labor*, 111.

5 "Call of Governor Seybold upon Assistant Secretary Cabot," U.S. Department of State, December 15, 1953, RG 59, 611.1913/12-1553, NARA.

6 "May Eliminate Native Workers from Residence on Canal Zone," *Panama Tribune*, March 14, 1954; "Local-Rate Site in New Cristobal—Rainbow City Families to Be Moved There," *Panama Star and Herald*, March 18, 1954.

7 "Seybold to Revise Local Rate Schools to Suit Panama Needs," *Panama Star and Herald*, March 19, 1954; "Gov. Explains Change Over in Schools," *Panama Tribune*, March 21, 1954; "Changes in Local-Rate School Setup Announced," *Nation*, March 26, 1954.

8 John S. Seybold, "Speech before Rotary Club of Panama," March 18, 1954, GWP 65/19, SCRBC.

9 Seybold, "Speech," 4–5, 8. For more on the school conversion, see Harper, *Tracing the Course*, chap. 5; Conniff, *Black Labor*, 121–24; and Jack Jamieson, "No Governor Has Stated U.S. Govt's Position as Clearly as Seybold," *Panama Tribune*, March 28, 1954.

10 Julio A. Salas et al., "Carta al Honorable Señor John S. Seybold," March 25, 1954, PJRC 191/540, ANP.

11 Julio A. Salas et al., "Telegrama a Presidente José A. Remón Cantera," April 14, 1954, PJRC 191/540, ANP.

12 Roberto Huertamatte, "Memorandum—Proyecto de alojar obreros zoneitas en Nuevo Cristóbal, enviado a Presidente Remón," May 3, 1954, PJRC 191/540, ANP.

13 Edward A. Gaskin, "Carta al Excelentísimo Señor Cor. José Remón Cantera, Presidente de la República," April 8, 1954, PJRC 191/540, ANP. Lloyd P. Vaughn, director of the CIO, also signed off on this letter, but based on Gaskin's previous correspondences with Remón and the press, the letter was likely largely authored by Gaskin.

14 Gaskin, "Carta al Excelentísimo," 3.

15 Gaskin, "Carta al Excelentísimo," 4. The higher cost of living in the republic (compared to the Canal Zone) was something recognized by Panamanian and Canal Zone officials. This difference in cost corresponded to the lower price of staples in zone commissaries and to fixed zone rental costs. The lack of any rental regulation in Panama City and Colón also contributed to this differential.

16 Edward A. Gaskin, "Carta al Excelentísimo Señor Presidente de la República Coronel José A. Remón Cantera," June 12, 1954, PJRC 177/503, ANP.

17 Seybold, "Speech," 4.

18 George W. Westerman, "New Spanish Program of Canal Zone Schools Is Most Commendable," *Panama Tribune*, February 21, 1954.

19 "Canal Zone Teachers Urge Study of Serious Aspects of Changes," *Panama Tribune*, March 28, 1954.

20 Gaskin, "Carta al Excelentísimo" (April 8, 1954), 2–3.

21 Gaskin, "Carta al Excelentísimo" (April 8, 1954), 3.

22 "Excluyese a los panameños de las escuelas para blancos en la Zona," *La Nación*, June 3, 1954.

23 Isabel E. de Cisneros, Jobita de Espinosa, et al., "Carta al Presidente Remón,"
    August 24, 1954, PJRC 191/540, ANP.

24 Cisneros et al., "Carta al Presidente Remón."

25 José Ramón Guizado, "Carta al Ing. Victor N. Julia, Secretario General de la
    Presidencia de la República," November 22, 1954, PJRC 191/540, ANP.

26 Ramón Guizado, "Carta al Ing."

27 Aníbal Sánchez, "La educación de los ciudadanos panameños en la Zona del
    Canal," *El Panamá América*, April 17, 1954.

28 Jack Jamieson, "Panama University Professors Discuss Exceptions to New C.Z.
    School Set-Up," *Panama Tribune*, June 20, 1954.

29 E.A.—A Panamanian parent of W.I. origin, "'Perfidy' Exposed," *Nation*, Sep-
    tember 14, 1954.

30 "Terminan las negociaciones del Nuevo Tratado con EE.UU.: Se firmará en
    Enero," *LED*, December 23, 1954.

31 "Se sugiere la negociación de un tratado comercial y reclamaciones por la inter-
    pretación del Tratado," *El Panamá América*, October 30, 1952.

32 Cámara de Comercio de Panamá, *Merchants of Panama*.

33 "Los instrumentos fueron firmados esta mañana en una solemne ceremonia," *El
    Panamá América*, January 25, 1955.

34 "Nearly 50,000 Persons in R.P. Enjoy C.Z. Coms'y Privileges," *Panama Tri-
    bune*, May 1, 1955. The article clarifies that Panamanian citizens made up 37,893
    of this total.

35 Two other Afro-Caribbeans, Fernando Bradley and Alfonso Giscombe, were
    alternates to principal deputies in the assembly.

36 "Treaty Discussion Air Grievances of Workers," *Panama Tribune*, February 27, 1955.

37 "Retirement," *Panama Tribune*, March 7, 1954; "In New York," *Panama Tri-
    bune*, June 27, 1954; "Leaves for US," *Panama Tribune*, November 14, 1954.

38 "Treaty Discussion Air Grievances."

39 "Treaty Discussion Air Grievances."

40 "'Los resultados del tratado son de positivos beneficios para Panamá,' Ricardo
    Arias E.," *El Panamá América*, January 25, 1955; "El nuevo tratado y los acuerdos
    adicionales," *El Panamá América*, January 25, 1955; George W. Westerman,
    "Treaty Strengthens Close Relations of Panama and U.S.," *Panama Tribune*,
    January 30, 1955. For more on the assassination of Remón, which remains
    unsolved to this day, see Guizado, *El extraño asesinato*; and Romeu, *Del caso
    Remón-Guizado*.

41 "Local 907 Made up of Non-Latins and Latins—Castillo," *Nation*, Septem-
    ber 23, 1954, 907; "Local 900, Not 907 Playing Politics—Castillo," *Nation*,
    September 22, 1954.

42 "RP Local 907 Presents Treaty Views to Solons," *Nation*, March 2, 1955.

43 Edward A. Gaskin, "Labor Day Address," September 5, 1955, GWP 46/11, 1,
    SCRBC.

44 Gaskin, "Labor Day Address," 2.

45 Gaskin, "Labor Day Address," 3.

46 Gaskin, "Labor Day Address," 4.

47 James F. Carroll to Jose de la Rosa Castillo C., President Local 907, December 21, 1955, GWP 51/5, SCRBC.

48 Carroll to Castillo C.

49 Edward A. Gaskin, "What the Locality Wage Rate Means!," *Nation*, January 29, 1956.

50 "Union Heads Ousted," *Panama Tribune*, February 19, 1956; "Local-Rate Union Is Placed under Administration Board," *Panama Star and Herald*, February 21, 1956.

51 "Gross Mishandling and Fraud Charged to Ex-Admin of Local 900," *Panama Tribune*, April 15, 1956.

52 "Blame National Office for Local 900's Plight," *Panama Star and Herald*, February 21, 1956.

53 "US Ducking Treaty," *Panama Star and Herald*, August 25, 1956.

54 "US Ducking Treaty."

55 The National Maritime Union (NMU) began operating in Panama, specifically in Colón, in 1963 and was recognized by the Panamanian government in 1967. The union focused on recruiting non-US workers employed by the military's maritime industry in the canal area. Lioeanjie, *Cuarenta años de lucha*, 23–24.

56 "Zone Employees Call for New Talks with US," *Panama Star and Herald*, October 18, 1956.

57 "Treaty Does Not Mean General CZ Wage Hike," *Sunday American*, August 19, 1956; Conniff, *Black Labor*, 119.

58 "Un problema muy grave," *El Día*, August 24, 1956.

59 "El denominador común: Los comisariatos," *El Panamá América*, August 27, 1956.

60 "El denominador común."

61 De la Guardia, *Segunda conversación*, 18–19.

62 De la Guardia, *Segunda conversación*, 19.

63 George W. Westerman, "Pensemos de nuestro país con orgullo," *El Mundo Gráfico*, July 20, 1957.

64 De la Guardia, *Tercera conversación*.

65 "RP Opposes CZ's Equal Wage Bill Interpretation," *Panama Star and Herald*, August 8, 1958.

66 Ernesto de la Guardia, "Discurso Ante la Asamblea Nacional," October 1, 1959, Presidencia Ernesto de la Guardia (PEDG) 277/639, ANP.

67 Hector Connor, "The Nationality Law Again and Again," *Atlantic*, September 26, 1953.

68 Pedro N. Rhodes, "Honorables Diputados de la Asamblea Nacional," February 12, 1955, GWP 63/18, SCRBC.

69 "Two Ex-Presidents Oppose Amendment to Lift Citizenship Rule," *Panama Tribune*, January 11, 1959.

70 "No Discrimination in Nationality Law," *Panama Tribune*, December 4, 1955; Westerman, *Los inmigrantes antillanos*, 100.

71 "Citizenship Amendment Measure Pigeon-Holed," *Panama Tribune*, January 7, 1961.

72 "End of Discriminatory Clause," *Panama Tribune*, February 11, 1961.

73 "A Great Act of Justice," *Panama Tribune*, February 25, 1961.

74 "Great Act of Justice."

Chapter Five: Panama in New York

1 Throughout this chapter I will refer to Leonor Jump as Leonor Jump Watson. This naming respects the naming practices that formed part of her life.

2 Las Servidoras, "Tenth Anniversary Scholarship Dinner-Dance of the Club Las Servidoras, Inc.," April 20, 1963, GWP 16/30, SCRBC.

3 "Sarah A. De Samuel," *Passenger and Crew Lists of Vessels Arriving at New York, New York, 1897–1957*, September 28, 1940, RG 85, Records of the Immigration and Naturalization Service, 1787–2004, NARA, Washington, DC; "Honored Here," *New York Amsterdam News*, January 11, 1941; interview with Grace Ingleton, Queens, New York, February 18, 2008.

4 The Dedicators Local, "First Dinner Program Tribute, The Dedicators Inc., Local, Honoring Mrs. Sarah Anesta Samuel and Mr. Henry Samuel," August 24, 1974, GWP 16/31, SCRBC.

5 US Department of Justice, *Annual Report* (1947, 1949, 1950).

6 "Ann Rose Mulcare (20 yo)," *Passenger and Crew Lists of Vessels Arriving at New York, New York, 1897–1957*, July 11, 1946, RG 85, Records of the Immigration and Naturalization Service, 1787–2004, NARA.

7 US Bureau of the Census, *Sixteenth Census*, La Boca, Balboa, Panama Canal, Enumeration District: 1-27, Sheet 6A; Fannie Keene, "On Brooklyn Society," *New York Amsterdam News*, June 24, 1950.

8 "Ann Rose Mulcare (20 yo)"; "Louisa J. Mulcare," *Passenger and Crew Lists of Vessels Arriving at New York, New York, 1897–1957*, July 11, 1946, RG 85, Records of the Immigration and Naturalization Service, 1787–2004, NARA.

9 Richards, *Maida Springer*; Pulido Ritter, "Notas sobre Eric Walrond"; S. S.-H. Lee, *Building a Latino Civil Rights*, 111–12; Watkins-Owens, *Blood Relations*, 156–57; J. Davis, *Eric Walrond*.

10 "E. B. Anderson Brooklyn," *New York Amsterdam News*, April 2, 1949, 37.

11 Connolly, *Ghetto Grows*, 73–74.

12 In 1955 George W. Westerman authored a study examining the deplorable state of housing options available to working-class Panamanians. His study resulted in a series of national lecture talks, but construction of new housing did not begin until after 1959, following the eruption of riots in Panama City. Wester-

man, *Urban Housing in Panama*; "Substandard Housing Cause of RP Diseases," *Panama Tribune*, January 22, 1956; "Housing Condition Here Subject of Lecture Series," *Panama Tribune*, April 22, 1956.

13   Paule Marshall's 1959 novel *Brown Girl, Brownstones* offered one of the first in-depth examinations of Caribbean life, particularly Anglophone Caribbean life in Brooklyn during the first half of the twentieth century. For more on Caribbean migrants in New York City during this period (most studies did not touch on Brooklyn until after the post-1965 immigration wave), see I. Reid, *Negro Immigrant*; Bryce-Laporte, "Black Immigrants"; James, *Holding Aloft*; and Watkins-Owens, *Blood Relations*.

14   Two rich studies on Puerto Rican migration to New York by the mid-twentieth century are Sánchez Korrol, *From Colonia to Community*; and Thomas, *Puerto Rican Citizen*. In Sánchez Korrol's study she also examines, albeit briefly, the presence of Puerto Ricans in Brooklyn (pp. 113–14, 206–8). Thomas makes fewer comments on the Puerto Rican presence in Brooklyn but does offer some analysis on the experiences of Black Puerto Ricans in 1940s New York City (pp. 91, 145). Jesús Colón is perhaps one of the most known Black Puerto Rican Brooklyn residents of this period. Some of his perspectives on being Puerto Rican and Black are found in Colón, *Puerto Rican in New York*.

15   As noted by historian Martha Biondi, notwithstanding local political successes, racial gerrymandering prevented Black residents in Brooklyn from voting a Black official into Congress until 1968. Biondi, *To Stand and Fight*, 221–22; Connolly, *Ghetto Grows*, 80–89; Wilder, *Covenant with Color*, 151, 184.

16   Wilder, *Covenant with Color*, 185–86, 193–94. For more on the coexistence of liberalist discourse and racial discrimination in 1950s and 1960s New York City, see C. Taylor, *Civil Rights in New York City*.

17   Wilder, *Covenant with Color*, 201–2, 210; Connolly, *Ghetto Grows*, 130–34; Biondi, *To Stand and Fight*, 230–35.

18   Wilder, *Covenant with Color*, 210–12, 214.

19   Most people of color from the Caribbean seeking to travel or immigrate to the United States in the first half of the twentieth century had to prove economic stability. This resulted in the most educated and trained Caribbean migrants, often in their twenties and early thirties, making the journey to the United States. I. Reid, *Negro Immigrant*, chap. 4; James, *Holding Aloft*, 78–79.

20   "Panamanian Theme Highlight of Gay Boro Surprise Party," *New York Amsterdam News*, June 7, 1952. The tamborito dance, a drums-based Afro-diasporic dance made popular during the Spanish colonial era, consisted of a "courting" couple led by the lyrics of a female vocalist and the clapping and singing of a participant audience. The pollera refers to a colonial-era embroidered dress, ranging in intricacy, which by the first decades of the twentieth century had come to be dubbed as the traditional dress of Panamanian women. Afro-descendant women designed and wore the earliest of these adornments but were largely uncredited in these early twentieth-century national narratives. For more on Afro-descendant pollera designers, see Molina Castillo, *La tragedia*.

The polleras used by tamborito dancers, usually during carnival, and mostly by light-skin mestiza women, were often very intricate and elegant. Head adornments, usually pearl clips, also formed part of the pollera ensemble. The montuno referred to the long-sleeved dress shirts (guayaberas), elegant straw hats, and leather sandals worn by the male dancers. These dancers were also, most often, light skin mestizo men.

21 Examples of such cultural producers included Ricardo Miró and Octavio Méndez Pereira. For more on the connections between folklorism and depicting a mestizo nation, see Szok, *Wolf Tracks*, chap. 1.

22 One public example of this understanding included a 1950 *Amsterdam News* piece on contributions by Caribbean migrants to New York. "To Their Adopted Home They Bring Many Gifts," *New York Amsterdam News*, September 8, 1951, 20.

23 "Joyce Daphnie Gumbs," *Index to Naturalization Petitions of the United States District Court of the Eastern District of New York, 1865–1957*, July 27, 1954, NARA Northeast Region. Based on her naturalization record, Gumbs was a Brooklyn resident since at least 1949.

24 The Dedicators Local, "First Dinner Program Tribute"; The Dedicators, "Celebration of Pioneering Women Committed to Excellence," May 20, 2001, Velma Armstrong Papers (VAP), the Dedicators, Inc. (TDI), New York.

25 The Dedicators, "Celebration of Pioneering Women."

26 The Dedicators Local, "First Dinner Program Tribute"; Priestley, "El sentido de la vida," 87–90; interview with Grace Ingleton, February 18, 2008.

27 Ingleton interview; Priestley, "El sentido de la vida," 89

28 The Dedicators, "Silver Anniversary, Seventh Spring Luncheon," June 11, 1978, Grace Ingleton Papers (GIP), TDI.

29 The Dedicators, "Silver Anniversary"; the Dedicators, "Celebration of Pioneering Women."

30 The Dedicators, "Silver Anniversary."

31 "Nella Gunning," *New York Passenger Lists*, 1820–1957, August 11, 1948, RG 85, NARA; "Leonard Oliver Gunning" *New York Passenger Lists*, 1820–1957, August 11, 1948, RG 85, NARA.

32 The Dedicators, "Silver Anniversary"; the Dedicators, "Celebration of Pioneering Women."

33 The Sarah Anesta Samuel Commemorative Society, "A Journey through the Legacy of Sarah Anesta Samuel" (2006), 5, VAP, TDI.

34 Valentina Robinson, "Untitled History of Las Servidoras," 1977, RBP, b3, SCRBC.

35 Based on their naturalization records, Gumbs resided in Brooklyn in the late 1940s, and Gunning started her residency in the borough in 1950 at the latest. "Joyce Daphnie Gumbs"; "Nella Brooks Gunning," *Petitions for Naturalization Filed in New York City, 1792–1989*, April 4, 1955, NARA Northeast Region.

36 "Esme Madelina Parchment," *Petitions for Naturalization Filed in New York City, 1792–1989*, NARA Northeast Region; Osborne, "Biographical Sketches," 16.

37 V. Robinson, "Untitled History," 1.

38 V. Robinson, "Untitled History," 2.

39 "Dr. Haughton in New Health Post," *New York Amsterdam News*, July 2, 1966.

40 On Black women and the beauty culture business in the Caribbean and the United States, see Candelario, *Black behind the Ears*; and Gill, *Beauty Shop Politics*.

41 V. Robinson, "Untitled History," 1–2.

42 Ingleton interview.

43 The Dedicators Local, "First Dinner Program Tribute."

44 Interview with Dorothy Haywood, February 18, 2011.

45 V. Robinson, "Untitled History," 1; "Las Servidoras to Dance at Diplomat," *New York Amsterdam News*, April 16, 1960. On the focus on African American and Puerto Rican juvenile delinquency in the late 1950s popular press, see Thomas, *Puerto Rican Citizen*, 194–96; and S. S.-H. Lee, *Building a Latino Civil Rights*, 55.

46 Ingleton interview.

47 Ingleton interview.

48 Marshall, "Black Immigrant Women," 84.

49 Ingleton interview.

50 Ingleton interview.

51 Interview with Velma Armstrong, Brooklyn, New York, February 29, 2009.

52 Armstrong interview.

53 Biondi, "Brooklyn College Belongs to Us."

54 Interview with Ruthwin Samuel, Queens, New York, February 18, 2008.

55 Samuel interview. As Biondi notes, white resistance to Black residents/homeowners was not as violent in New York as it was in Detroit and Chicago. New York's smaller white homeowner base was one key factor. The threat of violence was, however, very effective, something that Ruthwin Samuel could attest to decades later. Biondi, *To Stand and Fight*, 236

56 Purnell, "Taxation without Sanitation," 57. For more on how activists in Brooklyn engaged in community organizing that called out government neglect, see Purnell, *Fighting Jim Crow*.

57 Maloney, "El movimiento negro," 150; Priestley, "Etnia, clase y cuestión nacional," 59. According to historian Abdiel Zárate, protests among African American troops in the Canal Zone during the late 1960s inspired some of the Black organizations that emerged in Panama City, such as the *Asociación Afro-Panameña*. Zárate, "Los 500 años y los negros panameños," *La Prensa*, October 9, 1992, 6-A.

58 Marable, *Malcolm X*, 20–30; Vincent, "Garveyite Parents," 10–13.

59 Samuel interview. For more on social interactions between Afro-Caribbean Panamanians and African Americans (as well as other Latinx groups), see Opie, "Eating, Dancing, and Courting," 88–89, 93–94, 96, 99.

60 For more on Beecher's career in New York, see Corinealdi, "Creating Transformative Education."

61 The Dedicators Local, "First Dinner Program Tribute."

62 Ingleton interview; Armstrong interview.

63 In addition to Samuel, Gumbs, Parchment, Kirton, and Gunning had become naturalized US citizens. "Joyce Daphnie Gumbs"; "Esme Madelina Parchment"; "Edith Kirton," *Index to Petitions for Naturalization Filed in the United States District Court of the Eastern District of New York, 1865–1957*, November 11, 1954, NARA Northeast Region; "Nella Brooks Gunning."

64 Talk of denying birth-based citizenship to children born in the United States to undocumented parents has formed part of US political debate since at least 2010. This has not as yet included a call for the retroactive denial of said citizenship status. Alan Greenblatt, "Citizenship-by-Birth Faces Challenges," *National Public Radio*, May 25, 2010. As noted by Martha Jones in *Birth Right Citizens*, African Americans throughout the nineteenth century waged legal battles to have their birth-based citizenship recognized. Jones, *Birthright Citizens*.

65 Connolly, *Ghetto Grows*, chap. 7; Wilder, *Covenant with Color*, chap. 9.

66 Examples of such studies included Handlin, *Newcomers*; Glazer and Moynihan, *Beyond the Melting Pot*; Moynihan, *Negro Family*. Thomas, in *Puerto Rican Citizen*, 197–98, offers an incisive analysis of the problematic assumptions undergirding most social science research on Puerto Ricans during the 1950s and 1960s. For an analysis focused on the treatment of Black families and the Black poor within these studies, see Collins, "Comparison of Two Works"; and Paterson, *Freedom Is Not Enough*, among others. Sonia Song-Ha Lee offers a crucial counter-narrative to the emergence of these studies by examining how Puerto Rican and African American social workers and psychologists directly challenged "culture of poverty discourse." S. S.-H. Lee, *Building a Latino Civil Rights*, chap. 3. For an assessment of how Black scholars and cultural producers challenged the Moynihan report by articulating new forms of Black relationality, see King, "Black 'Feminisms' and Pessimisms."

67 Thomas, *Puerto Rican Citizen*, 217; S. S.-H. Lee, *Building a Latino Civil Rights Movement*, 53. Brian Purnell also offers the example of one family's specific legal case against the Board of Education on the grounds of inferior and segregated education. Purnell, *Fighting Jim Crow*, chap. 6.

68 Ingleton interview.

69 Las Servidoras, "Tenth Anniversary Scholarship Dinner-Dance."

70 Based on her naturalization records, Jump (Watson) was a resident of New York by at least 1947. "Leonor Jump," *Index to Naturalization Petitions of the United States District Court of the Eastern District of New York, 1865–1957*, April 29, 1952, NARA Northeast Region.

71 "Las Servidoras Chalks up Another New York Success," *Panama Tribune*, May 4, 1963. On the history of the Higher Horizons Program, see Wrightstone, *Evaluation of the Higher Horizons*; Thomas, *Puerto Rican Citizen*, 209–10; and C. Taylor, "Conservative and Liberal Opposition," 100. As Sonia

Song-Ha Lee has aptly argued, the Higher Horizons Program, while offering important support to students requiring additional academic assistance, was nonetheless part of a "compensatory education" platform that focused on improving students rather than addressing the wider inequities in the entire school system. It would be curious to hear from Jump Watson and others who were a crucial part of the program regarding what they understood to be their central mission as administrators, tutors, and counselors. S. S.-H. Lee, *Building a Latino Civil Rights Movement*, 172.

72   The reference to "Latin goups" in the cited quote corresponds to groups we would today define as Hispanic and/or Latina/o/x. "Las Servidoras Chalks up Another New York Success." For more on this idea of thinking as world citizens, see Corinealdi, "Envisioning Multiple Citizenships."

73   Las Servidoras, "Tenth Anniversary Scholarship Dinner-Dance."

74   "Las Servidoras Chalks up Another New York Success."

75   George Westerman to Ann Rose Mulcare, February 18, 1963, GWP 16/27, SCRBC.

76   "Photo Standalone 30—No Title," *New York Amsterdam News*, April 27, 1963.

77   Las Servidoras, "Tenth Anniversary Scholarship Dinner-Dance."

78   V. Robinson, "Untitled History," 10.

79   "Las Servidoras Chalks up Another New York Success."

80   The terms *cotillions* and *debutante balls* were used interchangeably by Las Servidoras throughout the 1960s. This was likely because of the range of age groups that participated in these events (debutantes, fifteen to twenty years old; escorts, sixteen to twenty-two years old; sub-debutantes, twelve to fourteen years old; junior escorts, thirteen to fifteen years old; flower girls, four to nine years old; heralds, four to nine years old; and post-debutantes, up to twenty-four years old). Las Servidoras, "Third Debutante Ball," September 16, 1967, GWP 16/31, SCRBC; the Dedicators, "1983 Debutante Cotillion, Guideline for Participants," 1983, Dorothy Haywood Papers (DHP), TDI.

81   The Dedicators, "Silver Anniversary"; Ingleton interview.

82   Haywood interview.

83   V. Robinson, "Untitled History," 2–3; Haywood interview.

84   Las Servidoras, "Third Debutante Ball"; the Dedicators, "1983 Debutante Cotillion."

85   The short-lived Reinado Soul in late 1960s Panama also addressed the absence of Black women in pageants and carnivals. Downer-Marcel, "*ARENEP*," 126–28.

86   Interview with Bernice Alder, Brooklyn, New York, July 30, 2008.

87   Alder interview.

88   Haywood interview.

89   "Debs Bow at Waldorf Astoria," *New York Amsterdam News*, October 2, 1965, 30; Las Servidoras, "Third Debutante Ball."

90   Las Servidoras, "Third Spring Luncheon Honoring Senator Waldaba Stewart and Mrs. Leonor Jump Watson," June 14, 1970, GWP 16/30, SCRBC.

91   V. Robinson, "Untitled History," 2–3.

92 Las Servidoras, "Las Servidoras Cordially Invites You to Its First Spring Luncheon," June 5, 1966, GWP 16/27, SCRBC.

93 Las Servidoras, "Second Spring Luncheon, Honoring Dr. George W. Westerman and Mr. Alvin L. Wilks," June 2, 1968, GWP 16/28, SCRBC; Ingleton interview.

94 "Las Servidoras Cordially Invites You"; Robert D. McFadden, "William Booth, Judge and Civil Rights Leader, Dies at 84," *New York Times*, December 27, 2006.

95 Las Servidoras, "Las Servidoras Cordially Invites You"; "Dr. Haughton in New Health Post."

96 V. Robinson, "Untitled History," 10.

97 Las Servidoras, "Third Spring Luncheon."

98 Las Servidoras, "Tenth Anniversary Scholarship Dinner-Dance"; *"Advertising Contract between the Panama Tribune* and Las Servidoras, Cotillion Dinner Dance, Sponsored by Las Servidoras, Inc, to Be Held Saturday Evening, September 16, 1967," 1967, GWP 16/27, SCRBC.

99 Las Servidoras, "Third Debutante Ball."

100 The concession spelled out in the Kennedy-Chiari accord came after several protests, including Operación Soberanía (Operation Sovereignty) in May 1958, led by high school and university students, and Operación Siembra de Banderas (Flag-Sowing Operation) in November 1959, led by university faculty and students. Both protests demanded recognition of the Panamanian flag in the Canal Zone. Zone officials responded violently to the second set of protests, evidencing some of the violence that would transpire in January 1964. For more on this first cycle of protests and on the 1964 protests and the response by US and Panamanian officials, see McPherson, "Rioting for Dignity"; del Cid Felipe, *Camino a la libertad*; and Jaén Suarez, *Panamá soberana*.

101 "Warns on Extremists, Militants Taking Over," *New York Amsterdam News*, June 8, 1968; "Panameños residentes en Nueva York rinden homenaje a Westerman," *El Panamá América*, June 11, 1968.

102 For more information on Bethune's career and activism, see Giddings, *When and Where I Enter*, chaps. 12–13; Broadwater, *Mary McLeod Bethune*; and Hanson, *Mary McLeod Bethune*.

103 Las Servidoras, "Second Spring Luncheon."

104 My use of *race men* borrows from Hazel V. Carby's text of the same name. Carby, *Race Men*.

105 Las Servidoras, "Second Spring Luncheon."

106 For more on Chisholm's personal biography, see Chisholm, *Unbought and Unbossed*; and Lynch, *Chisholm '72*. On the history of independence in Barbados and the connections between Bajans at home and in the diaspora, see Chamberlain, *Empire and Nation Building*. Curiously, even after independence, the Queen of England remained the Barbadian head of state. In 2020, the government of Barbados announced plans to remove the Queen from this position, with the aim of having Barbados become a formal republic by No-

vember 30, 2021. Julia Rawlins-Bentham, "PM Outlines Republic Journey for Barbados," *Barbados Government Information Service*, August 21, 2021, https://gisbarbados.gov.bb/blog/pm-outlines-republic-journey-for-barbados/.

107 "Warns on Extremists, Militants Taking Over." In the *New York Amsterdam News* coverage of Chisholm's speech, the paper chose to focus on her comments regarding extremists and militants (i.e., the need to "bring these groups to the fold") and less so on her comments regarding education and ongoing school debates. The newspaper also made little note of the group that had brought Chisholm, Westerman, Wilks, and at least one other political hopeful, Dollie L. Robinson, from Brooklyn, together. The article even misreported the name of the organization, calling them "Las Amigas" (The Friends). To the newspaper's credit, a correction did appear in the following week's issue. "Wrong Group," *New York Amsterdam News*, June 15, 1968, 17.

108 V. Robinson, "Untitled History," 10–11.

109 Las Servidoras, "Third Spring Luncheon."

110 Interview with Marcia Bayne Smith, March 2, 2011.

111 Bayne Smith interview.

112 Las Servidoras, "Third Spring Luncheon."

113 Leonor Jump Watson, "Acceptance Speech, Las Servidoras Third Spring Luncheon," June 14, 1970, GWP 16/29, SCRBC; capitalization in the original.

114 Las Servidoras, "Third Spring Luncheon." On Youth in Action, see Connolly, *Ghetto Grows*, 154–55. Connolly comments on Stewart's participation in Youth in Action and his eventual election to the New York Senate, but in his observations, he makes no mention of Stewart's upbringing in Panama. Connolly, *Ghetto Grows*, 155.

115 Las Servidoras, "Third Spring Luncheon."

116 "Panamanians Here on Goodwill Visit," *Daily Gleaner (Kingston, Jamaica)*, September 27, 1956; "Panamanians Here on Goodwill Tour," *Daily Gleaner*, September 28, 1957; "Panamanians Here Form Club," *Daily Gleaner*, June 21, 1958.

117 The Dedicators, "History of the Dedicators, Inc. 1953–1992," 1992, GIP, TDI; the Dedicators Local, "First Dinner Program Tribute."

Conclusion

1 For more on the military government of this period and the central role played by Omar Torrijos in this government, see Priestley, *Military Government*; and Materno Vásquez, *Omar Torrijos*. On how Torrijos made sovereignty over the Panama Canal a key platform of his political agenda, see Torrijos Herrera, *La quinta frontera*; Escobar Bethancourt, *Torrijos*; and Vargas, *Omar Torrijos Herrera*.

2 Maloney, "La contribución de Armando Fortune," 16.

3 Alberto Belinfante, "Panameños en EE.UU. tendrán conferencia," *El Panamá América*, May 3, 1974. Aminta Núñez, a historian and an anthropologist,

would also join the Universidad de Panamá faculty starting in the late 1970s. Agatha Williams, a sociologist, formed part of the faculty by the 1980s. Carlos "Cubena" Guillermo Wilson, "El aporte cultural de la etnia negra en Panamá," accessed December 15, 2020, http://diadelaetnia.homestead.com /cubena.html; Helkin Guevara, "Fallece la docente Aminta Núñez," *La Prensa*, January 25, 2017; Gólcher, Vázquez, and Camargo, *Cien mujeres por la vida*, 17–18, 163; Dedicators Local, "First Dinner Program Tribute." For a brief history of Black women academics in Panama and in the diaspora from the 1970s onward, see Hidalgo Villarreal, Warren, and Mendivil, "Panorama de la situación," 135–39. On inroads made by Afro-Caribbean Panamanian women in STEM fields, see Miller, "Experiences of Panamanian Afro-Caribbean Women in STEM."

4 Interview with Clarence Beecher, Chicago, September 11, 2008; Priestley, *Military Government*, chap. 4; Priestley, "¿Afroantillanos o afropanameños?," 195–96; Gandásegui, "Democracia y movimientos sociales," 44–45.

5 "Panamanians Open 3-Day Caucus in US," *Panama American*, May 17, 1974; Priestley, "¿Afroantillanos o afropanameños?," 198–201.

6 Panamanian Cultural Action Committee, "Proceedings of the First U.S. Conference," 1974, 5, GWP 20/9, SCRBC.

7 Gary Thomas, "Liberation Rally Draws Young Crowd," *New York Amsterdam News*, February 21, 1970; Carlos E. Russell, "Why Black Solidarity Day?," *New York Amsterdam News*, October 16, 1971; "Carlos Russell to Africa for Amsterdam," *New York Amsterdam News*, July 22, 1972.

8 Panamanian Cultural Action Committee, "Proceedings," 14. Freeing all Black political prisoners had likewise formed part of the Black Liberation Rally of 1971.

9 Panamanian Cultural Action Committee, "Proceedings," 16.

10 Panamanian Cultural Action Committee, "Proceedings," 16.

11 Panamanian Cultural Action Committee, "Proceedings," 11.

12 Priestley, *Military Government* 7; Materno Vásquez, *Omar Torrijos*, 142.

13 Panamanian Cultural Action Committee, "Proceedings," 19.

14 Panamanian Cultural Action Committee, "Proceedings," 19

15 Panamanian Cultural Action Committee, "Proceedings," 28.

16 Panamanian Cultural Action Committee, "Proceedings," 28.

17 Barrow, *No me pidas una foto*.

18 The 2010 census also revealed the gap in self-identification as Afro-descendant (Afrodescendiente) given the dominance of mestizo and raceless narratives in the country. Meneses Araúz, "Informe Sombra." For more on questions of personal and census identity among Afro-Caribbeans in late twentieth-century Panama, see Curtis, "Becoming More and More Panamanian." For more on opportunity programs in Brazil and Colombia, see Paschel, *Becoming Black Political Subjects*.

19 Maloney, "El movimiento negro"; Downer-Marcel, "ARENEP."

20 Panamanian Cultural Action Committee, "Proceedings," 30.

21 Priestley and Barrow, "The Black Movement in Panamá," 231, 245. Priestley and Barrow identify the 1974 US Conference of Panamanians as a political organization called the National Conference of Panamanians. This naming contradicts the published proceedings, although both the 2008 essay and the published proceedings converge on securing an absentee ballot.

22 Panamanian Cultural Action Committee, "Proceedings," 30.

23 Panamanian Cultural Action Committee, "Proceedings," 13.

24 Panamanian Cultural Action Committee, "Proceedings," 7–8.

25 "Decoration," *Sunday Republic*, June 27, 1982.

26 UNESCO, OEA/OAS (Organization of American States) and INAC (National Institute of Culture) also sponsored the congress. "Realizarán Congreso de Culturas Negras," *Matutino*, May 25, 1980; Maloney, "El movimiento negro," 155; Maloney, "Los afropanameños y la cultura nacional," 145; Tamayo G., "Congreso de la cultura negra."

27 "Realizarán Congreso."

28 Cedeño Cenci, *La recuperación de la identidad*, 8–9.

29 Abdiel Zárate, "Los 500 años y los negros panamaneños," *La Presna*, October 9, 1992; Downer-Marcel, "ARENEP," 128; interview with Aminta Núñez, Panama City, July 10, 2001; interview with Coralia Hassán de Yorente, Panama City, July 26, 2001.

30 SAMAAP, *SAMAAP Pamphlet*, 2000, author's personal collection; interview with Melva Lowe de Goodin, Panama City, July 13, 2001.

31 Ruben Dario Diaz C., "La población antillana y su contribución al desarrollo de la cultura del país," *La República*, April 8, 1984; Earl Patrick Watson, "The SAMAAP Fair," *Panama News*, March 24, 2000; Karla Jiménez Comrie, "Anuncian actividades en torno al Día de La Etnia Negra Nacional," *La Prensa*, May 6, 2015; Keila E. Rojas L., "Todo listo para celebrar la Gran Feria Afroantillana," *LED*, February 10, 2017. For recent studies on the work of SAMAAP, see Duke, "Black Movement Militancy in Panama," 75–83; and Davidson, "Among Spectators and Agents of History." On the historical work and architectural legacy of the Museo Afro-Antillano, see Osorio Ugarte, "El edificio del museo afroantillano," 133–53.

32 Williams, "La mujer negra y su inserción"; Williams, "Presencia de la mujer afropanameña," 71–80. For similar work in other parts of the Americas, see Gonzalez, "A mulher negra na sociedade brasileira"; Hull, Scott, and Smith, *All the Women Are White*; Brand, *No Burden to Carry*; Boyce Davies, *Black Women, Writing, and Identity*; Campbell, *Rotundamente negra*; and Rubiera Castillo, *Reyita, sencillamente*.

33 Eric Jackson, "George Westerman Center Opens with Tribute to Martin Luther King, Jr.," *Panama News*, January 2001. For an additional examination of activism spearheaded by Afro-Caribbean Panamanians and other Black Panamanians from the mid-1990s into the early twenty-first century, see Priestley and Barrow, "The Black Movement in Panama."

Bibliography

Archival Collections

Archivo Nacional de Panamá (ANP)
  Presidencia de Arnulfo Arias Madrid, 1940–1941 (PAAM)
  Presidencia de José Remón Cantera, 1952–1955 (PJRC)
  Presidencia de Ernesto de la Guardia, 1955–1959 (PEDG)
The Dedicators Inc., New York (TDI)
  Velma Armstrong Papers (VAP)
  Dorothy Haywood Personal Papers (DHP)
  Grace Ingleton Papers (GIP)
National Archives and Records Administration (NARA), College Park, Maryland
  Record Group 59—Records of the Department of State, Central Decimal Files
  Record Group 84—Records of the Foreign Service Posts of the Department of State
  Record Group 185—Records of the Panama Canal
National Archives and Records Administration (NARA), Northeast Region
  Index to Petitions for Naturalization filed in Federal, State, and Local Courts Located in New York City, 1792–1989
National Archives and Records Administration (NARA), Washington, DC
  Record Group 85—Records of the Immigration and Naturalization Service, 1787–2004
Schomburg Center for Research in Black Culture, New York Public Library (SCRBC)
  Robert H. Beecher Papers (RBP)
  Ewart Guinier Papers (EGP)
  George W. Westerman Papers (GWP)
Tamiment Library and Roger F. Wagner Labor Archives (TLRWLA), New York University
  American Business Consultants Inc.
  Abram Flaxer Papers (AFP)
  Edward K. Welsh Papers (EWP)

Government Reports, Publications, and Databases

Annual Report of the Governor of the Panama Canal. Washington, DC: United States Government Printing Office, 1934, 1936.

Arias, Arnulfo. *Discurso del Excelentísimo Doctor Arnulfo Arias M. al tomar posesión de la Presidencia de la República de Panamá.* Panama City: Imprenta Nacional, 1940.

Arias, Arnulfo. "El mejoramiento de la raza." *Boletín Sanitario* 1, no. 3 (1934): 3–5.

Censo Demográfico—República de Panamá. Panama City: Imprenta Nacional, 1931.

Central Intelligence Agency. CREST Reports.

de la Guardia, Ernesto. *Segunda conversacion con el pueblo panameño.* Panama City: Publicaciones de la Secretaría de Información de la Presidencia de la República, 1956.

de la Guardia, Ernesto. *Tercera conversacion con el pueblo panameño.* Panama City: Publicaciones de la Secretaría de Información de la Presidencia de la República, 1956.

Engelhardt, N. L. *Report of the Survey of the Schools of the Panama Canal Zone.* Mount Hope, Canal Zone: Panama Canal Press, 1930.

King, Margaret Lumpkin. *Education in the British West Indies.* Washington, DC: US Department of Health, Education, and Welfare, Office of Education, Division of International Education, 1955.

Memoria que el Ministro de Gobierno y Justicia presenta a la Honorable Asamblea Nacional en sus sesiones ordinarias. Panama City: Imprenta Nacional, 1943.

Memoria que el Secretario en el Despacho de Relaciones Exteriores presenta a La Asamblea Nacional en sus sesiones ordinarias. Panama City: Imprenta Nacional, 1932, 1934, 1936.

Panama Canal Commission. *Panama Canal Review.* Balboa Heights, Canal Zone: 1954–55.

República de Panamá. *Gaceta Oficial.* Panama City: Gobierno Nacional de Panamá, 1926–70.

US Bureau of the Census. *Sixteenth Census of the United States, 1940: Panama Canal Zone Population.* Washington, DC: National Archives and Records Administration, 1941.

US Department of Justice. *Annual Report of the Immigration and Naturalization Service.* Washington, DC: US Department of Justice, 1947, 1949, 1950.

Newspapers

Americas Daily (Miami)
Daily Gleaner (Kingston)
El Atlántico/The Atlantic (Colón)
El Mundo Gráfico (Panama City)
El País (Panama City)
El Panamá América/Panama American (Panama City)
La Estrella de Panamá/Star and Herald (Panama City)
La Hora (Panama City)
La Nación/The Nation (Panama City)
La Prensa (Panama City)
La República/The Republic (Panama City)

La Tribuna (Panama City)
Matutino (Panama City)
New York Amsterdam News (New York)
New York Times (New York)
Panama News (Panama City)
Panama Tribune/La Tribuna de Panamá (Panama City)

Interviews

Alder, Bernice. Brooklyn. July 30, 2008.
Armstrong, Velma. Brooklyn. February 29, 2009.
Bayne Smith, Marcia. Phone interview. March 2, 2011.
Beecher, Clarence. Chicago. September 11, 2008.
Haywood, Dorothy. Phone interview. February 18, 2011.
Hassán de Yorente, Coralia. Panama City. July 26, 2001.
Ingleton, Grace. Queens, New York. February 18, 2008.
Lowe de Goodin, Melva. Panama City. July 13, 2001.
Núñez, Aminta. Panama City. July 10, 2001.
Samuel, Ruthwin. Queens, New York. February 18, 2008.

Books, Articles, Dissertations, and Other Sources

Acosta, David. *Influencia decisiva de la opinión pública en el rechazo del Convenio Filos-Hines de 1947*. Panama City: Editorial Universitaria, 1994.

Alfaro, Olmedo. *El peligro antillano en la América Central: La defensa de la raza*. Panama City: Imprenta Nacional, 1924.

Altink, Henrice. *Destined for a Life of Service: Defining African-Jamaican Womanhood, 1865–1938*. Manchester: Manchester University Press, 2011.

Alvarez, Sonia E., and Kia Lilly Caldwell. "Promoting Feminist *Amefricanidade*: Bridging Black Feminist Cultures and Politics in the Americas." *Meridians* 14, no. 1 (2016): v–xi.

Anderson, Benedict. *Imagined Communities: Reflections on the Origin and Spread of Nationalism*. New York: Verso, 1991.

Anderson, Carol. "Bleached Souls and Red Negroes: The NAACP and Black Communists in the Early Cold War, 1948–1952." In *Window on Freedom: Race, Civil Rights, and Foreign Affairs, 1945–1988*, edited by Brenda Gayle Plummer, 67–114. Chapel Hill: University of North Carolina Press, 2003.

Andrews, George Reid. *Afro-Latin America, 1800–2000*. New York: Oxford University Press, 2004.

Aparicio, Fernando. *Liberalismo, federalismo y nación: Justo Arosemena en su contexto histórico*. Panama City: Editorial Portobelo, 1997.

Appelbaum, Nancy P. *Muddied Waters: Race, Region, and Local History in Colombia, 1846–1948*. Durham, NC: Duke University Press, 2003.

Appelbaum, Nancy P., ed. *Race and Nation in Modern Latin America*. Chapel Hill: University of North Carolina Press, 2003.

Araúz, Virgilio, ed. *Cien años de colonalismo monetario*. Panama City: Centro de Investigaciones Educativas y Nacionales, 2004.

Araúz Monfante, Celestino Andrés. *El imperialismo y la oligarquía criolla contra Carlos A. Mendoza*. Panama City: Órgano Judicial y Tribuna Electoral, 2009.

Araúz Monfante, Celestino Andrés. *Bocas del Toro y el Caribe Occidental: Periferia y margninalidad siglos XVI–XIX*. Panama City: INAC, 2006.

Araúz Monfante, Celestino Andrés, and Patricia Pizzurno. "Panamá bajo el imperio del panameñismo y la II Guerra Mundial." *Crítica* 23 (2003): 4–30.

Ariail, Cat. "Between the Boundaries: The Athletic Citizenship Quest of Carlota Gooden." *Journal of Sport History* 44, no. 1 (April 2017): 1–19.

Arnesen, Eric. "Civil Rights and the Cold War at Home: Postwar Activism, Anti-communism, and the Decline of the Left." *American Communist History* 11, no. 1 (2012): 5–44.

Barriteau, Violet Eudine. "The Relevance of Black Feminist Scholarship: A Caribbean Perspective." In *Feminist Africa 7: Diaspora Voices*, edited by Rhoda Reddock, 9–31. Cape Town: University of South Africa, 2006.

Barrow, Alberto. *No me pidas una foto: Develando el racismo en Panamá*. Panama City: Impresora Universal Books, 2001.

Barrow, Alberto, and George Priestley. *Piel oscura Panamá: Ensayos y reflexiones al filo del centenario*. Edited by Efigenia Cedeño G. Panama City: Editorial Universitaria, Carlos Manuel Gasteazoro, 2003.

Berg, Manfred. "Black Civil Rights and Liberal Anticommunism: The NAACP in the Early Cold War." *Journal of American History* 94, no. 1 (2007): 75–96.

Biesanz, John. "Cultural and Economic Factors in Panamanian Race Relations." *American Sociological Review* 14, no. 6 (1949): 772–79.

Biondi, Martha. "'Brooklyn College Belongs to Us': Black Students and the Transformation of Public Higher Education in New York City." In *Civil Rights in New York City: From World War II to the Giuliani Era*, edited by Clarence Taylor, 161–81. New York: Fordham University Press, 2011.

Biondi, Martha. *To Stand and Fight: The Struggle for Civil Rights in Postwar New York City*. Cambridge, MA: Harvard University Press, 2003.

Blain, Keisha, Asia Leeds, and Ula Y. Taylor, "Women, Gender Politics, and Pan-Africanism." *Women, Gender, and Families of Color* 4, no. 2 (2016): 139–45.

Bourgois, Philippe. *Ethnicity at Work: Divided Labor on a Central American Banana Plantation*. Baltimore, MD: Johns Hopkins University Press, 1989.

Boyce Davies, Carole. *Black Women, Writing, and Identity: Migrations of the Subject*. New York: Routledge, 1994.

Boyce Davies, Carole. *Left of Karl Marx: The Political Life of Black Communist Claudia Jones*. Durham, NC: Duke University Press, 2007.

Brand, Dionne. *No Burden to Carry: Narratives of Black Working Women in Ontario, 1920s–1950s*. Toronto: Women's Press, 1991.

Britton, Floyd. *Legado patriótico y revolucionario*. Panama City: Comité Nacional Organizador de los Actos del XX Aniversario del Asesinato de Floyd Britton, 1989.

Broadwater, Andrea. *Mary McLeod Bethune: Educator and Activist*. Berkeley Heights, NJ: Enslow, 2003.

Brown, Kimberly Juanita. *The Repeating Body: Slavery's Visual Resonance in the Contemporary*. Durham, NC: Duke University Press, 2015.

Brown, Patrice C. "The Panama Canal: The African American Experience." In "Federal Records and African American History," special issue, *US NARA Prologue Magazine* 29, no. 2 (1997). https://www.archives.gov/publications/prologue/1997/summer/panama-canal.

Brown Valdés, Carlos, and Manuel Castillero Cortés. "El afroantillano en la sociedad panameña." PhD diss., Universidad de Panamá, 1991.

Bryce-Laporte, Roy S. "Black Immigrants." In *Through Different Eyes: Black and White Perspectives on American Race Relations*, edited by Peter I. Rose, Stanley Rothman, and William J. Wilson, 44–61. New York: Oxford University Press, 1973.

Bryce-Laporte, Roy S. "Voluntary Immigration and Continuing Encounters between Blacks: The Post-Quincentenary Challenge." *Annals of the American Academy of Political and Social Science* 530 (November 1993): 28–41.

Burnett, Carla. "'Are We Slaves or Free Men?' Labor, Race, Garveyism, and the 1920 Panama Canal Strike." PhD diss., University of Illinois at Chicago, 2004.

Burnett, Carla. "'Unity Is Strength': Labor, Race, Garveyism, and the 1920 Panama Canal Strike." *Global South* 6, no. 2 (2013): 39–64.

Cámara de Comercio de Panamá. *The Merchants of Panama and the U.S. Commercial Agencies in the Canal Zone: Documents Relative to the Complaints of Panama Merchants and Industrialists over the Competitive Activities of Commissaries, Clubhouses, and Post Exchanges in the Canal Zone*. Panama City: n.p., 1952.

Campbell, Shirley. *Rotundamente negra*. San José, Costa Rica: Ediciones Perro Azul, 1994.

Candelario, Ginetta. *Black behind the Ears: Dominican Racial Identity from Museums to Beauty Shops*. Durham, NC: Duke University Press, 2007.

Cantón, Alfredo. *Desenvolvimiento de las ideas pedagógicas en Panamá, 1903–1926*. Panama City: Imprenta Nacional, 1955.

Carby, Hazel V. *Imperial Intimacies: A Tale of Two Islands*. New York: Verso, 2019.

Carby, Hazel V. *Race Men*. Cambridge, MA: Harvard University Press, 1998.

Carr, Barry. "Identity, Class, and Nation: Black Immigrant Workers, Cuban Communism, and the Sugar Insurgency, 1925–34." In *Marginal Migrations: The Circulation of Cultures within the Caribbean*, edited by Shalini Puri, 77–108. Oxford: Macmillan Caribbean, 2003.

Casey, Matthew. *Empire's Guestworkers: Haitian Migrants in Cuba during the Age of US Occupation*. Cambridge: Cambridge University Press, 2017.

Castillero Calvo, Alfredo. *Los negros y mulatos en la historia social panameña*. Panama City: Impresora Panamá, 1969.

Castillero Pimentel, Ernesto. *Panamá y los Estados Unidos*. Panama City: n.p., 1953.

Castillero R., Ernesto J. *El ferrocarril de Panamá y su historia*. Panama City: Imprenta Nacional, 1932.

Cedeño Cenci, Diógenes. *La recuperación de la identidad cultural del negro como una contribución a la paz mundial*. Panama City: Imprenta Universitaria, 1980.

Chamberlain, Mary. *Empire and Nation Building in the Caribbean: Barbados, 1937–66*. Manchester: Manchester University Press, 2010.

Chambers, Glenn A. *Race, Nation, and West Indian Immigration to Honduras, 1890–1940*. Baton Rouge: Louisiana State University Press, 2010.

Chirú Barrios, Félix J. "Liturgia al héroe nacional: El monumento a Vasco Núñez de Balboa en Panamá." *Cuadernos Inter.C.A.Mbio sobre Centroamérica y el Caribe* 9, no. 10 (2012): 71–99.

Chisholm, Shirley. *Unbought and Unbossed*. Boston: Houghton Mifflin, 1970.

Chomsky, Aviva. "'Barbados or Canada': Race, Immigration, and Nation in Early Twentieth-Century Cuba." *Hispanic American Historical Review* 80, no. 3 (2000): 415–62.

Chomsky, Aviva. *West Indian Workers and the United Fruit Company in Costa Rica, 1870–1940*. Baton Rouge: Louisiana State University Press, 1996.

Colby, Jason M. *The Business of Empire: United Fruit, Race, and U.S. Expansion in Central America*. Ithaca, NY: Cornell University Press, 2011.

Collins, Patricia Hill, ed. *Black Feminist Thought: Knowledge, Consciousness, and the Politics of Empowerment*. 2nd ed. New York: Routledge, 2000.

Collins, Patricia Hill. "A Comparison of Two Works on Black Family Life." *Signs* 14, no. 4 (1989): 875–84.

Colón, Jesús. *A Puerto Rican in New York and Other Sketches*. New York: Mainstream Press, 1961.

Conniff, Michael L. *Black Labor on a White Canal: Panama, 1904–1981*. Pittsburgh, PA: University of Pittsburgh Press, 1985.

Connolly, Harold X. *A Ghetto Grows in Brooklyn*. New York: New York University Press, 1977.

Conte-Porras, Jorge. *Arnulfo Arias Madrid*. Panama City: Litho-Impresora Panamá, S.A., 1980.

Corinealdi, Kaysha. "Being Fully Human: Linda Smart Chubb and the Praxis of Black Feminist Internationalism." *Signs: Journal of Women in Culture and Society* 47, no. 4 (forthcoming, Summer 2022).

Corinealdi, Kaysha. "Creating Transformative Education: Robert Beecher and Thinking through Race and Empire from Panama to New York City." *International Journal of Africana Studies* 18, no. 2 (2017): 74–94.

Corinealdi, Kaysha. "Envisioning Multiple Citizenships: West Indian Panamanians and Creating Community in the Canal Zone Neocolony." *Global South* 6, no. 2 (2013): 87–106.

Corinealdi, Kaysha. "Redefining Home: West Indian Panamanians and Transnational Politics of Race, Citizenship, and Diaspora, 1928–1970." PhD diss., Yale University, 2011.

Corinealdi, Kaysha. "A Section for Women: Journalism and Gendered Promises of Anti-Colonial Progress in Interwar Panama." *Caribbean Review of Gender Studies*, no. 12 (2018): 95–120.

Craft, Renée Alexander. "'Una Raza, Dos Etnias': The Politics of Becoming/Performing Afropanameño." *Latin American and Caribbean Ethnic Studies* 3, no. 2 (2008): 123–47.

Crawford, Sharika. "A Transnational World Fractured but Not Forgotten: British West Indian Migration to the Colombian Islands of San Andrés and Providence." *New West Indian Guide / Nieuwe West-Indische Gids* 85, nos. 1–2 (2011): 31–52.

Cullather, Nick. *Secret History: The CIA's Classified Account of Its Operations in Guatemala, 1952–54.* Stanford, CA: Stanford University Press, 2006.

Curtis, Ariana. "Become More and More Panamanian: Contemporary Constructions of West Indian Identity in Urban Panama." PhD diss., American University, 2012.

Davidson, Emily. "Among Spectators and Agents of History: Navigating through Memory Sites of the Panama Canal." *Global South* 6, no. 2 (2013): 130–53.

Davis, James. *Eric Walrond: A Life in the Harlem Renaissance and the Transatlantic Caribbean.* New York: Columbia University Press, 2015.

Davis, Raymond Allan. "West Indian Workers on the Panama Canal: A Split Labor Market Interpretation." PhD diss., Stanford University, 1981.

de la Rosa Sánchez, Manuel. "El negro en Panamá." In *Presencia africana en centroamérica*, edited by Luz María Martinez Montiel, 217–89. Mexico City: Consejo Nacional Para la Cultura y las Artes, 1993.

del Cid Felipe, José Alberto. *Camino a la libertad: Realidad histórica de los hechos que rodearon; Antes y después, la gesta patriótica del 9 de Enero de 1964.* Panama City: Imprenta de la Universidad de Panamá, 2014.

del Vasto Rodríguez, César Enrique. *Historia del Partido Comunista de Panamá (1930–1943).* Panama City: Universal Books, 2002.

del Vasto Rodríguez, César Enrique. *Historia del Partido del Pueblo, 1943–1968.* Panama City: Editorial Universitaria Carlos Manuel Gasteazoro, 1999.

Dixon, Kwame, and John Burdick, eds. *Comparative Perspectives on Afro-Latin America.* Gainesville: University Press of Florida, 2014.

Donoghue, Michael E. *Borderland on the Isthmus: Race, Culture, and the Struggle for the Canal Zone.* Durham, NC: Duke University Press, 2014.

Donoghue, Michael E. "Imperial Sunset: Race, Identity, and Gender in the Panama Canal Zone, 1939–1979." PhD diss., University of Connecticut, 2006.

Donoghue, Michael E. "Race, Labor, and Security in the Panama Canal Zone: The 1946 Greaves Rape Case, Local 713, and the Isthmian Cold War Crackdown." In *Race, Ethnicity, and the Cold War: A Global Perspective*, edited by Phillip E. Muehlenbeck, 63–90. Nashville, TN: Vanderbilt University Press, 2012.

Downer-Marcel, Joseph M. "ARENEP—Acción Reinvidicadora Del Negro Panameño: A Community Grass Roots Organization (and Social Movement)." PhD diss., Michigan State University, 1997.

Du Bois, W. E. B. *The Correspondence of W. E. B. Du Bois.* Vol. 3, *Selections, 1944–1963.* Edited by Herbert Aptheker. Amherst: University of Massachusetts Press, 1997.

Duke, Dawn. "Black Movement Militancy in Panama: SAMAAP's Reliance on an Identity of West Indianness." *Latin American and Caribbean Ethnic Studies* 5, no. 1 (2010): 75–83.

Duncan, Quince. "El negro en Panamá." In *El negro en centroamérica: Panamá, Costa Rica, Nicaragua, Honduras, Guatemala, Belice*, edited by Santiago Valencia Chala, 66–75. Quito, Ecuador: Centro Cultural Afro-Ecuatoriano (Ed-Abya-Yala), 1986.

Durling Arango, Virginia. *La inmigración prohibida*. Panama City: Publicaciones Jurídicas de Panamá, 1999.

Edmondson, Belinda. *Caribbean Middlebrow: Leisure Culture and the Middle Class*. Ithaca, NY: Cornell University Press, 2009.

Edwards, Brent Hayes. *The Practice of Diaspora: Literature, Translation, and the Rise of Black Internationalism*. Cambridge, MA: Harvard University Press, 2003.

Escobar, Felipe Juan. *Arnulfo Arias o el credo panameñista, 1903–1940*. Panama City: Imprenta La Academia, 1942.

Escobar Bethancourt, Rómulo. *Torrijos: Colonia Americana, No!* Bogotá: Carlos Valencia Editores, 1981.

Estrella, Amarilys. "Muertos Civiles: Mourning the Casualties of Racism in the Dominican Republic." *Transforming Anthropology* 28, no. 1 (2020): 41–57.

Euraque, Dario. "The Threat of Blackness to the Mestizo Nation: Race and Ethnicity in the Honduran Banana Economy, 1920s and 1930s." In *Banana Wars: Power, Production, and History in the Americas*, edited by Steve Striffler and Mark Moberg, 229–52. Durham, NC: Duke University Press, 2003.

Euraque, Dario, Jeffrey Gould, and Charles R. Hale, eds. *Memorias del mestizaje: Cultura política en centroamérica de 1920 al presente*. Antigua, Guatemala: Centro de Investigaciones Regionales de Mesoamérica, 2004.

Evangelista, Javiela. "Reshaping National Imaginations in the Midst of Civil Genocide: Denationalization in the Dominican Republic and Transnational Activism." PhD diss., The Graduate Center—City University of New York, 2016.

Ewing, Adam. "Caribbean Labour Politics in the Age of Garvey, 1918–1938." *Race and Class* 55, no. 1 (2013): 23–45.

Finchelstein, Federico. *Transatlantic Fascism: Ideology, Violence, and the Sacred in Argentina and Italy, 1919–1945*. Durham, NC: Duke University Press, 2010.

Fortune, Armando. *Obras selectas*. Edited by Gerardo Maloney. Panama City: Instituto Nacional de Cultura, 1994.

Franks, Julie. "Property Rights and the Commercialization of Land in the Dominican Sugar Zone, 1880–1924." *Latin American Perspectives* 26, no. 1 (1999): 106–28.

Frederick, Rhonda. *"Colón Man a Come": Mythographies of Panama Canal Migration*. Lanham, MD: Lexington Books, 2005.

Fuente, Alejandro de la, and George Reid Andrews, eds. *Afro-Latin American Studies: An Introduction*. Cambridge: Cambridge University Press, 2018.

Gandásegui (hijo), Marco A. "Democracia y movimientos sociales en Panamá en el centenario de la República." *Latin Americanist* 47, nos. 1–2 (2003): 35–70.

García B., Pantaleón. "Chiarismo vs. Acción Comunal: 2 de Enero de 1931." *Revista Cultural Lotería*, no. 527 (2016): 6–26.

García B., Pantaleón. *La doctrina Monroe, el destino manifiesto, el ferrocarril de Panamá y las rivalidades anglosajonas por el control de la América Central: Ensayos sobre las relaciones entre Panamá y los Estados Unidos*. Panama City: Imprenta de la Universidad, 1998.

García Ferreira, Roberto. *La CIA y el caso Arbenz*. Guatemala: Universidad de San Carlos de Guatemala, Centro de Estudios Urbanos y Regionales, 2009.

García-Peña, Lorgia. *The Borders of Dominicanidad: Race, Nation, and Archives of Contradiction.* Durham, NC: Duke University Press, 2016.

Garvey, Marcus. *The Marcus Garvey and Universal Negro Improvement Association Papers.* Vol. 12, *The Caribbean Diaspora, 1910–1920.* Edited by John Dixon, Mariela Haro Rodriguez, Anthony Yuen, and Robert A. Hill. Durham, NC: Duke University Press, 2014.

Gaskin, Edward A. *Blacks Played Significant Role in Improving Life on the Isthmus of Panamá.* Balboa, Ancon: Gebsa de Panama, 1984.

Geggus, David. "The Sounds and Echoes of Freedom: The Impact of the Haitian Revolution." In *Beyond Slavery: The Multilayered Legacy of Africa in Latin America and the Caribbean,* edited by Darién J. Davis, 19–36. Lanham, MD: Rowman and Littlefield, 2007.

Giddings, Paula J. *When and Where I Enter: The Impact of Black Women on Race and Sex in America.* New York: Morrow, 1996.

Gill, Tiffany M. *Beauty Shop Politics: African American Women's Activism in the Beauty Industry.* Urbana: University of Illinois Press, 2010.

Gilroy, Paul. *The Black Atlantic: Modernity and Double Consciousness.* Cambridge, MA: Harvard University Press, 1993.

Giovannetti-Torres, Jorge L. *Black British Migrants in Cuba: Race, Labor, and Empire in the Twentieth-Century Caribbean, 1898–1948.* Cambridge: Cambridge University Press, 2019.

Giovannetti-Torres, Jorge L. "The Elusive Organization of 'Identity': Race, Religion, and Empire among Caribbean Migrants in Cuba." *Small Axe* 10, no. 1 (2006): 1–27.

Glazer, Nathan, and Daniel P. Moynihan. *Beyond the Melting Pot: The Negroes, Puerto Ricans, Jews, Italians, and Irish of New York City.* Cambridge, MA: MIT Press, 1963.

Gleijeses, Piero. *Shattered Hope: The Guatemalan Revolution and the United States, 1944–54.* Princeton, NJ: Princeton University Press, 1991.

Goffe, Tao Leigh. "Albums of Inclusion: The Photographic Poetics of Caribbean Chinese Visual Kinship." *Small Axe* 22, no. 2 (2018): 35–56.

Gólcher, Ileana, Margarita Vázquez, and Juana Camargo. *Cien mujeres por la vida y la dignidad nacional.* Panama City: Universidad de Panamá, Facultad de Humanidades, 2005.

Gonzalez, Lélia. "A mulher negra na sociedade brasileira." In *O lugar da mulher: Estudos sobre a condição feminina na sociedade actual,* edited by Madel T. Luz, 87–106. Rio de Janeiro: Edições Graal, 1982.

Gonzalez, Lélia. "Racismo e sexismo na cultura brasileira." In *Movimientos sociais urbanos, minorias étnicas e outros estudos,* edited by Luis Antônio Machada da Silva, 233–44. Brasília: Associação Nacional de Pós-Graduação e Pesquisa em Ciências Sociais, 1983.

Grandin, Greg. *The Last Colonial Massacre: Latin America in the Cold War.* Chicago: University of Chicago Press, 2011.

Greene, Julie. *The Canal Builders: Making America's Empire at the Panama Canal.* New York: Penguin, 2009.

Gudmundson, Lowell, and Justin Wolfe, eds. *Blacks and Blackness in Central America: Between Race and Place.* Durham, NC: Duke University Press, 2010.

Gudmundson, Lowell, and Justin Wolfe. Introduction to Gudmundson and Wolfe, *Blacks and Blackness in Central America*, 1–23.

Guizado, José Ramón. *El extraño asesinato del Presidente Remón*. Barcelona: Editorial Linomonograph, 1964.

Guridy, Frank Andre. *Forging Diaspora: Afro-Cubans and African Americans in a World of Empire and Jim Crow*. Chapel Hill: University of North Carolina Press, 2010.

Hall, K. Melchor Quick. *Naming a Transnational Black Feminist Framework*. New York: Routledge, 2020.

Hall, Stuart. "Cultural Identity and Diaspora." In *Identity, Community, Culture, Difference*, edited by Jonathan Rutherford, 222–37. London: Lawrence and Wishart, 1990.

Handlin, Oscar. *The Newcomers: Negroes and Puerto Ricans in a Changing Metropolis*. Cambridge, MA: Harvard University Press, 1959.

Hanson, Joyce Ann. *Mary McLeod Bethune and Black Women's Political Activism*. Columbia: University of Missouri Press, 2003.

Harpelle, Ronald. "Bananas and Business: West Indians and United Fruit in Costa Rica." *Race and Class* 42, no. 1 (2000): 57–72.

Harpelle, Ronald. "Cross Currents in the Western Caribbean: Marcus Garvey and the U.N.I.A. in Central America." *Caribbean Studies* 31, no. 1 (2003): 35–73.

Harpelle, Ronald. *The West Indians of Costa Rica: Race, Class, and the Integration of an Ethnic Minority*. Montreal: McGill-Queen's University Press, 2001.

Harper, Alda. *Tracing the Course and Growth and Development of Educational Policy for the Canal Zone Colored Schools, 1905–1955*. Ann Arbor: University of Michigan School of Education, 1979.

Herman, Rebecca. "The Global Politics of Anti-Racism: A View from the Canal Zone." *American Historical Review* 125, no. 2 (2020): 460–86.

Hidalgo Villarreal, Verónica, Nyasha Warren, and Lina Lay Mendivil. "Panorama de la situación de las mujeres afrodescendiente en las ciencias: El caso de Panamá." *Revista Debates Insubmissos* 3, no. 10 (2020): 129–44.

Hintzen, Amelia. "'A Veil of Legality': The Contested History of Anti-Haitian Ideology under the Trujillo Dictatorship." *New West Indian Guide / Nieuwe West-Indische Gids* 90, nos. 1–2 (2016): 28–54.

Hoffnung-Garskof, Jesse. "The Migrations of Arturo Schomburg: On Being Antillano, Negro, and Puerto Rican in New York, 1891–1938." *Journal of American Ethnic History*, no. 21 (2001): 3–49.

Hoffnung-Garskof, Jesse. *Racial Migrations: New York City and the Revolutionary Politics of the Spanish Caribbean*. Princeton, NJ: Princeton University Press, 2019.

Hooker, Juliet. "'Beloved Enemies': Race and Official Mestizo Nationalism in Nicaragua." *Latin American Research Review* 40, no. 3 (2005): 14–39.

Howe, James. *A People Who Would Not Kneel: Panama, the United States, and the San Blas Kuna*. Washington, DC: Smithsonian Institution Press, 1998.

Hull, Gloria T., Patricia Bell Scott, and Barbara Smith, eds. *All the Women Are White, All the Blacks Are Men, but Some of Us Are Brave: Black Women's Studies*. New York: Feminist Press, 1982.

Iber, Patrick. *Neither Peace nor Freedom: The Cultural Cold War in Latin America.* Cambridge, MA: Harvard University Press, 2015.

Jaén Suarez, Omar. *La presencia africana en Panamá.* Vol. 7. Panama City: Biblioteca de la Cultura Panameña, 1981.

Jaén Suarez, Omar. *Panamá soberana, el 9 de enero de 1964: Sus causas, los eventos y sus consecuencias.* Panama City: Expedición del Istmo, 2013.

James, Winston. *Holding Aloft the Banner of Ethiopia: Caribbean Radicalism in Early Twentieth-Century America.* London: Verso, 1998.

Jiménez Román, Miriam, and Juan Flores, eds. *The Afro-Latin@ Reader: History and Culture in the United States.* Durham, NC: Duke University Press, 2010.

Jones, Martha S. *Birthright Citizens: A History of Race and Rights in Antebellum America.* Cambridge: Cambridge University Press, 2018.

Joseph, Gilbert M., and Greg Grandin, eds. *A Century of Revolution: Insurgent and Counterinsurgent Violence during Latin America's Long Cold War.* Durham, NC: Duke University Press, 2010.

Katagiri, Yasuhiro. *Black Freedom, White Resistance, and Red Menace: Civil Rights and Anticommunism in the Jim Crow South.* Baton Rouge: Louisiana State University Press, 2014.

Kelley, Robin D. G. *Freedom Dreams: The Black Radical Imagination.* Boston: Beacon, 2002.

King, Tiffany Lethabo. "Black 'Feminisms' and Pessimism: Abolishing Moynihan's Negro Family." *Theory and Event* 21 no. 1 (2018): 68–87.

King H., Thelma. *El problema de la soberanía en las relaciones entre Panamá y los Estados Unidos de América.* Panama City: Ministerio de Educación, 1961.

Knapp, Herbert, and Mary Knapp. *Red, White, and Blue Paradise: The American Canal Zone in Panama.* San Diego, CA: Harcourt Brace Jovanovich, 1984.

Korrol, Virginia E. Sánchez. *From Colonia to Community: The History of Puerto Ricans in New York City.* Berkeley: University of California Press, 1983.

La Boca Normal Training School. *The Thinker—1944.* Yearbook. La Boca, Canal Zone: La Boca Normal Training School, 1944.

La Boca School. *La Bocan.* Yearbook. Panama City: Star and Herald, 1940.

LaFeber, Walter. *The Panama Canal: The Crisis in Historical Perspective.* New York: Oxford University Press, 1978.

Lasso, Marixa. *Erased: The Untold Story of the Panama Canal.* Cambridge, MA: Harvard University Press, 2019.

Lasso, Marixa. "Nationalism and Immigrant Labor in a Tropical Enclave: The West Indians of Colón City, 1850–1936." *Citizenship Studies* 17, no. 5 (2013): 551–65.

Lasso, Marixa. "Race and Ethnicity in the Formation of Panamanian National Identity: Panamanian Discrimination against Chinese and West Indians in the Thirties." *Revista Panameña de Política* 4 (2007): 61–92.

Lawson, A. L. *Panamá y sus hijos negros.* Panama City: n.p., n.d.

Lee, Ana Paulina. *Mandarin Brazil: Race, Representation, and Memory.* Stanford, CA: Stanford University Press, 2018.

Lee, Erika. "The 'Yellow Peril' and Asian Exclusion in the Americas." *Pacific Historical Review* 76, no. 4 (2007): 537–62.

Lee, Sonia Song-Ha. *Building a Latino Civil Rights Movement: Puerto Ricans, African Americans, and the Pursuit of Racial Justice in New York City*. Chapel Hill: University of North Carolina Press, 2014.

Leeds, Asia. "Toward the 'Higher Type of Womanhood': The Gendered Contours of Garveyism and the Making of Redemptive Geographies in Costa Rica, 1922–1941." *Palimpsest: A Journal on Women, Gender, and the Black International* 2, no. 1 (2013): 1–27.

Lee-Loy, Anne-Marie. "An Antiphonal Announcement: Jamaica's Anti-Chinese Legislation in Transnational Context." *Journal of Asian American Studies* 18, no. 2 (2015): 141–64.

Lioeanjie, René Charles. *Cuarenta años de lucha de la National Maritime Union of America: AFL-CIO a favor de los trabajadores del área del Canal de Panamá, 1963–2003*. Panama City: Imprenta Novo Art, 2003.

Lizcano, Francisco. "La población negra en el istmo centroamericano." In *Presencia africana en centroamérica*, edited by Luz María Martínez Montiel, 31–59. Mexico City: Consejo Nacional Para la Cultura y las Artes, 1993.

Lowe de Goodin, Melva. *Afrodescendientes en el Istmo de Panamá, 1501–2012*. Panama City: Editora Sibauste, 2012.

Lowe de Goodin, Melva. *De Barbados a Panamá: From Barbados to Panama*. Panama: Editora Géminis, 1999.

Lowe de Goodin, Melva. "La fuerza laboral afroantillana en la construcción del Canal de Panamá." Edición Especial, *Revista Cultural Lotería* 1 (July 1999): 121–44.

Lynch, Shola, dir. *Chisholm '72: Unbought and Unbossed*. Documentary. Calabasas, CA: Lantern Lane Entertainment and REALside Production, 2004.

MacPherson, Anne. "Colonial Matriarchs: Garveyism, Maternalism, and Belize's Black Cross Nurses, 1920–1952." *Gender and History* 15, no. 3 (2003): 507–27.

Makalani, Minkah. *In the Cause of Freedom: Radical Black Internationalism from Harlem to London, 1917–1939*. Chapel Hill: University of North Carolina Press, 2011.

Maloney, Gerardo. *El Canal de Panamá y los trabajadores antillanos*. Panama City: Universidad de Panamá, 1989.

Maloney, Gerardo. "El movimiento negro en Panamá." *Revista Panameña de Sociología*, no. 5 (1989): 144–58.

Maloney, Gerardo. "La contribución de Armando Fortune al estudio y comprensión del negro en Panamá." In *Obras Selectas*, by Armando Fortune, edited by G. Maloney, 9–34. Panama City: Instituto Nacional de Cultura, 1993.

Maloney, Gerardo. "Los afropanameños y la cultura nacional." In *Visiones del sector cultural en centroamérica*, edited by Jesús Oyambun, 409–18. San José, Costa Rica: Centro Cultural de España, 2000.

Maloney, Gerardo. "Significado de la presencia y contribución del afro antillano en la nación panameña." In *Historia General de Panamá*, 152–71. Panama City: Comité Nacional del Centenario, 2004.

Marable, Manning. *Malcolm X: A Life of Reinvention*. New York: Viking, 2011.

Marable, Manning, and Vanessa Agard-Jones, eds. *Transnational Blackness: Navigating the Global Color Line*. New York: Macmillan, 2008.

Marco Serra, Yolanda. "El movimiento sufragista en Panamá y la construcción de la mujer moderna." In *Historia de los movimientos de mujeres en Panamá en el siglo XX*, edited by Fernando Aparicio, Yolanda Marco Serra, Miriam Miranda, and Josefina Zurita, 45–132. Panama City: Agenda del Centenario, Universidad de Panamá, 2002.

Marco Serra, Yolanda. "Los debates acerca de la condición femenina y el feminismo en Panamá, 1911–1922." *Revista del CESLA: International Latin American Studies Review* 21 (2018): 89–102.

Marshall, Paule. "Black Immigrant Women in *Brown Girl, Brownstones*." In *Caribbean Life in New York City: Sociocultural Dimensions*, edited by Constance R. Sutton and Elsa Chaney, 81–85. New York: Center for Migration Studies, 1987.

Marshall, Paule. *Brown Girl, Brownstones*. New York: Random House, 1959.

Martinez H., Milton. "Luchas populares en Colón (1850–1980)." In *Colón al calor de sus luchas: Aporte a la historia popular*, 63–144. Panama City: Centro de Estudios y Acción Social de Panamá (CEASPA), 1983.

Martínez Mauri, Mónica. *La autonomía indígena en Panamá: La experiencia del pueblo kuna (siglos XVI–XXI)*. Quito: Ediciones Abya-Yala, 2011.

Materno Vásquez, Juan. *Omar Torrijos*. Panama City: Litografía e Imprenta LIL, 1987.

May McNeil, Dorothy. "Traducción de la correspondencia epístolar de los emigrantes antillanos en el istmo de Panamá en el siglo XIX." *Boletín de la Academia Panameña de la Historia*, nos. 29–30 (1981): 5–61.

McDuffie, Erick. *Sojourning for Freedom: Black Women, American Communism, and the Making of Black Left Feminism*. Durham, NC: Duke University Press, 2011.

McGraw, Jason. *The Work of Recognition: Caribbean Colombia and the Postemancipation Struggle for Citizenship*. Chapel Hill: University of North Carolina Press, 2014.

McGuiness, Aims. *Path of Empire: Panama and the California Gold Rush*. The United States in the World. Ithaca, NY: Cornell University Press, 2008.

McKittrick, Katherine. *Demonic Grounds: Black Women and the Cartographies of Struggle*. Minneapolis: University of Minnesota Press, 2006.

McLean Araúz, Mauricio. *Xenofobia: En las cuatro primeras décadas de la república de Panamá*. Panama City: Editorial Universitaria Carlos Manuel Gasteazoro, EUPAN, 2016.

McLean Petras, Elizabeth. *Jamaican Labor Migration: White Capital and Black Labor, 1850–1930*. Boulder, CO: Westview Press, 1988.

McLeod, Marc C. "'Sin Dejar de Ser Cubanos': Cuban Blacks and the Challenges of Garveyism in Cuba." *Caribbean Studies* 31, no. 1 (2003): 75–105.

McLeod, Marc C. "Undesirable Aliens: Race, Ethnicity, and Nationalism in the Comparison of Haitian and British West Indian Workers in Cuba, 1912–1939." *Journal of Social History* 31, no. 3 (1998): 599–623.

McPherson, Alan. "Rioting for Dignity: Masculinity, National Identity and Anti-US Resistance in Panama." *Gender and History* 19, no. 2 (2007): 219–41.

McPherson, Alan. *Yankee No! Anti-Americanism in U.S.-Latin American Relations*. Cambridge, MA: Harvard University Press, 2003.

Mendeita, Adela, and Rogelio Husband. "Contribución del afro-antillano a la identidad nacional." Master's thesis, Universidad de Panamá, 1997.

Meneses Araúz, Eunice. "Informe Sombra Ante El CERD Panama." Panama City: Coordinadora Nacional de Organizaciones Negras Panameñas, February 11, 2010.

Milazzo, Marzia. "White Supremacy, White Knowledge, and Anti–West Indian Discourse in Panama: Olmedo Alfaro's *El Peligro Antillano En La América Central*." *Global South* 6, no. 2 (2013): 65–86.

Miller, Beverly A. King. "The Experiences of Panamanian Afro-Caribbean Women in STEM: Voices to Inform Work with Black Females in STEM Education." PhD diss., University of New Mexico, 2013.

Mirabal, Nancy Raquel. *Suspect Freedoms: The Racial and Sexual Politics of Cubanidad in New York, 1823–1957*. New York: New York University Press, 2017.

Molina Castillo, Mario José. *La tragedia del color en el Panamá colonial, 1501–1821: Panamá, una sociedad esclavista en el período colonial*. Panama City: Impresos Modernos, 2011.

Moreno Vega, Marta, Marinieves Alba, and Yvette Modestin, eds. *Women Warriors of the Afro-Latino Diaspora*. Houston: Arte Público Press, 2012.

Morris, Courtney Desiree. "Becoming Creole, Becoming Black: Migration, Diasporic Self-Making, and the Many Lives of Madame Maymie Leona Turpeau de Mena." *Women, Gender, and Families of Color* 4, no. 2 (2016): 171–95.

Moynihan, Daniel P. *The Negro Family: The Case for National Action*. Washington, DC: Department of Labor / US Government Printing Office, 1965.

Múnera, Alfonso. *Fronteras imaginadas: La construcción de las razas y de la geografía en el siglo XIX Colombiano*. Bogotá: Editorial Planeta Colombia, 2005.

Murphy, Patricia Gill. "Antillean Pioneers: Migrant Education and Social Change." Paper Presented at Caribbean Studies Association Conference, Santo Domingo, Dominican Republic, May 25–29, 1983.

Myers Asch, Chris. *Chocolate City: A History of Race and Democracy in the Nation's Capital*. Chapel Hill: University of North Carolina Press, 2017.

Navarro, Alfredo Figueroa. *Dominio y sociedad en el Panamá Colombiano (1821–1903)*. Panama City: Impresora Panamá, 1978.

Newton, Velma. *The Silver Men: West Indian Labour Migration to Panama, 1850–1914*. 3rd ed. Kingston, Jamaica: Ian Randle, 1984.

Ngai, Mae M. *Impossible Subjects: Illegal Aliens and the Making of Modern America*. Politics and Society in Modern America. Princeton, NJ: Princeton University Press, 2004.

Noer, Thomas. "Segregationists and the World: The Foreign Policy of the White Resistance." In *Window on Freedom: Race, Civil Rights, and Foreign Affairs, 1945–1988*, edited by Brenda Gayle Plummer, 141–62. Chapel Hill: University of North Carolina Press, 2003.

Nwankwo, Ifeoma C. K. "Bilingualism, Blackness, and Belonging: The Racial and Generational Politics of Linguistic Transnationalism in Panama." In *Black Writing, Culture, and the State in Latin America*, edited by Jerome C. Branche, 171–92. Nashville, TN: Vanderbilt University Press, 2015.

Nwankwo, Ifeoma C. K. *Black Cosmopolitanism: Racial Consciousness, and Transnational Identity in the Nineteenth-Century Americas*. Philadelphia, PA: University of Pennsylvania Press, 2005.

Opie, Frederick Douglass. *Black Labor Migration in Caribbean Guatemala, 1882–1923*. Gainesville: University Press of Florida, 2009.

Opie, Frederick Douglass. "Eating, Dancing, and Courting in New York Black and Latino Relations, 1930–1970." *Journal of Social History* 42, no. 1 (2008): 79–109.

O'Reggio, Trevor. *Between Alienation and Citizenship: The Evolution of Black West Indian Society in Panama, 1914–1964*. Lanham, MD: University Press of America, 2006.

Osborne, Alfred E. "Biographical Sketches of Pioneers." In *Pioneers in Canal Zone Education*, edited by George Westerman, 12–20. La Boca, Canal Zone: La Boca Occupational High School Shop, 1949.

Osorio Ugarte, Katti. "El edificio del museo afroantillano de Panamá: Importante legado cultural e histórico construido en madera." *Canto Rodado* 8 (2013): 133–53.

Parker, Jason. "'Capital of the Caribbean': The African American–West Indian 'Harlem Nexus' and the Transnational Drive for Black Freedom, 1940–1948." *Journal of African American History* 89, no. 2 (2004): 98–118.

Parker, Jeffrey W. "Sex at the Crossroads: The Gender Politics of Racial Uplift and Afro-Caribbean Activism in Panama, 1918–1932." *Women, Gender, and Families of Color* 4, no. 2 (2016): 196–221.

Paschel, Tianna. *Becoming Black Political Subjects: Movements and Ethno-Racial Rights in Colombia and Brazil*. Princeton, NJ: Princeton University Press, 2016.

Paterson, James T. *Freedom Is Not Enough: The Moynihan Report and America's Struggles over Black Life: From LBJ to Obama*. New York: Basic Books, 2010.

Patterson, Tiffany Ruby, and Robin D. G. Kelley. "Unfinished Migrations: Reflections on the African Diaspora and the Making of the Modern World." *African Studies Review* 43, no. 1 (2000): 11–45.

Paulino, Edward. "Erasing the Kreyol from the Margins of the Dominican Republic: The Pre- and Post-Nationalization Project of the Border, 1930–1945." *Wadabagei: A Journal of the Caribbean and Its Diasporas* 8, no. 2 (2005): 35–71.

Pearcy, Thomas L. "Panama's Generation of '31: Patriots, Praetorians, and a Decade of Discord." *Hispanic American Historical Review* 76, no. 4 (1996): 691–719.

Peña, Concha. *José Antonio Remón Cantera: Ensayo de biografía con notas de mi cuaderno de periodista*. Panama City: Editora La Nación, 1955.

Pérez Pimentel, Rodolfo. "Olmedo Alfaro Paredes." In *Diccionario Biográfico Ecuador*, edited by R. Pérez Pimentel, 8–17. Guayaquil: Editorial Universidad de Guayaquil, 1994.

Pippin, Larry LaRae. *The Remón Era: An Analysis of a Decade of Events in Panama, 1947–1957*. Stanford, CA: Stanford University Press, 1964.

Pizzurno Gelós, Patricia. *El discurso eugenésico en Panamá: Herencia, pobreza y raza, 1920–1960*. Panama City: Editoral Portobelo, 2018.

Pizzurno Gelós, Patricia. *Memorias e imaginarios de identidad y raza en Panamá, siglos XIX y XX*. Panama City: Editorial Mariano Arosemena, 2011.

Porras, Hernán F. *Papel histórico de los grupos humanos de Panamá*. Panama City: Biblioteca de la Nacionalidad, 1999.

Priestley, George. "¿Afroantillanos o Afropanameños?: La participación política y las políticas de identidad durante y después de las negociaciones de los tratados

Torrijos-Carter." In *Piel oscura Panamá: Ensayos y reflexiones al filo del centenario*, 185–227. Panama City: Editorial Universitaria, Carlos Manuel Gasteazoro, 2003.

Priestley, George. "El sentido de la vida, la identidad y el corazón de la Tía Anesta." In *Piel oscura Panamá: Ensayos y reflexiones al filo del centenario*, 87–90. Panama City: Editorial Universitaria, Carlos Manuel Gasteazoro, 2003.

Priestley, George. "Etnia, clase y cuestión nacional en Panamá: Análisis de estudios recientes." Translated by Velma Newman. *Tareas*, no. 67 (1987): 35–62.

Priestley, George. *Military Government and Popular Participation in Panama*. Boulder, CO: Westview, 1986.

Priestley, George. "Raza y nacionalismo: George Westerman y la 'cuestión' antillana 1940–1960." In *Piel oscura Panamá: Ensayos y reflexiones al filo del centenario*, 93–131. Panama City: Editorial Universitaria, Carlos Manuel Gasteazoro, 2003.

Priestley, George, and Alberto Barrow. "The Black Movement in Panama: A Historical and Political Interpretation." *Souls* 10, no. 3 (2008): 227–55.

Priestley, George, and Gerardo Maloney. "El grupo antillano en el proceso político panameño." *Tareas*, no. 33 (1975): 11–27.

Pulido Ritter, Luis. "Notas sobre Eric Walrond, la inmigración caribeña y la transnacionalidad literaria en Panamá: Una excursión por las calles de la memoria, la reflexión y los espacios en movimiento." *Cuadernos Inter.C.A.Mbio sobre Centroamérica y el Caribe* 5, no. 6 (2008): 175–80.

Purcell, Trevor W. *Banana Fallout: Class, Color, and Culture among West Indians in Costa Rica*. Los Angeles: Center for Afro-American Studies, University of California, 1993.

Purnell, Brian. *Fighting Jim Crow in the County of Kings: The Congress of Racial Equality in Brooklyn*. Lexington: University Press of Kentucky, 2013.

Purnell, Brian. "'Taxation without Sanitation Is Tyranny': Civil Rights Struggles over Garbage Collection in Brooklyn, New York, during the Fall of 1962." In *Civil Rights in New York City: From World War II to the Giuliani Era*, edited by Clarence Taylor, 52–76. New York: Fordham University Press, 2011.

Putnam, Lara. "Circum-Atlantic Print Circuits and Internationalism from the Peripheries in the Interwar Era." In *Print Culture Histories beyond the Metropolis*, edited by James J. Connolly, Patrick Collier, Frank Felsenstein, Kenneth R. Hall, and Robert G. Hall, 216–39. Toronto: University of Toronto Press, 2016.

Putnam, Lara. "Citizenship from the Margins: Vernacular Theories of Rights and the State from the Interwar Caribbean." *Journal of British Studies* 53, no. 1 (2014): 162–91.

Putnam, Lara. "Eventually Alien: The Multigenerational Saga of British West Indians in Central America, 1870–1940." In *Blacks and Blackness in Central America: Between Race and Place*, edited by Lowell Gudmundson and Justin Wolfe, 278–306. Durham, NC: Duke University Press, 2010.

Putnam, Lara. *Radical Moves: Caribbean Migrants and the Politics of Race in the Jazz Age*. Chapel Hill: University of North Carolina Press, 2013.

Putnam, Lara. "Sidney Young, the Panama Tribune, and the Geography of Belonging." Paper presented at American Historical Association Annual Meeting, Washington, DC, January 2–5, 2014.

Queeley, Andrea. "El Puente: Transnationalism among Cubans of English-Speaking Caribbean Descent." *African and Black Diaspora: An International Journal* 5, no. 1 (2012): 105–22.

Queeley, Andrea. *Rescuing Our Roots: The African Anglo-Caribbean Diaspora in Contemporary Cuba.* Gainesville: University Press of Florida, 2015.

Rabe, Stephen G. *Eisenhower and Latin America: The Foreign Policy of Anticommunism.* Austin: University of Texas Press, 1988.

Ransby, Barbara. *Eslanda: The Large and Unconventional Life of Mrs. Paul Robeson.* New Haven, CT: Yale University Press, 2013.

Reggiani, Andres H. "Depopulation, Fascism, and Eugenics in 1930s Argentina." *Hispanic American Historical Review* 90, no. 2 (2010): 283–318.

Reid, Ira de Augustine. *The Negro Immigrant: His Background, Characteristics, and Social Adjustment, 1899–1937.* New York: Columbia University Press, 1939.

Reid, Roberto. "Don Pedro N. Rhodes." *The Silver People Chronicle* (blog), January 12, 2009. http://thesilverpeoplechronicle.com/2009/01/don-pedro-n-rhodes.html.

Rhenals Doria, Ana Milena, and Francisco Javier Flórez Bolívar. "Escogiendo entre los extranjeros 'indeseables': Afro-antillanos, sirio-libaneses, raza e inmigración en Colombia, 1880–1937." *Anuario Colombiano de Historia Social y de la Cultura* 40, no. 1 (2013): 243–71.

Richards, Yevette. *Maida Springer: Pan-Africanist and International Labor Leader.* Pittsburgh, PA: University of Pittsburgh Press, 2000.

Rivera-Rideau, Petra R., Jennifer A. Jones, and Tianna S. Paschel, eds. *Afro-Latin@s in Movement: Critical Approaches to Blackness and Transnationalism in the Americas.* New York: Palgrave Macmillan, 2016.

Robeson, Paul, Jr. *The Undiscovered Paul Robeson: Quest for Freedom, 1939–1976.* New York: Wiley, 2001.

Robinson, William Francis. "The Arias Madrid Brothers: Nationalist Politics in Panama." PhD diss., Auburn University, 2000.

Robinson, William Francis. "Panama for the Panamanians: The Populism of Arnulfo Arias Madrid." In *Populism in Latin America*, edited by Michael L. Conniff, 184–200. Tuscaloosa: University of Alabama Press, 2012.

Romeu, José Vicente. *Del caso Remón-Guizado.* Panama City: INAC, Editorial Mariano Arosemena, 2000.

Rosa Sanchez, Manuel de la. "El negro en Panamá." In *Presencia africana en centroamérica*, edited by Luz María Martínez Montiel, 217–89. Mexico City: Consejo Nacional Para la Cultura y las Artes, 1993.

Rubiera Castillo, Daisy. *Reyita, sencillamente: Testimonio de una negra cubana nonagenaria.* Havana: Pro Libros World Data Research Center, 1997.

Russell, Carlos E. *An Old Woman Remembers . . . : The Recollected History of West Indians in Panama, 1855–1955.* Brooklyn: Caribbean Diaspora Press, 1995.

Salabarría Patiño, Max. *El Colón de ayer, 1926–1950.* Panama City: La Impresora de la Nación, 1994.

Salabarría Patiño, Max. *La ciudad de Colón en los predios de la historia.* Panama City: Litho Editorial Chen, 2002.

Samudio, César. *El Canal de Panamá 1903–1955.* Panama City: Imprenta Nacional, 1992.

Sanders, James E. *Contentious Republicans: Popular Politics, Race, and Class in Nineteenth-Century Colombia*. Durham, NC: Duke University Press, 2004.

Senior, Olive. "The Colon People." *Jamaica Journal* 11, no. 3 (1978): 62–71.

Senior, Olive. *Dying to Better Themselves: West Indians and the Building of the Panama Canal*. Kingston, Jamaica: University of West Indies Press, 2014.

Shoaff, Jennifer L. "The Right to a Haitian Name and a Dominican Nationality: La Sentencia (TC 168–13) and the Politics of Recognition and Belonging." *Journal of Haitian Studies* 22, no. 2 (2016): 58–82.

Sigler, Thomas, Kali-Ahset Amen, and K. Angelique Dwyer. "The Heterogenous Isthmus: Transnationalism and Cultural Differentiation in Panama." *Bulletin of Latin American Research* 34, no. 2 (2014): 229–44.

Siu, Lok C. D. *Memories of a Future Home: Diasporic Citizenship of Chinese in Panama*. Stanford, CA: Stanford University Press, 2005.

Smart Chubb, Linda. "Will Trinidad Spurn the Call? (October 13, 1927)." In *Isthmian Echoes: A Selection of the Literary Endeavors of the West Indian Colony in the Republic of Panama*, edited by Sidney A. Young, 139–41. Panama City: Benedetti Hnos, 1928.

St. Clair Drake, John Gibbs, and Horace R. Cayton. *Black Metropolis: A Study of Negro Life in a Northern City*. New York: Harcourt, Brace, 1945.

Stephens, Michelle. *Black Empire: The Masculine Global Imaginary of Caribbean Intellectuals in the United States, 1914–1962*. Durham, NC: Duke University Press, 2005.

Sullivan, Frances Peace. "'Forging Ahead' in Banes, Cuba: Garveyism in a United Fruit Company Town." *New West Indian Guide / Nieuwe West-Indische Gids* 88 (2014): 231–61.

Szok, Peter A. *La Última Gaviota: Liberalism and Nostalgia in Early Twentieth-Century Panama*. Westport, CT: Press, 2001.

Szok, Peter A. *Wolf Tracks: Popular Art and Re-Africanization in Twentieth-Century Panama*. Jackson: University Press of Mississippi, 2012.

Tam, Juan. "Huellas Chinas en Panamá." *Revista Cultural Lotería*, no. 459 (March–April 2005): 1–45.

Tamayo G., Eduardo. "Congresos de la cultura negra de las Américas." In *Afroamericanos: buscando raíces, afirmando identidad*. Vol. 4. Quito: ALAI, 1995. https://www.alainet.org/es/active/999.

Taylor, Clarence, ed. *Civil Rights in New York City: From World War II to the Giuliani Era*. New York: Fordham University Press, 2011.

Taylor, Clarence. "Conservative and Liberal Opposition to the New York City School-Integration Campaign." In *Civil Rights in New York City: From World War II to the Giuliani Era*, 95–117. New York: Fordham University Press, 2011.

Taylor, Ula Yvette. *The Veiled Garvey: The Life and Times of Amy Jacques Garvey*. Chapel Hill: University of North Carolina Press, 2002.

Thomas, Lorrin. *Puerto Rican Citizen: History and Political Identity in Twentieth Century New York City*. Chicago: University of Chicago Press, 2010.

Tinker, Keith L. *The Migration of Peoples from the Caribbean to the Bahamas*. Gainesville: University Press of Florida, 2011.

Torrijos Herrera, Omar. *La quinta frontera: "Partes" de la batalla diplomática sobre el Canal de Panamá*. Ciudad Universitaria Rodrigo Facio, Costa Rica: EDUCA-Editorial Universitaria Centroamericana, 1978.

Trouillot, Michel-Rolph. *Silencing the Past: Power and the Production of History*. Boston: Beacon, 1995.

Turits, Richard L. "A World Destroyed, a Nation Imposed: The 1937 Haitian Massacre in the Dominican Republic." *Hispanic American Historical Review* 82, no. 3 (2002): 589–635.

Turner Yau, Anayansi. *La constitución de 1946 y la constituyente que le dio origen: Análisis del proceso de la formación de las normas constitucionales de 1946*. Panama City: Litho Editorial Chen, 2014.

Vargas, Dalys. *Omar Torrijos Herrera y la patria internacional*. Panama City: Fundación Omar Torrijos, 2004.

Vincent, Ted. "The Garveyite Parents of Malcolm X." *Black Scholar* 20, no. 2 (1989): 10–13.

Vinson, Ben, III. "African (Black) Diaspora History, Latin American History." *Americas* 63, no. 1 (2006): 1–18.

Von Eschen, Penny. *Race against Empire: Black Americans and Anticolonialism, 1937–57*. Ithaca, NY: Cornell University Press, 1997.

Watkins, Patricia. "Los aspectos socio-políticos en la trilogia canalera de Joaquín Beleño." PhD diss., Florida State University, 1996.

Watkins-Owens, Irma. *Blood Relations: Caribbean Immigrants and the Harlem Community, 1900–1930*. Bloomington: Indiana University Press, 1996.

Watson, Sonja Stephenson. *The Politics of Race in Panama: Afro-Hispanic and West Indian Literary Discourses of Contention*. Gainesville: University Press of Florida, 2014.

Westerman, George W. *Blocking Them at the Canal: Failure of the Red Attempt to Control Local Workers in the Vital Panama Canal Area*. Panama City: Imprenta de la Academia, 1952.

Westerman, George W. "Gold vs. Silver Workers in the Canal Zone." *Common Ground* 9, no. 2 (1948): 92–95.

Westerman, George W. "Historical Notes on West Indians on the Isthmus of Panama." *Phylon* 22, no. 4 (1961): 340–50.

Westerman, George W. *Los inmigrantes antillanos en Panamá*. Panama City: La Impresora de la Nación (INAC), 1980.

Westerman, George W. *A Minority Group in Panama: Some Aspects of West Indian Life—Un grupo minoritario en Panamá: Algunos aspectos de la vida de los antillanos*. 1st ed. Panama: Liga Cívica Nacional/National Civic League, 1950.

Westerman, George W., ed. *Pioneers in Canal Zone Education*. La Boca, Canal Zone: La Boca Occupational High School Shop, 1949.

Westerman, George W., ed. *A Plea for Higher Education of Negroes on the Canal Zone*. Panama City: El Panamá América, 1942.

Westerman, George W. *Urban Housing in Panama and Some of Its Problems*. Panamá City: Institute for Economic Development, 1955.

Whitney, Robert, and Graciela Chailloux Laffita. *Subjects or Citizens: British Caribbean Workers in Cuba, 1900–1960*. Gainesville: University Press of Florida, 2013.

Wilder, Craig Steven. *A Covenant with Color: Race and Social Power in Brooklyn.* New York: Columbia University Press, 2000.

Williams, Agatha. "La mujer negra y su inserción en la sociedad panameña." *Tareas* 57 (March 1984): 83–91.

Williams, Agatha. "Presencia de la mujer afropanameña en el istmo." *Revista Cultural Lotería*, no. 411 (April 1997): 71–80.

Wilson, Carlos Guillermo. "Aspectos de la prosa panameña contemporánea." PhD diss., University of California, Los Angeles, 1975.

Wrightstone, Jacob Wayne. *Evaluation of the Higher Horizons Program for Underprivileged Children.* New York: Bureau of Educational Research, Board of Education, 1964.

Young, Kevin A., ed. *Making the Revolution: Histories of the Latin American Left.* Cambridge: Cambridge University Press, 2019.

Young, Sidney A., ed. *Isthmian Echoes: A Selection of the Literary Endeavors of the West Indian Colony in the Republic of Panama.* Panama City: Benedetti Hnos, 1928.

Zenger, Robin Elizabeth. "West Indians in Panama: Diversity and Activism, 1910s–1940s." PhD diss., University of Arizona, 2015.

Zien, Katherine. "Race and Politics in Concert: Paul Robeson and William Warfield in Panama, 1947–1953." *Global South* 6, no. 2 (Fall 2013): 107–29.

Zien, Katherine. *Sovereign Acts: Performing Race, Space, and Belonging in Panama in the Canal Zone.* New Brunswick, NJ: Rutgers University Press, 2017.

Zumoff, Jacob A. "The 1925 Tenant's Strike in Panama: West Indians, the Left, and the Labor Movement." *Americas* 74, no. 4 (2017): 513–46.

Index

Anglophone Caribbean, 1, 8, 40, 44, 96, 119, 136; education in, 64, 72; and Las Servidoras, 160, 163; migrants from, 72, 76, 114, 153, 200n4, 223n13; repatriation to, 51–53; and the *Tribune*, 31, 35–36, 51. *See also* English (language)
Angola, 184
anti-African legislation, 19
anti-Asian legislation, 19, 45–46
anti-Blackness, 6, 31–32, 180, 185–86, 188; anti-Black nationalism, 3, 5, 16, 24, 26, 37, 47, 119–20, 133, 149, 193–94; and mestizaje, 13–19, 21, 44–45, 48, 217n62
anticommunism, 3, 83–96, 99, 101, 117, 120, 192, 212n107
Antigua, 78, 151
anti-imperialism, 26, 37, 102, 122, 184, 194
Antilles, 16
anti-Semitism, 47
anti–West Indian sentiment, 16–17, 19, 25, 48, 115
Aparicio, Fernando, 196n20
Arango, José Agustín, 12
Arango L., C. A., 48
Araúz, Francisco, 82
Arbenz, Jacobo, 117
Archibold P., Eduardo, 116
Argentina, 48, 95
Arias, Arnulfo, 57–64, 73, 103, 156, 158, 205n4, 207n33; 1931 coup, 16, 47, 62, 70; removal from office, 67, 97; second term, 88, 97–98, 157, 214n14
Arias, Harmodio, 47, 49–50, 148
Arias, Ricardo, 137
Arias Paredes, Francisco, 47, 70; 1931 coup, 70
Armstrong, Velma Brown, 161–62, 164
Arosemena, Justo, 146, 196n20
arrabaleros, 10
Asch, Chris Myers, 108
A. S. G., 43–44
Ashwood, Amy, 8
Asian people, 18, 19, 45–46, 58, 195n7. *See also* anti-Asian legislation
Asociación Afro-Panameña, 163, 188, 225n57

assimilation, 4, 20, 31, 56, 149, 163; alleged failures of, 18, 26, 71, 115, 118–20, 130; and the LCN, 68
Azuero, Panama, 13

Bajans, 162, 176, 193, 228n106
Balboa, Panama, 15, 152
Balboa High School, 174
Baptists, 160
Barbados, 7, 9, 24, 31, 40, 151, 153, 157, 176, 228n106
Barbados Advocate, 53
Barletta, Nicolás Ardito, 47
Barrow, Alberto, 231n21
Bayne Smith, Marcia, 176–77
Bazán, José Dominador, 104, 147–49
Bedford-Stuyvesant Youth in Action, 178
Beecher, Clarence, 182–83
Beecher, Robert H., 74, *131*, 159, 164, 182
Beleño, Joaquín, 121, 142; "A Sieve of In-accuracies," 113; "Clear Proof of Criollo Sectarianism," 111–19; *Luna Verde*, 217n62
Belgium, 108, 112
Bell, Albert E., 76
Berrocal, Manuel J., 115
Bethune, Mary McLeod, 175
Bethune-Cookman School, 175
bigotry, 48, 91, 115, 117, 133, 148–49, 185, 194. *See also* anti-Semitism; nativism; racism; xenophobia
bilingualism. *See* multilingualism
Binnom, Rosa, 156–57
Biondi, Martha, 87, 223n15, 225n55
Black internationalism. *See* internationalism
Black Liberation Rally (1971), 184, 230n8
Black Panamanian (term), 27
Black Power movement, 163
Black press, 3, 21, 36–37, 160. *See also indi-vidual journalists and publications*
Black solidarity, 24, 184
Black Solidarity Day, 184
blanqueamiento, 13
Bocas del Toro, Panama, 7, 19, 61, 195nn10–11
Bolivia, 95

chombos (term), 11, 48, 51, 194

Christianity, 159–60. *See also* Baptists; Catholicism; Episcopalians; Protestantism

circum-Caribbean world, 2, 5, 28

Citizens Committee to End Silver-Gold Jim Crow in Panama, 83

citizenship, 6, 191, 205n4, 220n34; activism around, 25–27, 57–92, 102–11, 120–22, 147, 192–93; and assimilation, 120–21; colonial, 8, 31; conditional, 122–23, 126, 147, 149; and the Constitution, 32, 59–73, 78–80, 97, 151, 186; and criollos, 111–16, 142; and depopulation, 122–30; dual citizenship, 186, 189; and dual wage system, 14–15, 83, 99–100, 122–23, 197n29, 198n32; exclusion from, 2–3, 20–21, 26, 32, 59–62, 97, 103, 122–26, 185–86; gendered, 208n45; jus sanguinis (lineage-based), 70, 78; jus soli (birth-based), 5, 20, 32, 56, 58–72, 91, 112, 144, 149, 156–58, 164, 226n64; and New York-based Panamanians, 151–52, 155–58, 161, 164–66, 174, 176; questionable, 92, 123, 127, 135, 140, 161; republican, 31; and ser panameño discourse, 134–39, 146–49; and the *Tribune*, 31–32, 37, 205n6; US, 14–15, 17, 23, 78, 80–81, 83, 94, 99–100, 105, 107, 123–24, 130, 146, 156, 164–66, 174, 198n32, 226n64; vernacular, 5, 195n7; and whiteness, 14–15, 17, 83, 100, 123, 146, 156. *See also* denationalization; prohibited immigrants

civil rights, 33; activism, 3, 24, 107, 166, 172, 178

Clark, Kenneth B., 152

Clarke de Martin, Marion, 182

Club Alpha, 159

Coalición Patriótica Nacional, 102, 109

Cold War, 82, 87–88, 105, 165

Colombia, 10–12, 187, 190, 196n20

Colombian Congress, 10

Colón, Jesús, 223n14

Colón, Panama, 23, 36, 64, 69, 71, 83, 90, 146, 155; activism in, 33, 164, 174, 189, 221n55; Afro-Caribbeans in, 7–9, 15–16, 19, 31, 125, 139; employment in, 17, 44,

51; government representatives for, 61, 147–48; housing in, 153, 219n15; and the Hull-Alfaro Treaty, 102; Local 900 union rally in, 103–4; New Cristóbal, 124–26, 154; public hygiene campaigns in, 13; radio broadcasts in, 100, 116; schools in, 157

Colón Federal Credit Union, 8

colonialism/imperialism, 2, 4, 20, 28, 51, 135, 176, 180, 182, 186; and anti-Blackness, 15, 17, 24, 110, 114; British, 6–8, 43, 49–50, 53, 114, 200n4; and citizenship, 5, 8, 31; French, 6–7; Ottoman, 198n42; Portuguese, 184; Spanish, 12–13, 18, 185, 193, 223n20; US, 3, 15–16, 23–24, 94, 143, 153, 185, 200n59. *See also* anti-imperialism; decolonization; neocolonialism

Colón Municipal Council, 64, 147

Columbia University, 175; Teacher's College, 43, 72

Comité Pro-Reforma Constitucional, 66–67, 69, 71

Common Council for American Unity, 211n93

Common Ground, 87, 211n93

communism, 47, 123; and hemispheric diplomacy, 26, 47, 93–121; and labor activism, 82–92, 210n82. *See also* anticommunism

Communist Party, 83

Confederación de Trabajadores Latino Americanos (CTLA), 82

Congress of Industrial Organizations (CIO), 81–89, 92–93, 103–4, 106, 116, 139, 141–42, 210n72, 216n49, 219n13. *See also* AFL-CIO; United Public Workers of America (UPWA)/Local 713 UPWA-CIO

Conniff, Michael, 17, 200n59

Connor, Hector, 39, 52, 147, 148

Costa Rica, 19–20, 35

cotillions, 166, 169–74, 179, 227n80

coups, 105; 1931 (Acción Comunal), 47, 62, 70; 1941 (Ricardo Adolfo de la Guardia Arango), 67; 1951 (José Antonio Remón Cantera), 97; 1968 (Omar Torrijos), 181–82

English (language), 120, 152, 155, 160–61, 190, 197n28; campaigns against, 10, 17, 88, 111–16, 118–19, 133, 142, 183; in education, 24, 40, 42–44, 116, 129–30, 157; English-language press, 8, 16, 25, 29, 31–32, 35–36, 54–56, 69, 98, 107, 124; as language of colonization, 193. *See also* Anglophone Caribbean; *Panama Tribune*

English-language private schools (West Indian schools), 40, 44

Episcopalians, 160, 166

Escobar, Felipe Juan, 65–66, 207n25

Escobar Bethancourt, Rómulo, 183, 185

Escuela Normal de Institutoras, 41

Esteñoz, Ernesto, 104

eugenics, 5, 13, 16, 19, 58. *See also* sterilization

Eurocentrism, 11

Europe, 3–4, 11, 13, 37, 94, 114, 190

Evans, John, *133*

Executive Decree No. 59 (1942), 64–65

expulsion, 4, 46–47, 88, 124, 185

Fábrega, Ricardo, 48

Fábrega-Wilson Treaty (1942), 207n33

fascism, 59, 66. *See also* Hitler, Adolf; Mussolini, Benito; Nazis

Federación de Estudiantes Panameños, 66–67, 98

Federación Sindical de Trabajadores de Panamá, 98

Federoff, Anthony J., 141

feminism, 22, 33, 46, 95

Filos-Hines Convention (1947), 102

First US Conference of Panamanians (1974), 27, 180–90, 231n21

Flaxer, Abram, 83, 85

Fortune, Armando, 182

Fortune, Thomas, 178

France, 6–7, 11, 155, 171, 197n29, 217n62

Frederick, Rhonda, 51

French (language), 190

French Caribbean, 6–7

Frente Patriótico de la Juventud, 66

Gadpaille, Hector, *2*

Galindo, Juan A., 61

Gardner, Barbara, 173, 176

Garvey, Amy Jacques, 201n23

Garvey, Marcus, 8–9, 37–38, 51–52

Garvey Day, 38

Gaskin, Edward A., *77*, 91–92, 94, 102, 135, 144, 149; in CZCTA, 76, 78, 81; English-language speech, 118–20, 133, 142; on La Boca library committee, 74, 76; in Local 713, 82, 88; in Local 900, 89, 93, 99, 103–11, 117–21, 126–28, 141, 216n49; on Remón-Eisenhower Treaty, 138–41; on Seybold, 100–101

Gatun, Panama, 36, *133*

Gatun Literary and Debating Society, 36

gender, 2, 5, 49, 67–68, 81, 103, 180, 182; in activism, 22, 27, 150–79; in citizenship, 208n45; in education, 22, 41–42, 72, 76, 124, 208n45, 208n49; patriarchy, 22, 190; at the *Tribune*, 1, 33–34, 37, 41–42, 44, 46–47, 55, 71, 175; in the US Conference of Panamanians, 190; in US-Panama relations, 95. *See also* feminism

Germany, 47–48, 59–60

Girl's Friendly Society, 160

Goethals, George, 218n2

Goffe, Tao Leigh, 195n7

gold and silver rolls system, 14–15, 83, 87, 99, 116, 194, 197n29, 203n54, 210n72, 213n10

Goldsmith, Len, 210n82

González Revilla, Nicolas, 183

Government and Civic Employees Organizing Committee, Local 900, 89, 93, 99–100, 103–9, 117–20, 126–27, 137–38, 140–42, 147, 216n49

Grace, Catherine, 156, 158

Gran Feria Antillana, 191

Great Britain, 115, 148, 197n22; British imperialism, 6–8, 43, 49–50, 53, 114, 200n4; British slavery, 18. *See also* Anglophone Caribbean; British Caribbean; British Legation (Panama); England

Greene, Julie, 200n59

Greenidge, C., 51–52

Grenada, 163

Griffith, Edward, 189

Thomas, George, *2*
Thomas, Lorrin, 223n14, 226n66
Thompson, Ruby, *133*
Thompson, William, 50–51, 53
Tom Boys of Red Tank, 36
Torres de Araúz, Reina, 191
Torrijos, Omar, 182, 184–85, 188, 229n1
Trouillot, Michel-Rolph, 21
Trujillo, Rafael, 59
Truman, Harry S., 83
Turkish people, 18, 45
Turks (term), 198n42
Turpeau de Mena, Maymie Leona, 4

UNESCO, 90, 108, 112
Unión de Afro-Panameños, 188
United Brotherhood of Maintenance of
    Way Employees and Railroad Shop
    Laborers: 1920 strike, 9–10, 39, 76
United Fruit Company, 6, 19
United Nations (UN), 145, 168, 173, 183.
    See also UNESCO
United Public Workers of America
    (UPWA)/Local 713 UPWA-CIO, 81–82,
    84–89, 92, 99, 118, 210n82, 212n102;
    "Jim Crow Discrimination against U.S.
    Employees in the Canal Zone," 83
United Rubber Workers of America,
    216n49
United States, 21, 37, 67, 103, 108–9,
    114–15, 200n59, 226nn63–64; Afro-
    Caribbean immigration to, 9, 22, 24,
    27, 64, 78, 150–79, 181, 183–90, 194,
    223n19; and Afro-Caribbean world
    making, 2–3, 6–7, 23–26, 119, 150, 193;
    and anticommunism, 3, 82–83, 86–90,
    95–101, 105, 117, 123, 210n82, 212n107;
    canal building, 11–12, 200n4; compa-
    nies, 6; and depopulation, 123–26; and
    dual wage system, 14–17, 76, 83, 99–101,
    138–45, 197n29, 198n32, 213n10; and
    education, 78–80, 128–29, 189–89;
    expansionism of, 195n11, 196n20; and
    eugenics, 13; hegemony in Canal Zone,
    7, 58, 111, 135, 145, 153, 217n62; and im-
    migration, 19–20, 46, 203n57, 223n19;
    and labor organizing, 9, 26, 81–92, 99,

104–7, 116–17, 137, 140–46, 210n72,
210n82; and racial segregation, 14–15,
39, 79, 83, 85, 97, 123–24, 128–30, 185–
87, 211n86; and repatriation, 49–50,
54, 148; sovereignty in Panama, 12, 14,
94, 102, 120, 174, 197n28; stock market
crash (1929), 45; treaty negotiations,
102–7, 111, 120, 122–27, 135–36, 138–40,
207n33, 216n45; the *Tribune* in, 35, 87;
US citizenship in Panama, 23, 78, 83,
100, 123–24, 156; and whiteness, 31–32,
80–82, 92, 123–30, 146, 156, 210n72.
See also Canal Zone; US empire; Zonians; *individual states and cities*
Universal Negro Improvement Associa-
    tion (UNIA), 8–10, 37–38, 51–52, 163,
    191, 196n14. See also *Negro World*
Universidad de Panamá, 73, 80, 111, 132,
    182–83, 190, 217n62, 229n3
University of Chicago: International
    House, 94
University of Nebraska, 76
US Armed Forces, 137
US Army, 99, 161, 164
US Congress, 50, 83, 88, 123, 141, 145, 163,
    210n82, 223n15; *Congressional Record*,
    107; House Sub-Committee on Educa-
    tion and Labor, 87; Senate, 99, 138
US Department of Defense, 90, 94
US Department of State, 99, 106
US empire, 3, 15–16, 23–24, 28, 94, 143, 153,
    155, 185, 200n59
US House Un-American Activities Com-
    mittee (HUAC), 82
US Supreme Court, 65–66, 128

Varela, José M., 61
Vasco Núñez de Balboa medal, 93, 108–9,
    113, 116, 190
Vega, Simón, 61
Velarde, Fabián, 205n4, 206n12
Venezuela, 19
Vietnam War, 164

Walker, Robert C., 100, 106
Walrond, Eric, 152
Walrond, Hubert N., 9, 31

Walter, Claude L., *2*

Washington, DC, 12, 45, 86, 90, 104–6, 108, 111, 115–17, 128, 146, 176, 183

Watkins, Daphne, *132*

Welsh, Edward (Ed) K., 89, 104, 106–7, 216n49

Westerman, George, *2*, 68, 168; "Fifty Years of Treaty Negotiations Between Panama and the United States," 107; "Gold vs. Silver Workers in the Canal Zone," 87; role at the *Tribune*; 1, 80, 84–88, 95, 97, 173; "Sore Spots in United States–Panama Relations," 94; on working-class housing, 222n12

West Indian Panamanian (term), 27

West Indians, 71–72, 188, 191, 193, 207n25; anti–West Indian prejudice, 16–19, 25, 46–52, 69, 115, 118, 148–49; in education, 40, 43–44, 130–32; and labor activism, 75–76, 81; in Panamanian press, 8; terminology, 27, 79; West-Indian press, 8, 29–32, 54. *See also* Panama Canal West Indian Employees Association (PCWIEA)

West Indian schools. *See* English-language private schools (West Indian schools)

West Indies, 28

White, Walter, 90

White House, 49, 216n45

whiteness, 10, 18, 69, 71, 97, 104, 141, 148, 156, 182; and citizenship, 15; and depopulation, 123–26; and education, 44, 74, 80, 127–35, 146; and Iberian-focused identity, 13, 16–17, 19, 185; and immigration policy, 144; and labor, 14–15, 31, 39, 45, 81–86, 100, 123–24, 186, 210n72; in New York, 161–63, 225n55; and PPP, 47; and racial segregation, 15, 42, 74, 83, 109, 123–24, 128, 130, 134, 154, 211n86;

and unions, 9, 92, 210n72; white European migration, 4, 36; white oligarchy, 11; white press, 32, 48

white supremacy, 5–6, 37, 91, 198n36. *See also* racism

Wiley, John C., 106

Wilkins, Roy, 90

Wilks, Alvin K., 173–74, 229n107

Williams, Agatha, 192, 229n3

Williams, Harold W., *2*

Williams, L. Christy, 33, *35*

Williams, Leslie, 118, 133

Women's Hour, The, 157, 159

Women's Life Problem Association, 201n16

Women's Missionary Society of Red Tank, 36

Workman, 8–9, 31, 55, 192, 201n16, 201n19, 201n21

World War II, 70, 79, 100, 102

xenophobia, 3, 50. *See also* nativism

Yergan, Max, 83

Young, David, 1, *2*

Young, Sidney, 51–52, 69, 85, 209n67; in 1948 presidential election, 97; on citizenship, 60, 67–68; on education, 40–41, 119; *Isthmian Echoes*, 30, 32–33; Parque Young, 1, *2*, 156, 180; on repatriation, 46–49; role at the *Tribune*, 1, 29–33, 37–38, 46–49, 59–61, 97; on *Tribune*'s Spanish edition, 55. See also *Panama Tribune*

Zárate, Abdiel, 225n57

Zien, Katherine, 197n31, 200n59

Zonians, 15, 31, 124, 186, 197. *See also* Canal Zone